FACILITATING 5-MEO-DMT
AN ANTHOLOGY OF APPROACHES TO SERVING
THE GOD MOLECULE

MARTIN W. BALL, PH.D.
EDITOR

Facilitating 5-MeO-DMT:
An Anthology of Approaches to Serving The God Molecule

By Martin W. Ball, Ph.D., editor

Kyandara Publishing

Ashland, Oregon

© 2022

ISBN: 9798437179420

Disclaimer: This book is for educational and philosophical purposes and is not intended to encourage illegal or irresponsible behavior.

Dedication: This book is dedicated to everyone everywhere throughout all space and time – may we all find our way home to The Universal Self with an open and loving heart.

Thanks: In addition to extending my thanks to everyone who contributed to this book and made it a reality, I also extend my thanks to the eagles and other fine feathered friends who allowed me to photograph them and use their images in the art featured in this book.

Cover art and interior art ©2022 by Martin W. Ball   www.fractalimagination.com

*A note on author names: due to legal issues, or simply a concern for privacy, not all the authors featured in this book are using their real names. This choice was left to each individual contributor. Also, contributors were given the freedom to either discuss/share their personal background, or not. For this reason, bios are not specifically provided for all contributors or their contact information or how to find them either online or in real life as tends to be standard in anthologies such as this. This is done to provide them with privacy and should not be taken as a disregard of acknowledgement for their contributions to this work.

TABLE OF CONTENTS:

EDITOR'S INTRODUCTION	1
WELCOME TO THE TEMPLE OF AWAKENING DIVINITY	30
DRINKING TEA WITH GOD AND THE PATH TO SURRENDER	47
EXPERIENCE AS THE TRUE TEACHER	66
LESS IS MORE FOR WORKING ONE-ON-ONE	86
ON THE RESPONSIBILITIES OF THOSE SERVING 5-MEO-DMT	98
IN EVOLUTIONARY SYNC	104
THE LOGOS PORTAL	107
THE ENTHEOGENIC SUCHNESS OF BEING	116
FROM TRAUMA TO SELF-REALIZATION	128
FRACTAL EXPRESSIONS OF THE ONE	139
FROM INITIATION TO FACILITATION	153
HEART-CENTERED INTEGRATION AND SUPPORT	160
WHO DO YOU SERVE?	173
THE ULTIMATE UN-CONDITIONING	187
SUGGESTIONS FOR FUTURE RESEARCH	204
APPENDIX A: INTEGRATING 5-MEO-DMT	222
APPENDIX B: A RECOMMENDED MODEL FOR BEST PRACTICES	231
APPENDIX C: A CONVERSATION WITH HAL FROM T.O.A.D.	257
APPENDIX D: 5-MEO-DMT AND THE OBSOLESCENCE OF TRADITIONAL THEOLOGY	271
ABOUT THE AUTHOR/EDITOR:	284

Editor's Introduction

Back in early 2008, when I had my first "full-release" dose experience of 5-MeO-DMT, I knew a grand total of *one person* in the entire world who facilitated with this powerful entheogenic molecule. At that time, even in psychedelic culture, very few people had ever heard of 5-MeO-DMT, and back then, when mentioning it to others in the community, they'd almost always respond with, "You mean DMT?"

No.

Not even close!

Back in 2008, the world was hot for DMT.

Heavily influenced by Terence McKenna and his proclamation that DMT was the most powerful psychedelic available, along with his (in my opinion), patently absurd musings on "machine elves," "2012," "the end of history," the "transcendental object at the end of time," UFOs, the "alien other," and speculations on "translinguistic matter," the psychedelic community was basically of the opinion that DMT was *the thing*, and not only that, but that the world was heading toward some kind of apocalyptic transformation that would come about in 2012 and it was all related to DMT, in one manner or another. There was even widespread speculation on the internet that Dec 21st, 2012, would feature a magnetic pole shift on earth which (somehow) would trigger a global release of DMT in the pineal glands of all humans on earth simultaneously, ushering us all collectively into the new age of… who-knows-what.

Obviously, nothing of the sort ever happened because it was all nonsense and pure psycho-babble to begin with. No UFOs manifested to deliver humanity into the arms of the galactic community, there was no grand ascension, and the "transcendental object at the end of time" never materialized. The DMT-infused fantasy was a grand dud and a great big nothing.

With the exception of fantasy and sci-fi epics where fulfillment of prophecy is central to plot and character development (Paul, Anakin, Harry, Rand, Ciri, Miraanni), that's how all real-life "prophecies" tend to play out. Lots of hype. Not much reality.

McKenna favored DMT over 5-MeO-DMT because, as he put it, 5-MeO-DMT only produced "a feeling," whereas, far more significantly to his mind and personal tastes, he really "hallucinated" on DMT, at a level that was far beyond any other psychedelic, and therefore, he proclaimed it to be the "the heart" of the psychedelic experience.

From the vantage point of 2022, a full decade beyond the supposed "end of history" of 2012, I think that many (though my thoughts were completely dismissed by the larger psychedelic community at the time in 2008) would now agree that McKenna completely missed the point, and while his metaphysics enjoyed widespread support pre-2012, with the complete failure of anything actually happening, his views can now be looked at as quaint, entertaining, amusing, perhaps inspiring, but certainly not grounded in any kind of objective reality.

Furthermore, back in 2008, Rick Strassman's 2001 book, *DMT: The Spirit Molecule*, was just being made into a widely-viewed film by the same name, narrated by Joe Rogan. Strassman's work was ground-breaking primarily in the sense that he was the first researcher to be granted permission by the U.S. federal government to perform human-subject research with an illegal psychedelic substance in over two decades, helping to usher in a new age of scientific research on psychedelics.

Over the course of his research, Strassman developed his somewhat confusing and physics-challenging interpretation of DMT as allowing a "tuning in to channel dark matter." Similar to the endemic insertion of theoretical physics into spirituality and psychedelic theory-building, Strassman speculated that DMT allows humans to "tune in" to dark matter – a theoretical concept in astrophysics that has been introduced to account for the fact that a large portion of the mass of the universe appears to be missing from the observable electromagnetic spectrum. In other words, there seems to be a vast amount of "stuff" out there that is undetectable by scientific

Facilitating 5-MeO-DMT

instruments, yet appears to shape and mold the structure of the observable universe. Thus: "dark matter."

Those who espouse spiritual, religious, and metaphysical views have been eager to bolster their beliefs and interpretations with cutting-edge science ever since the advent of modern science. Pick up any book by a contemporary "New Age" author, and you're almost guaranteed that there will be some reference made to quantum mechanics, multiple-universes, dark matter, and the like, making the presentation sound "sciency" without actually being scientific, at all. You could also pick up any writings from over a hundred years ago by spiritualists and you'll see the exact same phenomenon, just with cutting-edge scientific terms from that era. Heck – America even has an entire religion devoted to this wedding of "science" to religion: Christian Scientists!

In the Philosophy of Science and Religion, this called the "God of the gaps" problem, where something that is not proven in religion or spirituality is bolstered by its supposed connection to something that is not understood in science – a gap in knowledge. This has been a tendency in Western thought ever since the Enlightenment and rational science was distinguished from the faith of religion and separate areas of knowledge were carved out for each domain. Because the domain of rational science has been seen as dominant and authoritative, religion and spirituality have sought to bolster their own reality claims by importing spurious understandings of science into religion and spirituality. This is an endemic problem and far more akin to science fiction and fantasy than actual science. Lest anyone get the wrong idea, I fully support the use of science to help us understand the nature of reality and the nature of consciousness, but I don't ever support the use of "God of the gaps" because it simply isn't scientific at all. It just appears that way to the uninformed.

Strassman's presentation follows this model by speculating that various "beings" and "other realms" exist in "dark matter" (or also possibly in "multiple realities/multiverses") that individuals can experience and perceive when consuming DMT. I don't think you'd find a single astrophysicist who'd agree with this idea because astrophysicists are pretty clear about dark matter: they have *no idea what it is, how it behaves, or what it's made of*. So, the idea that it's filled with beings and realms we can tune into via DMT must be baffling to them.

But, it sounds cool: DMT gives you access to other beings and other realms, and ...science!

Strassman went further, and speculated that, because DMT is a natural mammalian neurotransmitter, it was responsible for the "entry" of "the spirit" to connect to the physical body in utero, which he correlated with the Tibetan Buddhist belief that individuated consciousness reincarnates by entering into a fetus 49 days after death (after having traversed the *bardo* – the in-between state of consciousness after death and prior to re-birth as is detailed in the book of relatively minor importance in Tibetan Buddhism, the *Bardo Thodol*).

For all these reasons, Strassman dubbed DMT "The Spirit Molecule," and his, along with McKenna's views, became the gold standard in psychedelic discourse around DMT being the world's most significant psychedelic compound. Though Strassman is ultimately far more scientifically grounded than the wild tales and speculations produced by McKenna, and he was doing his best to make sense of the data and experiences he was collecting from his test subjects and grappling with how to take them at face value, together, their views cemented the idea in the psychedelic community that DMT must be very special, and it would be hard for anything else to compete with that specialness.

To challenge this dominant narrative, back in 2008, I proclaimed on my podcast and in my writings that, "If DMT is 'The Spirit Molecule,' then 5-MeO-DMT is 'The God Molecule.'" The idea went as follows: if DMT experiences are filled with all kinds of crazy psychedelic content of beings and realms, then by comparison, it's a lesser-order experience to the sense of experiencing God as made accessible via 5-MeO-DMT – you know, that "feeling" McKenna was referring to but had nothing meaningful to say about. By putting the word "God" in there, I thought it would be the best short-hand reference for the beyond-words profound magnitude of the experience and make its distinction from DMT unambiguous, clear, and easily referenced. I don't know if I would have decided to call 5-MeO-DMT "The God Molecule" if Strassman hadn't dubbed DMT "The Spirit Molecule" and have that term widely adopted by psychedelic culture, but he did, so I did, and both terms have stuck, culturally-speaking.

It was at this point that I also started referring to 5-MeO-DMT as the "Crown Jewel of Entheogens" and specifically identified what it made it so profoundly unique: it, more than any other psychedelic molecule, granted reliable access to nondual states of consciousness. At that time, the terms nondual and nonduality were almost never used in psychedelic discourse. The world was far more fascinated by decidedly dualistic phenomena: beings, realms, spirits, etc. – experiences that *persevered, amplified, and accented* the perceiving subject, perceived object, relationship, and apparent *otherness*.

In my work, I've taken pains to distinguish between what I call the "shamanic model" of psychedelic experience in contrast with what I've articulated as the "nondual model" of psychedelic experience. The shamanic model is all about spirits, realms, and otherness, whereas the nondual model is about recognizing that *all appearances are manifestations of one universal self, consciousness, or being.*

The world of self and other, me and the spirits, here and there, heaven and earth, physical and spiritual, and other such metaphysical dichotomies is dualistic in nature. Nondual means *not that*. Nondual means that reality, at its foundation, is unitary in nature and that all duality is merely apparent, but not fundamentally "real" in an absolute sense.

The nondual position could be stated thusly: there is, in reality, only ONE being/consciousness that exists, and everything that we sense, perceive, and experience, including ourselves, is this ONE being experiencing itself in different guises and forms, but in actuality, is still just ONE.

From this perspective, there's no such thing as "otherness" in psychedelic experiences: it is all an experience of oneself.

Furthermore, the individuated sense of self, the egoic identity, is fundamentally a character through which the Universal Consciousness expresses and experiences itself.

To put it bluntly, as I like to do, the only thing that *actually exists is God*.

And that means that each and every one of us is a direct manifestation and embodiment of this ONE universal consciousness and being. In fact, everything that exists is this ONE universal being, parceled out into apparent subjects and objects, yet still fundamentally ONE.

That's what happened to me upon that first full-release dose of 5-MeO-DMT back in 2008: I experienced *everything*, my apparent individuated and egoic-identified self, included, as being ONE universal consciousness that was primarily made of the universal energy of unconditional love and awareness. It's also my view (and experience) that this also means that we don't need to introduce concepts like souls or spirits, or even reincarnation, because everything already is one being, and the only thing that creates individuated perspectives is bodies (not spirits or souls), which I like to refer to as vehicles for the universal consciousness to experience and perceive itself through.

I experienced *myself* as *God*, and since this was true for me, and as I wasn't fundamentally different from anyone else, this *must be equally true for everyone and everything*. If I, in my true nature, am God, then so is everyone else.

So, I started making waves in the psychedelic world about the profound, and unique, significance of this amazing molecule, 5-MeO-DMT. One of the first hurdles was the push-back against the designation of DMT as being the "top" psychedelic, as, to my mind, it very clearly and obviously wasn't. Second, was to articulate just what the

5-MeO-DMT experience was and how profoundly different it was from not just DMT, but other entheogens and psychedelics, as well. Third, was the injection of the language of nonduality into psychedelic discourse, and, to open up the conversation in the psychedelic world around the concept of "God," which was almost completely absent in psychedelic discourse at the time.

Today, some 14 years after my first full experience with 5-MeO-DMT, we live in a very different world. The terms I first introduced around 5-MeO-DMT, such as "The God Molecule," and "The Crown Jewel of Entheogens" are now widely-used around the world when discussing 5-MeO-DMT. While there is still some confusion around the idea that 5-MeO-DMT is *not* DMT, it is much more widely understood that these are two very different molecules and that the experiences they make accessible to human consciousness bear very little resemblance to each other. Additionally, well-known individuals such as the son of the President of the U.S., Hunter Biden, and celebrities such as Mike Tyson, have professed how their lives were transformed by 5-MeO-DMT, via the use of the secretions of the Sonoran Desert toad (also known as the Colorado River toad), and articles about this molecule can now be found across the media spectrum, so there's much more awareness of 5-MeO-DMT than ever. Though he did not enjoy the experience at all, it was also featured in Michael Pollan's book, *How to Change Your Mind,* which, ironically, is one of the best-selling books in the world about psychedelics, though written by someone who was a virtual newbie to the psychedelic scene. In the process, 5-MeO-DMT has now come to eclipse interest in DMT, and it's a decidedly *hot* topic world-wide.

In contrast to 2008, I now personally know of numerous individuals (and countless more I don't know) around the world who work with and facilitate experiences with 5-MeO-DMT. Most are relatively new to the practice. Some have been at it for a while. The "old guards" in the psychedelic world intentionally kept quiet about 5-MeO-DMT, in part to reserve it for elite circles of psychonauts, and also to keep it off the radar of federal drug warriors. 5-MeO-DMT was shared in closely-guarded circles, and even some churches, but it wasn't talked about openly. It was extra-super-double top secret, and very few had access to it, or even knew what it was.

But the world is very different now. I, not being connected to the "old guard" in any way, after my first experience with 5-MeO-DMT, started belting out about it from the proverbial rooftops. It became a regular topic on my podcast, *The Entheogenic Evolution* (which I started in early 2008) and was featured prominently in my 2008 book of the same name. Shortly thereafter, James Oroc's book, *Tryptamine Palace,* was published in 2009. At that point, the toad was out of the bag, and the world was

Facilitating 5-MeO-DMT

destined to learn about 5-MeO-DMT whether the old psychedelic guard wanted it to, or not.

For their own reasons, legislators in the federal government of the U.S. decided to designate 5-MeO-DMT a schedule 1 illegal substance in this country, effective Jan 19th of 2011. It's been reported that one of the issues under consideration was an unverified report that *one person* had died while consuming 5-MeO-DMT in the form of secretions of the Sonoran Desert toad, so, you know, gotta protect the children! Or something like that.

Some countries have followed suit, and others have not sought to make access to 5-MeO-DMT illegal. Currently, there's a patchwork of legal access to and illegal prohibition of 5-MeO-DMT around the world. For example, it's an illegal felony here in the United States, but not across the boarders in either Mexico or Canada – two places where facilitation of the 5-MeO-DMT experience have flourished. It's flourished here in the U.S., too, but it's mostly underground, secret, and protective of facilitators and participants alike. There are a few "above ground" churches where toad secretions are served as a religious sacrament, but they have yet to be tested in court on the question of whether the federal government needs to extend religious freedom exemptions to them under the umbrella of the Religious Freedom Restoration Act.

Personally, I see access to 5-MeO-DMT, and psychedelics in general, as a universal human right. This is especially so with 5-MeO-DMT because, as "The God Molecule," it provides access to the most profound experience available to human beings: the experience of absolute ONENESS and our inherent divinity as manifestations of God. To my mind, I can't think of a more fundamental human right than this.

Not everyone "goes all the way" with 5-MeO-DMT, and elsewhere, I've articulated all the various ways that the ego (out of resistance or even necessity) can get in the way of the full experience. But, the *potential* is there, and there in a way that we don't generally find with other psychedelics, except in exceptional circumstances. In theory, though not always in practicality, *anyone* can smoke or vaporize 5-McO-DMT and, within mere *seconds*, can have a direct experience of their true nature as God or the Unitary Being and Universal Consciousness. That's pretty fucking profound. It doesn't matter what your background is, what you believe, what religion you belong to, what spirituality you follow, what you want, or don't want, to be true. It just presents this absoluteness to the one experiencing it: This IS IT!

Entire religions and spiritual traditions have been built around developing methodologies to help people experience this profound state of consciousness and embodied awareness. That a mere molecule can do, in a few seconds, what even a lifetime of spiritual practice may or may not achieve, is a pretty profound thing, and a potential game-changer for humanity. Just imagine: *anyone can have this experience*. If ever a great equalizer were available to humanity, this is it. All one needs is access, and hopefully, skillful facilitation.

To say that experiencing 5-MeO-DMT can be monumental and profoundly life-changing is not in any way hyperbole or overstatement. If there's anything on Earth that is truly and reliably mind-blowing, this is it, and in spades. The context in which one is served can have a deep impact on how the experience is received, processed, and integrated. It can swing wildly from profoundly liberating and ecstasy-inducing to deeply traumatic and horrifying. There are a lot of "it depends" in there. As I like to say, even with something as reliably nondual as 5-MeO-DMT, results vary. Other than an unfathomably massive influx and amplification of energy, there are no guarantees.

As such, education, preparation, set, setting, and facilitation are all extremely important. But, with 5-MeO-DMT, unlike the case of iboga, ayahuasca, San Pedro, peyote, and mushrooms, there are no long-standing traditions of how to serve or work with this molecule. While there have been Central American Indigenous cultures that have traditionally used a snuff made with seeds that contain 5-MeO-DMT (*yopo*), the smoking and vaporizing of 5-MeO-DMT is a decidedly modern phenomenon, and is how the majority of individuals are introduced to this powerful molecule. It can also be taken nasally (depending on the form of the molecule), or anally, yet the most widespread use is through smoking or vaporizing where the experience begins within a few heartbeats and things very quickly go from zero to infinity. And while there are *now* a number of Indigenous cultures in the Americas who have been introduced to "toad medicine" by Dr. Octavio Rettig, and subsequently adopted its use into their ceremonies and cultures, it's just as new there as it is anywhere else. While some of the cultures Rettig has introduced to toad medicine do have prior use of entheogens, many don't, and none have had a clear or unambiguous historical use of 5-MeO-DMT prior to his introduction.

Elsewhere, primarily in my 2017 book, *Entheogenic Liberation*, I discuss what I've learned to be the significant factors for working with 5-MeO-DMT and the energetic process it engenders in relation to the energetic patterning and structures of the human ego. While more books and writings about 5-MeO-DMT and the Sonoran Desert toad have appeared over the years, *Entheogenic Liberation* is the most comprehensive about just what the experience is, and how to work with it. In writing that book, I set out to create the guidebook that I didn't have when I was going through my own process with 5-MeO-DMT, and used my years as a facilitator of working

Facilitating 5-MeO-DMT

energetically one-on-one with clients with this powerful tool as the source material for all that is presented in it.

This book here has a very different aim. I urge the reader to take this as something of an anthropological or sociological survey that is not intended as being overtly evaluative or instructive, though various contributors to this volume do offer their own perspectives on what is best and what isn't. Because the serving of 5-MeO-DMT is fast becoming a global phenomenon, what I've done is invited various facilitators to share with the reader what their practices, concerns, philosophies, and methods are. This should not be considered an endorsement of anything presented within this book. This is not an attempt to articulate what's best, or how it should be done, or a guide for those who want to start facilitating. It is, however, an attempt to relate just a small sample of what's happening out there in the world with 5-MeO-DMT. It is by no means comprehensive. It's just a snapshot. It is a window into the thoughts and practices of various 5-MeO-DMT facilitators from around the world.

In putting this book together, I sent out a proposal to many of the 5-MeO-DMT facilitators whom I personally knew, and also invited them to forward the book proposal on to others that they might know. I also put out an open call on social media. The result is that some of the entries in this book come from people I know personally, and others are from people I've never met or even spoken to. Of all the submissions, only one comes from someone I've personally experienced 5-MeO-DMT with, and this is Hal from the Temple of Awakening Divinity. My own personal feeling is that the only real way to evaluate anyone's approach to working with a psychedelic medicine is to participate in their unique way of facilitating, and therefore direct experience is *fundamental and necessary* to evaluating anyone's practice in any truly meaningful sense. In other words, if you haven't experienced it, with this particular person, in this particular context, then you don't *really know* what it's like.

Given that I only have direct experience with one of the individuals featured in this book, it should be clear that I'm not offering any kind of evaluation, or endorsement of anything presented by contributors. I'm allowing them the space and opportunity to speak for themselves and present how they go about doing what they do, why, and how they came into the practice. While I presented potential contributors with a series of questions for them to consider, I also made it clear that individuals could represent themselves and their practices in any way they wanted, and they had the freedom to focus on and articulate what's important to them. Some contributors answered the questions I asked, and others created their own statement or followed their own format. The overriding concern was that everyone speaks from their own experience and practice, and to take this as an opportunity to tell their stories as they saw fit.

Martin W. Ball, Ph.D., Editor

The question prompts I provided to potential contributors were as follows:

- How were you introduced to 5/Toad? What was your experience?
- How did you become a facilitator and why?
- What, if any, training did you receive?
- How do you conduct sessions?
- How would you describe your approach: nondual, shamanic, ceremonial, therapeutic...?
- Do you work one-on-one, in groups, in retreats, at a center, with a team...?
- What do you see as the purpose of working with 5?
- If you use unconventional or controversial methods, what is the rationale? In your own view, how does it serve your practice?
- How do you handle issues of informed consent?
- What do people get out of their sessions/experiences?
- Do you provide pre-session information, screening, prep? If so, what?
- What are some of the best results you've seen?
- What are some of the difficulties you've encountered with patients/clients?
- What are your recommendations for integration and post-experience processing?
- What resources do you use or recommend to clients?
- How many people have you served, and what kinds of people have you worked with? (drug addicts, spiritual seekers, vets, ages, genders, occupations, interests, nationalities/ethnicities)
- Do you see different issues between serving men and women, old and young, healthy and those with medical issues?
- What do you feel are the responsibilities of those serving 5?
- Do you have an opinion on synthetic vs. "natural"?
- If you choose to work with toad, what's your take on sustainable harvesting, toad protections, and related ethical questions?
- How do you feel 5 works with other entheogenic medicines? What are their relationships?
- Who should take 5? Who shouldn't?
- What role do you see for 5 in the global community?
- What are the lessons you've learned from serving 5?

FACILITATING 5-MEO-DMT

- Do you see serving 5 as being different from serving other entheogenic medicines? How? Why?
- What concerns, if any, do you have about the surging interest in 5 globally, and the sharp increase in demand for the experience (and its possible negative impacts on toads)?
- What hopes do you have with 5 and the experiences it makes possible for people?
- Have you been public about your work with 5? (ie, presented at conferences, WBAC, given interviews, etc.) If so, how do you navigate being public?

I also presented a third possibility as an alternative to either formatting their own submission or answering the questions listed above: the submission could come in an interview format. The logic behind this third option is that my podcast, *The Entheogenic Evolution*, has been a home to having discussions about 5-MeO-DMT since its inception in 2008. I made the offer of either transcribing a previous interview that had been featured on my podcast, or alternatively, having contributors come on the podcast for an interview that would then be transcribed and used in this book. Both options have been taken by contributors, so some of the entries are in conversation format between myself and the contributors or a re-worked version of the conversation into an individual presentation.

Because I've been very prolific over the years since 2008 in writing about, sharing about, and conversing about 5-MeO-DMT, many of the submissions in this collection mention me or my work, as I've been the source of information for many people first discovering 5-MeO-DMT or entering into the world of 5. This was not intentional on my part, but it was probably inevitable, given how much I've focused on this molecule, how it works, and how to work with it. Readers will also probably note that many submissions refer to nonduality and nondual states of consciousness, which is also, at least in part, due to my influence on the discourse.

At times, there are references to pre-existing nondual traditions, meanings, interpretations, and teachings. For myself, my nondual take on 5-MeO-DMT, and subsequently, on reality in general, came directly from my experiences with this molecule. When I wrote my 2009 book, *Being Human*, I first articulated there what I described as my "radical nonduality," and the worldview that had arisen via my personal experiences, which I've named "the entheological paradigm." Something that I've often argued is that while the nondual experience is the nondual experience, and at the deepest levels, it doesn't really matter how it was accessed, I am also of the view that 5-MeO-DMT is its own unique energetic vehicle, and as such, have preferred not to make reference to any pre-existing nondual traditions or teachings. In my opinion, the maps of consciousness and being generated by such traditions do not necessarily "fit" with either the 5-MeO-DMT experience in particular, or psychedelic states in general. So, my nonduality doesn't come from any nondual religion or spiritual tradition, though some who facilitate 5-MeO-DMT do seek to use traditional nonduality as a lens through which to explore and understand the 5-MeO-DMT experience.

From the traditional perspective, nonduality is most closely associated with religious and spiritual traditions that developed in India. However, once we get into the various traditions of India, what becomes clear is that the maps, methods, and conceptualization of the process of attaining nondual states varies tremendously, and even while many such religions make use of similar terms, they mean very different things in different traditions. For example, most religions originating from India contain the concept of "karma," but the *meaning* of this term is radically different from one religion, or even sect or branch, to another, so making the assumption that they're using the same terms so they must have a similar meaning is entirely incorrect. Jains, Buddhists, and Hindus all have *very* different views of what karma is, how it is accumulated, how one gets rid of it, and what the process and experience of liberation and enlightenment are. And even making a statement like "Hindus believe karma is X . . ." is highly problematic as there are so many versions of "Hinduism," let alone Buddhism.

One such term, which makes its appearance in these pages in different submissions is the Sanskrit word, *samadhi*. Samadhi has been adopted as a nickname for 5-MeO-DMT within the wider culture. In the religions of India, *samadhi* is used to refer to the highest states of meditative awareness, often with an emphasis on nonduality, but not always. It is a word that is used across numerous traditions, but can have radically different meanings depending on context, historical development, cultural interactions, and adaptations. Buddhist *samadhi* is not necessarily equivalent to Hindu *samadhi*, or Jain *samadhi*, or yogic *samadhi*, or Sikh *samadhi*. And within religions, Zen Buddhist *samadhi* isn't necessarily the same as Tantric Buddhist *samadhi*. Or within Hinduism, we also have the various Vedantic schools that span from nondual, qualified-nondual, to dual. So, do you see the problem? When *we,* in the 5-MeO-DMT community use the term *samadhi*, what, precisely, do *we* mean?

This is why I've preferred to use the language of energy to describe the process of working with 5-MeO-DMT, without reference to any pre-existing concepts or traditions. In my opinion, it's cleaner and less burdened by cultural conceptuality,

FACILITATING 5-MEO-DMT

tradition, and doctrine. That's why I'm a self-described "radical nondualist." My nonduality comes from myself and my direct experience, not something that came before that may or may not be an ideal fit and weighed down by hundreds or even thousands of years of interpretation and re-interpretation.

But of course, everyone here, in this book, has been welcomed to approach these issues from whatever their own perspective is. I appreciate that where contributors use the term *samadhi*, they provide what they take its meaning to be.

However, I will leave this part of the discussion with one example that should be illuminating, and hopefully pique some curiosity. In the nondual meditation religions of India, the universally-taught and promoted body posture is that of seated meditation in lotus position with the legs crossed over themselves and hands held together with one overlapping the other, positioned at the navel. If *samadhi* is a state of consciousness experienced in meditation, then we can assume that fully energetically embodied experience is not relevant for the attainment of *samadhi*, and in fact, *samadhi* is generally articulated as *an experience of consciousness* where the body has been *transcended*. In contrast, when someone has a full-release nondual experience on 5-MeO-DMT, individuals almost universally open their bodies in a "spread-eagle" or "star" position, mainly due to the fact that they are experiencing infinite levels of energy coursing through their beings during that phase of the experience. I've written and shared much more about this phenomenon elsewhere, so I won't belabor the point here, yet this is an obvious and clear presentation of *energetic difference* between meditation and the energetic expansion that is the experience of 5-MeO-DMT. *They are not the same thing, as is made clear by how the experiences are embodied and articulated through body posture, movement, and expression. There's something very different going on here, energetically, and this is obvious by how the experience is directly expressed in the body.*

Speaking of differences, let's return to the topic of 5-MeO-DMT in comparison to DMT, and other tryptamines. As there is still confusion in the world about these differences, it's worthwhile exploring to some degree here where we have an opportunity to clear up some confusion. The other day, I was reading an article about how "rich people" were "smoking toad," and in the article, 5-MeO-DMT was referred to as "toad DMT." 5-MeO-DMT *is not* "toad DMT." Nor is it "frog DMT," as it is sometimes called. 5-MeO-DMT *is not* DMT.

There are a wide variety of tryptamines that exist in the world, both out there in "nature," as well as a diverse array that have been created in curious chemists' laboratories, such as was the case with the famed Sasha Shulgin. Without getting in-depth into the chemistry, a tryptamine is a molecule with a basic structure to which other elements can be added at various positions on the base molecule, and with each transformation of the base molecule, different biological, mental, emotional, and physical effects are generated. In mammals, tryptamines function as neurotransmitters and interact with receptor sites throughout the body: the brain, the heart, and the gut (all of which are comprised of neural tissue and networks and are in communication with each other). Naturally occurring tryptamines in humans include serotonin, melatonin, DMT, and 5-MeO-DMT. In the lab, chemists have created other tryptamines, such as 5-MeO-MiPT, 4-ACO-DMT, 5-MeO-DALT, and many, many others. As someone who's made it a point to try out many of these molecules, I can personally assure you that *they're all very different from each other*, though they also do bear some "family resemblance" to one another.

Beyond humans, tryptamines occur in all mammals. They are also found in a wide diversity of plants with different concentrations in different parts, such as seeds, leaves, roots, or bark. Curiously, toads also produce tryptamines in their protective secretions from their glands. All toads produce bufotenine, 5-HO-DMT, which tends to function as a nerve toxin, thereby making toads nasty meals for any would-be predators. One toad, however, *Bufo alvarius,* (whose correct Latin name is *Incilius alvarius,* though since this is less-often used, and "bufo" has come to be a shorthand for the secretions of this toad, the term "bufo" will be used throughout this book) in addition to producing 5-HO-DMT, also produces 5-MeO-DMT. This *the only toad in the world* that does so and is the "toad" referred to when discussing 5-MeO-DMT. However, the amount of 5-MeO-DMT produced by the Colorado River toad (also known as the Sonoran Desert toad) varies, comprising around only 5-15% of the total secretions, so there's a complex array of other tryptamines and toxins present. Yet, the *one and only reason anyone ever uses toad secretions* is because it contains 5-MeO-DMT. While there may be some kind of entourage effect with toad secretions, the fundamental ingredient is 5-MeO-DMT, and it is this molecule, and its effects, which dominate the experience. The result is that you can get *the same effects* from lab-made 5-MeO-DMT, in terms of energetic experience and potential for nondual access, and there is no clear or unambiguous advantage to using toad secretions, other than placating the desire to work with something "natural" as opposed to something made in a lab. The question of the "entourage effect" is addressed more thoroughly in the final chapter of "Suggestions for Future Research."

So, 5-MeO-DMT is a *form* of DMT, but it is not at all the same as DMT. The base molecule of DMT has a methoxylated addition on the 5 position, which is where we get the "5-MeO" part of its name. At times, 5-MeO-DMT is referred to simply as "5-MeO," or even just "5," but when the broader spectrum of tryptamines is taken into consideration, this can be confusing as there are a number of other psychedelic

Facilitating 5-MeO-DMT

molecules that also have a methoxylated addition at the 5 position. However, since 5-MeO-DMT is far more well-known and considered to be of special importance, we can get away with calling it "5" or "5-MeO," as virtually no one comes back with a response of, "You mean 5-MeO-MiPT?" When we say "5-MeO," it's generally understood what we're referring to.

But the confusion with "regular" DMT persists. So, let's clear some of that up. DMT and 5-MeO-DMT are *extremely different molecules* from a phenomenological perspective. They do have some commonalities, however. They are both extremely fast-acting, when smoked or vaporized, are both extremely powerful, and also relatively short-acting, lasting more in the range of minutes as compared to hours, as is common for many psychedelic molecules. However, the similarities end there, and the differences are far starker and striking than any superficial similarity they share.

DMT, for one, is *far weaker*, in the sense that you need to use 10 times more molecule for a "full" experience than you do of 5-MeO-DMT. For example, a 10mg experience of 5-MeO-DMT is more potent than 100mg of DMT. DMT is also much shorter-acting, where a full DMT experience lasts 5-15 minutes compared to a full 5-MeO-DMT experience of 10-40 minutes.

While the experience of both molecules includes the phenomenology of experiencing intense levels of energy in one's being (which can be somatic, mental, visual, emotional, cognitive, etc.), the energetic experience of DMT tends to amplify the ego, whereas 5-MeO-DMT holds the potential to completely dissolve the energetic structures of the ego. Part of the difference could be related to the fact that DMT is far more visual in nature than 5-MeO-DMT, and this visual augmentation (explosion, really) perhaps preserves the subject/object relationship of the ego in that it is so radically occupied with *looking at really weird shit* on DMT: aliens, space stations, spirits, deities, machine elves, UFOs, etc. In other words, the ego, on DMT, is highly preoccupied with the question of, "What the fuck is *that!?*"

To say that DMT is highly visual is a vast understatement. As McKenna praised it, "It's the only psychedelic where I really hallucinate!" Visually, DMT is simply over-the-top, and in that respect, we can safely say that it's about the most "psychedelic" (in the colloquial sense) of all the psychedelics out there. Visually, it's extraordinarily colorful, engrossing, and highly geometric and fractal, and certainly very infinite. It's crazy. It's beautiful. It's terribly complex. It's engrossing, and captivating.

But, it preserves and augments the ego.

And then, it's gone.

5-MeO-DMT, on the other hand, is *not* defined by its visual nature. Some people get no noticeable visual effects from 5-MeO-DMT, and those who do tend to describe it as being pure white, or golden, light, that has fractal edges with iridescence in slight rainbow colors. This is *extremely different* from the hyper-saturated neon-bright colors of DMT. For some, 5-MeO-DMT presents as "The Void," where all perception is completely empty of content, and this "void" may appear as either completely black, or as filled with scintillating light (yet still paradoxically empty of any perception of "thingness"). And though there can be strong visual effects with 5-MeO-DMT, a common assessment (after the fact, when the ego comes back online) is that visually, it is "crystal clear," and this refers not only to its visual quality, but also to the sense of gnostic revelation and sense of being that is made accessible via this molecule.

Both molecules can produce a "near-death" like experience, but even here, there are profound differences. With DMT, it's most common for people to experience themselves as "dying," and then travelling out to *some other place*, which might be rationalized as some kind of after-life realm. However, with 5-MeO-DMT, people experience themselves as "dying," and then, as the ego falls away and dissolves, suddenly find that *they are the Universal Consciousness and Being that is everyone and everything*. In other words, people tend to "travel out" on DMT, whereas with 5-MeO-DMT, they tend to "go" to "the center" of all existence and being and, in that state, recognize the fundamental nature of reality as being identical with themselves, without separation. In other words, DMT is predominately dualistic in nature, whereas 5-MeO-DMT is fundamentally nondualistic in nature.

What becomes clear from the nondual perspective is that *all dualistic experiences wherein the ego is preserved, in some fashion, are a lesser-order experience and not as fundamentally "true" as the sense of unitary being discovered in nonduality*. To put it bluntly, DMT seems more of a "show" and "projection" that is experienced by the (often) confused and awed ego, whereas 5-MeO-DMT presents as the *fundamental nature of being and reality*.

That, to me, seems like a pretty darn big difference, and gets us well beyond McKenna's dismissive "5-MeO-DMT is just a feeling" versus how much he hallucinates on DMT. There's a reason 5-MeO-DMT is sweeping the globe, and it's precisely because of this "feeling" that McKenna was unable to identify or articulate anything meaningful about.

So, if you want to blow your mind and have a wild, psychedelic, highly hallucinatory ride (which, for the record, can be great fun, so don't think I'm dissing on it), then DMT is what you're looking for. However, if you want to get to the very heart of being and all of reality, and truly know yourself at the deepest and most intimate level, and also have an opportunity to process and release all your egoic trauma and residue either on the way up or back down, then you'd never choose DMT over 5-

FACILITATING 5-MEO-DMT

MeO-DMT. In this matter, one is *clearly superior* to the other. They are not comparable, and they are not interchangeable. And for those few who still proclaim that DMT is more powerful than 5-MeO-DMT, I'm sorry, but I think you're profoundly mistaken. As far as I'm concerned, there's no real debate or question here.

Which brings us to the question of why 5-MeO-DMT is considered to be so therapeutically significant. While both DMT and 5-MeO-DMT hold the potential to generate new neural networks, increase neuroplasticity, and reduce inflammation, 5-MeO-DMT is therapeutically (and also "spiritually") more significant precisely because of the work it does on the human ego. For example, when it comes to trauma, parts of one's prior experience are blocked by protective mechanisms of the ego, which tend to trap the effects of trauma in one's psyche, emotional body, and physical body. By dissolving the structures of the ego, as 5-MeO-DMT does in spades, unprocessed, unconscious, and unresolved material is given an opportunity to rise to the surface and process out. This is why, when people consume 5-MeO-DMT, there can be so much screaming, crying, vomiting, and even full-body orgasms, taking place. The experience allows for a profound energetic cleansing and re-set. DMT rarely accomplishes this, and this is why researchers are focusing far more on the therapeutic potential of 5-MeO-DMT than DMT.

Furthermore, in scientific studies done on psychedelics, it has been found that the "mystical" experience tends to have the most therapeutic benefits for patients. "Mystical" can be defined in various ways, but in general, "mystical" is tended to mean a sense of being in the presence of God, of feeling unconditional love, of transcending all space and time, a sense of union with the divine, or, as articulated through nonduality, a sense of *being one with all of reality and as being identical with the universal consciousness*. Hands down, 5-MeO-DMT is by far *the most mystical* of any psychedelic substance. It also, more reliably than any other psychedelic, gives access to mystical and nondual states of awareness. It also works much more quickly than other psychedelics, in this regard. For example, someone could have a 6-hour deep mushroom trip, and might only catch a glimpse of the mystical experience for a few minutes or seconds, and if this aspect of the experience is the more therapeutically beneficial, then why not get right to it with a fast-acting compound such as 5-MeO-DMT that can get you "there" within seconds, rather than an hours-long experience that might not ever get you there, and also allows for deep egoic processing on the way up and on the way down, all fit within a 20-40 minute time frame? It is *precisely* for this reason that many companies and researchers around the world are currently working on developing therapeutic delivery methods for 5-MeO-DMT. You could potentially treat far more patients in a shorter period of time, and with more reliable results, than the day-long attention and care it takes to work with psilocybin or MDMA.

It is important to note, however, that all psychedelic therapy carries the risk of trauma. This is probably least concerning with MDMA, to which most people react very favorably as it's, in most cases, an extremely feel-good experience. However, a powerful mushroom journey at doses powerful enough to give access to a mystical experience can be hellish and deeply traumatizing for hours for someone who is having a difficult experience or resisting. The same holds true for 5-MeO-DMT. The experience is simply so powerful, so profound, so incredibly overwhelming that some people find it to be deeply traumatic, confusing, and producing lasting difficulties, post-experience. And this can occur even in the most carefully regulated ceremonial or therapeutic space with well-trained facilitators. While context can contribute to a traumatic experience, it's mostly an internal phenomenon and often caused by the individual's inability to trust, surrender, and let go fully into the experience and allow the energy to process naturally. It's important to note that this is not necessarily an easy process, so it isn't to blame anyone for "not doing it right," as this is BIG medicine, and not everyone can process the experience cleanly.

And here's the thing: you never know what you're going to get. Some people, such as in some of the submissions included in this book, are of the opinion that only those with significant prior psychedelic experience, or those who are well-grounded in a spiritual or meditative tradition, should attempt to experience 5-MeO-DMT, because it is so monumental and powerful. However, from my own experience, I'd say that neither prior psychedelic experience, or experience with spiritual or meditative traditions, has any real bearing on one's chances of surrendering and allowing the experience of 5-MeO-DMT to unfold without resistance by the ego. In my direct experience, I've seen people with years of prior psychedelic and meditative experience have total freak-outs on 5-MeO-DMT where it's scared the shit out of them, and have also seen people with zero psychedelic or meditative experience do beautifully on 5-MeO-DMT.

When it comes to the question of *who should take 5-MeO-DMT?*, my personal answer is: anyone who wants to get to the heart of being and is willing to take the risks involved. No prior experience is necessary, and it's important to note that because the experience of 5-MeO-DMT is so radically powerful and unique, no prior experience can really prepare anyone for it. Because I see 5-MeO-DMT as an equal-opportunity nondual agent, I do recommend that people learn as much about the potentials of the experience as possible prior to attempting to experience or work with it. For me, the best preparation is education, which is precisely why I've dedicated so much of my

FACILITATING 5-MEO-DMT

work around providing the world with detailed and comprehensive information about all aspects of working with 5-MeO-DMT from an insider's perspective. And while this book here obviously goes beyond my personal perspective and experience, it's following along with the same intent: to educate people around the topic of how different individuals facilitate 5-MeO-DMT and what they perceive, from their experience, as defining features of working with this profound molecule and entheogenic agent.

Something that I'm sure everyone included here would agree with is the requirement that anyone looking to facilitate 5-MeO-DMT, whether it be ceremonially, therapeutically, or spiritually, *must have ample experience with the molecule first*. This is one of those things that *if you don't know it from the inside, then you literally have no idea*. The non-5-MeO-DMT-initiated mind *cannot, in any way, understand what the experience is like*. If it helps, think of it this way: every "idea" you have is a product of your ego. If, as is generally held in the 5-MeO-DMT community, this molecule effectively dissolves your ego, then you literally *cannot* have an idea of the experience that is accurate. You can use words, concepts, and language to discuss it *after the fact*, but prior to "going in," you have *no idea* what you're getting into.

Part of the problem is the fundamentally paradoxical nature of reality and being. As is revealed by the nondual experience of 5-MeO-DMT, we are all, simultaneously, the person we think we are and identify as, yet are also all the Universal Consciousness and Being (God). We are simultaneously *this one, right here*, and also everything and everyone else, and also *no-thing*, and universal, without separation or boundaries. As an analogy, it's kind of like how things are in quantum physics where "objects" exist as both discrete particles and waves, simultaneously. At the thoroughly dualistic and particalized end of spectrum, we appear to *just* be this person, right here. At the thoroughly universal waved end of the spectrum, we are everything and nothing, we are God. Yet, somehow, paradoxically, *both are true, simultaneously*. We are both "this," and "that," and also "nothing," all at once.

Talk about a mind-bender!

If that doesn't pull the proverbial rug out from underneath your experience of reality, then I don't know what will.

The ego doesn't necessarily like this situation. The ego, as expressed through conceptuality, likes things to either be "this" or "that," but not both, at the same time.

The key, to my mind, is about finding *balance, centeredness, and authentic embodiment*. Such, however, is not about adopting the right beliefs, ideas, doctrine, or ideology. Balance, centeredness, and authentic embodiment *must be found within*. It cannot come from outside the individual. And this is precisely why 5-MeO-DMT is such a powerful agent: it gives one the opportunity to explore this directly, energetically, and in an intimately embodied way. It's not about what you think or believe. It's about *how you are being*. And in order to get there, you'll most likely need to process, release, and transmute a great deal of personal (egoic and individual life-history) material along the way. And the route to get there via 5-MeO-DMT is much faster and more reliable than any other methodology available to humanity. I take up this topic again in the first appendix to this volume where I discuss how embodiment is crucial to what we can understand as genuine "integration" of 5-MeO-DMT that goes beyond standard wellness protocols for integrating psychedelic experience.

5-MeO-DMT, simply put, is not only a game-changer, I think it's also *the* game-changer. It's the greatest molecular technology available to humanity for personal transformation and self-awareness. *That's* the reason I like to call it "The Crown Jewel of Entheogens." And again, I think "The God Molecule" captures its spirit rather nicely, as well.

Now that 5-MeO-DMT is out in the world, there are some common terms and phrases that are in use around it that we can delve into here for those reading this collection of accounts who are perhaps unfamiliar with some of the terminology that has become standard for those of us on the inside of the 5-MeO-DMT universe.

First, there are some phrases that are associated with different levels of the 5-MeO-DMT experience, and also related to doses (though this is from the experiential level and cannot be clearly demarcated by dose or milligram weight, as different people react differently to different doses at different days and times – always remember: results vary!).

The "handshake" dose: this is generally meant to indicate that the person being served is receiving what is expected to be a small, introductory dose, and not one that is intended to dissolve the ego and grant access to a nondual state. I like to say that the ego is like a gravity well in spacetime: unless enough energy is introduced, everything near it will fall into its orbit. With enough energy, you can reach "escape velocity," and break free of the gravity well. 5-MeO-DMT does this, but only when "enough" has been provided (and this varies, so there's no magic number that is universally applicable). With the "handshake," the idea is that the participant can "dip their toes" into the 5-MeO-DMT experience without having their ego threatened with total annihilation.

It's important to note that different facilitators have very different opinions about first introducing clients/patients/initiates to the molecule with a low dose such as this. For some, it is important to gradually work individuals up to higher doses, whereas for others, this is seen as potentially misleading, as the ego can develop the idea of, "Oh,

Facilitating 5-MeO-DMT

this isn't so radical! I can manage this!" and cause it to freak out even more when it finally reaches the nondual threshold at a higher dose.

Some people who facilitate never go beyond these low doses as they don't want to have to manage the explosive potential of what takes place at higher doses. Some facilitators see these low doses as a waste of time, and medicine. So, opinions differ.

The "hug" dose: this would be a "level" above the "handshake" where the individual is given a bit more (when working with the pure molecule, this can be the difference of only a milligram or two more) and afforded a deeper and more enveloping 5-MeO-DMT experience. At this level, the ego is still largely intact, but the overall energy of the experience is noticeably increased. The energy of 5-MeO-DMT has a steep logarithmic climb, so things get more powerful very quickly when increasing the dose. But at this level, since the ego isn't fully dissolved, it can actually be more confusing for some individuals than a larger dose. It's not easy to turn off the ego, which always thinks it should be *doing* something, and in these intermediate dose ranges, it often has no idea what to do with itself, so it gets confused, attempts to control, and struggles to intellectualize what it is experiencing. But, at this point, it's starting to get the idea that what might be coming next, with a larger dose, will be well out of its comfort zone of prior experience or frame of reference.

The "full release," "full surrender," or "complete embrace" dose: this is used for a dose that holds the potential for a full nondual experience, with the understanding that even at these levels, it is still possible for the ego to hold on, resist, avoid, or otherwise co-opt the experience, so a nondual experience isn't guaranteed. Just like to escape the gravity well of a planet, a rocket needs enough fuel, though merely having enough fuel isn't a guarantee that that rocket won't exploded upon lift off, go off course, or crash. The same holds true for higher doses of 5-MeO-DMT. There's no guarantee. However, the expectation, at this level, is that the one taking it has the potential to completely dissolve the egoic structures and enter "full absorption" in an infinitely-expanded energetic state. At this stage, there are no perceptions of separation, boundaries, or limits. There is no longer an observing self or that which is observed as there is no longer a distinction between subject and object and it is the experience of the immediate "suchness" of being. It is beyond concepts, beyond belief, and is overwhelming, ecstatic, and for many, blissful and loving.

Which brings us to our next term: that of the "white-out," or, alternatively, the "black-out." At high doses, many, especially those who are just beginning their explorations with 5-MeO-DMT, are unable to maintain conscious awareness of their experience and therefore have a discontinuity in consciousness. This is most likely due to the fact that 99% of all humans have zero reference for experience that is not filtered through the ego, and therefore the self-identified person and egoic consciousness is rendered unaware of the nondual experience. For some, as the energy of the medicine opens up, everything turns to white light, the ego "dies," and then, once the energy starts to wane, the ego comes back online, and the person describes how everything turned to light and then ... the next thing they know, they find themselves "back" in their body and egoic awareness, and they might have zero recall of what their experience over the last 10 minutes or so was. Similarly, for some, everything goes dark, and they "black-out," and then "regain" consciousness (via the re-appearance of the ego) at a later time.

While such an event can indicate that a person had "too much," this is not necessarily the case. Often, it's an experience that transforms over time as the individual becomes more experienced with maintaining awareness, where it can distinctly be observed that the ego very clearly comes and goes, but awareness remains. Furthermore, it's common that aspects of the experience of a white or black-out filter back into awareness over subsequent days and months in a process that is very similar to how one might not remember a dream upon waking, only to have bits and pieces of a significant dream come back into awareness as events or situations trigger recall due to something appearing or feeling familiar to something that was present within the dream.

Somewhat the opposite of the white or black-out is the phenomenon that has been labeled as a "spontaneous reactivation." This is where a 5-MeO-DMT experience, where no 5-MeO-DMT has actually been consumed, breaks open into everyday consciousness and experience, post-experience of having consumed the molecule. Back in 2008, after my second 5-MeO-DMT experience, the following day I was sitting in meditation and as I was exhaling, I knew that, somehow, if I just followed my breath all the way, I'd go back "in" to the 5 experience. And that's exactly what happened. What followed was indistinguishable between what was happening to me right then and there and the experience of taking a hit of 5-MeO-DMT. It then happened every day for the next two weeks.

When I informed the person who had facilitated for me, he'd never heard of this happening. So, I was the first person that I'd ever heard of having this kind of experience. A few months later, when I'd started a new relationship and was taking my new partner for her own experiences with the Temple of Awakening Divinity, she started waking up between 2 and 3 am in the morning, after her second or third experience with the medicine, fully back "in the medicine," and for her, it was jarring, scary, and extremely uncomfortable. She was the first person the 3 of us (herself, me, and our facilitator) where we'd seen this kind of reaction.

FACILITATING 5-MEO-DMT

Now that many more people have experienced 5-MeO-DMT and reported their own experience of after-effects, we now know that both of these situations are relatively common, though not universal, post-5-MeO-DMT experience. Some people find that their meditation is suddenly far more powerful and energetic than ever, and easily slip into a 5-MeO-DMT-like experience in meditation. And for many others, waking up, most often between 2 and 3 am in the morning (or for others, immediately upon transitioning from being awake to falling asleep), and having a full 5-MeO-DMT-like experience, which, in the moment, appears indistinguishable from the "real" thing, is also very common. And just like my then-partner (and now-wife) and myself, these "spontaneous reactivations" tend to subside within a couple of weeks once they start.

At the time in 2008, this was new to all of us. We know now that this is rather common, and such events have been come to be called "spontaneous reactivations," or simply "reactivations." At times, some people refer to these events as "flashbacks," but this term doesn't really capture the experience. You're not "flashing back," because it's all happening *right here, right now,* and need not mirror or imitate your actual experience with 5-MeO-DMT. For example, my second experience with 5-MeO-DMT was one of releasing years of pent-up and repressed emotional pain that came out in the form of wailing, screaming, and crying. In my reactivations, I never "flashed back" to that releasing of pain. Rather, my reactivations were ecstatic, expansive, and energetically powerful. While they had a decidedly 5-MeO-DMT feel to them, they were not echoes of my most recent 5-MeO-DMT experience. Regardless, it is this kind of "breaking-through into ordinary reality" that is referred to by the use of the term "reactivation." Not everyone gets this, but many do. In some instances, it's an indication that the energy of the 5-MeO-DMT has not been fully expressed and processed. In others, it just means someone is available to go deeper into the moment of being and not necessarily a manifestation of unprocessed energetic materials.

As has been mentioned, individuals can experience a great deal of "releasing" and "purging" on either the way up to the pinnacle of nonduality, or on the descent back down into the ego. These can take all manner of forms: vibrations and tremors in the body, vomiting, drooling, screaming, crying, involuntary body movements, somatic processing, emotional outbursts, acting out (fighting, trying to run away, flopping around, becoming hyper-sexual), etc. This is another area where we find a great deal of diversity, and also see how deeply personal each experience is, as it is always a reflection of the individual's energetic state in that very moment. This is where unconscious patterns, choices, and limitations come to the surface to be sorted, expressed, released, and transformed. This is where a lot of the "juice" of working with 5-MeO-DMT is found. It is through such energetic processing that individuals are effectively able to recalibrate their energetic being as restricted through the confines of the ego, and is also an indication that someone is not merely engaging in "spiritual bypassing," where the difficult aspects of being human are pushed aside and ignored for the desire to attain bliss and perfection. Being human is a messy, difficult business, and *everyone* has energetic blocks and residuals to process through if they are truly seeking to transform, empower, and recalibrate themselves into a cleaner, more centered and authentic vehicle for the One Universal Consciousness to experience itself through.

No, no one actually "smokes toad." This phrase gets tossed around a lot, but it isn't literally accurate. When people say they "smoked toad," what they mean is that they smoked (or more often, vaporized) the secretions of *Bufo alvarius*. In the 5-MeO-DMT community, this is simply referred to as bufo, toad, toad medicine, and sometimes bufo toxin. Furthermore, no one "licks" toads. While it's a fun song, Thomas Dolby's song featuring Imogen Heap, "The Toad Lickers," doesn't reference anything anyone anywhere actually does. Secretions from the toad are collected, dried, and then vaporized. And while it's cool that Neil Gaiman has one of his characters in *American Gods* vaporizing "synthetic toad skins," that's about as far off from reality as anyone can get when it comes to toad and 5-MeO-DMT.

When individuals specifically reference 5-MeO-DMT, 5-MeO, or simply 5, they are generally referring to what we could broadly classify as the "pure molecule," which might reference something either made in a lab or extracted from various plants and grasses that naturally contain this molecule. For lab-made 5-MeO-DMT, it is often referred to as "synthetic," which, while technically accurate, is often so labeled dismissively by those who's egoic preference is for what they categorize as "natural" and therefore "better." This bias, at times, is so extreme that there have been facilitators who have claimed that synthetic is completely inferior to "natural toad medicine" and even proclaimed it to be ineffective. As someone who does not share this bias, and as someone who has experienced toad medicine, extracted 5-MeO-DMT, and lab-made 5-MeO-DMT, it's my opinion that they are *all equally effective and there is no fundamental difference.*

Nonduality itself presents a challenge to this distinction between "natural" and "synthetic," because at the foundation, all of reality is experienced as one unitary being, and therefore *everything* that exists in the dualistic world is all equally God. From this perspective, there is no fundamental difference between a molecule found in "nature" or one created in a lab. They both have an identical molecular structure and are made of the same elements. It's only their origin that is different, and when it comes to chemicals, origin is largely irrelevant (unless one chooses to project various spiritual

Facilitating 5-MeO-DMT

metaphysics onto chemistry). *How* a molecule is made does not affect its efficacy in my experience and perspective.

Contrary to those who espouse the virtues of "natural over synthetic," based on online surveys and self-reporting, synthetic or pure molecule 5-MeO-DMT seems to produce fewer negative reactions and traumatic experiences than toad. Because toad contains a variety of other compounds, it is more likely to have complex interactions with an individual's biochemistry. Furthermore, it is impossible to measure exact dosage with toad, whereas it is quite simple with the pure molecule.

The treatment of toads and their possible exploitation (and harm) is something that is of interest within the 5-MeO-DMT community. Though it is illegal to collect and harvest toads in the U.S., it isn't in Mexico, and with the surging interest in "toad medicine," more and more people are going out into the desert in the monsoon months to collect toad secretions. Ironically, this situation has been made worse by making 5-MeO-DMT illegal in the U.S. Prior to Jan 19th, 2011, it was extremely easy to get the pure molecule from chemical laboratories in the U.S. All it took was going online, placing an order, and then awaiting its arrival in one's mailbox. Pretty simple. Now, however, anyone in the U.S. who wants to work with the pure molecule must turn to the black market and illegal underground, and for many, taking a trip out to the desert to catch some toads is a more ideal option. Additionally, people in Mexico now advertise the selling of toad secretions to a global marketplace on social media. It's not unreasonable to ask what effect this is having on the toads and their viability and overall well-being as individuals and as a species. Yes, it's cool that this one toad has the world's most potent entheogen in it just waiting to be squeezed out and collected and made available to humans (as a character in one of my novels expresses, "No one suspects a toad!"), but do our interests in 5-MeO-DMT justify how the toads are treated? Honestly, humans don't have a very good track record with use of natural resources, particularly in the modern era. Ethically, and practically speaking, it might be best if everyone used synthetic 5-MeO-DMT, which, to reassert, is perfectly effective and is in no way inferior to toad. We can love "nature," leave it alone, and still have access to the experience that we're looking for.

If only we could ask the toads what they think…

Which is another aspect of the toad phenomenon. There are those in the 5-MeO-DMT community who do claim to speak for the toads, or for their spirit, and consider themselves as in communication with toad intelligence. Personally, I'm someone who is thoroughly skeptical of any and all spiritual claims, and from my position as a nondualist, it's all "you" anyway, so I tend to view such claims as a form of psychological projection and transference. However, there are those who come from more of a shamanic background or perspective who like to talk about the spirit of the toad. This can be harmless, but it can also delve into spiritual doctrine or ideology, and that's where I get concerned. Once we start getting into what people "believe," things start to get messy, and metaphysics almost always come into play. If the goal is to be grounded in "what is," metaphysics is always a leap beyond "what is" to "what I think it is," and here it opens up all kinds of ontological and epistemological questions that most are not really equipped to engage with in a meaningful way other than to state their beliefs.

There are a few other terms and phrases that are worthwhile to attend to before I let you go and dive into the anthology. As different people facilitate in different ways and different contexts, the person being facilitated for might be referred to in various forms. For some, the person is a client. For others, it might be a patient. And for still others, it might be participant or even an initiate.

Furthermore, for some facilitators, the act of serving others 5-MeO-DMT is a session, and the session might be divided into several "rounds" of consuming the medicine. For others, it's a ceremony, and it might be the serving of communion. For some, it's a "medicine," and for others, it might be "drug." It all depends on context and perspective, and purported aims of the event. As the editor, I've sought to keep some uniformity in language and terms, but also allow each contributor to speak in their own language and terminology.

As editor, my hand is at play in various ways throughout these contributions. Many have come from individuals whose first language isn't English, and in some cases, editing has been extensive to make the entry easily readable in English. I've also converted any non-American English spellings into American English. In the case of transcribed interviews, these have been edited for clarity and readability. Most of us don't speak the way we write, or vice versa, so there's always massaging that happens with transcriptions to avoid incomplete sentences, interjections, run-ons, or what-have-you. Also, at times where I, as editor, felt that some background information could be relevant, have occasionally inserted clearly-labeled editor's notes.

Though I am no longer a facilitator of 5-MeO-DMT, I was, and practiced for 7 years. My take-away from what I learned in those years became the source for my book, *Entheogenic Liberation*. Anyone who isn't familiar with that work and who wants to know how I saw the practice of facilitating 5-MeO-DMT from my own perspective is welcome to read that book. Because I've written and shared about this so thoroughly and comprehensively there, I'm not including any kind of entry about facilitation from myself in this collection. This is an opportunity for others to share their views, methods, and concerns.

Facilitating 5-MeO-DMT

To conclude this introduction, I'd like to reiterate that this collection is not meant to be evaluative. This is not a book about *how one should or should not* facilitate 5-MeO-DMT. It's a book about how different people approach working with this molecule in the practice of serving others, and their concerns and perspectives. As I wrote above, being included in this collection is not an endorsement. As you'll find, there's a wide variety of perspectives and practices covered in the material that follows. There are highly-structured ceremonial procedures, and more therapeutic and non-spiritual perspectives. There are entries from individuals who have been facilitating for years, and others from those who are relatively new to their practice. It's all welcome here, as a survey of what people are doing and what they think of what they're doing. There's been no criteria for who is "qualified" to participate in this book versus who isn't.

Regardless of how anyone *thinks* facilitating 5-MeO-DMT *should happen*, the reality is that different people have different perspectives, values, and methods. And when it comes to recipients or participants, some people are very comfortable with a large group ceremony that lasts hours, and others are entirely disinterested in such. Some people like being in a group, or going on a retreat, and others would like to work one-on-one, get in, get their experience, and go home. Some people want to be part of a larger community of spiritual seekers, and others just want to overcome their childhood trauma and move on with their lives. Just as there is diversity among facilitators, so too is there among the potential clientele. There are spiritual seekers, and people seeking healing. There are those who are committed to personally discovering the truth of existence and the nature of being, and those who are curious about what all the hype about this molecule is. In my view, there's room enough for all of us. Hopefully, this collection reflects this.

In contrast with much of what is presented in this volume, upon invitation, I have included an appendix that has been submitted by "The Conclave," which is an anonymous collection of 5-MeO-DMT facilitators, educators, and enthusiasts. Here The Conclave has produced a document concerning the topic of "best practices" when it comes to the facilitation of 5-MeO-DMT. As the document recognizes that there are many approaches, it fits well with this collection, and adds some perspective on what certain members of the 5-MeO-DMT community collectively consider to fall within the scope of best facilitation for all involved.

To get us started, we'll begin where I began: with the Temple of Awakening Divinity. This is purely for the fact that it was at the Temple of Awakening Divinity that I was first able to really experience the fullness of what 5-MeO-DMT had to offer, so it seems a fitting place to begin this anthology. As I've mentioned, at the time, in 2008, this was *only* context in which I personally knew that 5-MeO-DMT was being facilitated. It's far more structured than most, and personally, it's not my style. But, it did provide me with the opportunity to explore 5-MeO-DMT over the course of an extremely transformative period of my life, and therefore, in mirror of my own experience, it is where we'll get started.

For those of you who have contributed to this collection: THANK YOU! Obviously, this book wouldn't be happening without your willingness to share, be open, and be vulnerable. I hope you have found creating your contribution to be worthwhile, enjoyable, and an opportunity to deeply express and share yourself and your passion.

For those of you reading, I hope you enjoy this collection and find it informative.

May your path lead to the only place there really is to go: yourself, in all your infinite glory.

Welcome to the Temple of Awakening Divinity

by Hal Lucious Nation

I am the Snake that giveth Knowledge & Delight and bright glory,
and stir the hearts of men with drunkenness.
To worship me take wine and strange drugs
whereof I will tell my prophet, & be drunk thereof! They shall not harm ye at all.
It is a lie, this folly against self. The exposure of innocence is a lie.
Be strong, o man! lust, enjoy all things of sense and rapture:
fear not that any God shall deny thee for this.

– Liber AL vel Legis, The Book of the Law, Ch. 2 v. 22

Beloved Initiates, Aspirants, Allies & Friends,
Greetings and Peace,

Facilitating 5-MeO-DMT

As we move powerfully into the 15th year since the inception and establishment of the Temple of Awakening Divinity, it is our sincerest honor to offer you, dear reader, this small glimpse into our process of bringing the Entheogenic Gnosis forward into humanity.

When we began this collective endeavor back in December of 2007e.v., it was our sincerest hope and belief that our sacred Work would provide a rapid and profound shift in the consciousness of humanity that would stimulate a new paradigm of enhanced spiritual awareness and expanded human consciousness. And, that this paradigm would spark a movement toward establishing global peace, responsible planetary stewardship, greater levels of love, an increased sense of community, human understanding and enhanced well-being for all life on Earth. Perhaps we were overly enthusiastic or somewhat naïve at that time. We had envisioned that, culturally, we might be a bit further along in this process by now, in terms of this global shift in consciousness. The wheels of progress continue to turn slowly, if not seemingly grinding completely to a halt.

Divine Consciousness is definitively awakening within our world. Yet, humanity, clearly entrenched within its persistent cultural, egoic ways of being, seems to be holding on even tighter than we had originally anticipated. Old habits, indeed, die hard. And the contending forces of tyranny, superstition and oppression are extremely resistant in loosening their choke hold on the personal freedoms and cognitive liberty of the greater populace. And yet, we remain ever steadfast in our commitment to assisting in fostering this global awakening; even in the face of the rapid decline in our ecological systems and the exponential rise in environmental devastation due to global warming and climate change that ravages our planet; a disastrous, ongoing world-wide pandemic and the massive trauma it has engendered, the real potential of yet another World War now unfolding within eastern Europe, once again threatening humanity with mutual nuclear destruction. And those are simply the current headlines from this week. I digress.

I am deeply grateful to my friend and ally, Dr. Martin Ball, who has traveled this path with me, nearly since its inception. It was my sincere honor to be the one to introduce him to our sacred Eucharist and to have him participate in our Temple ceremonies for over a year, leading to the publishing of his seminal work on the subject, *The Entheogenic Evolution*, which prominently features our Temple's particular approach to this Work. And while our specific practical and philosophical approaches to this Work are vastly different, this has not impacted our mutual love and respect for one another in this process.

Martin W. Ball, Ph.D., Editor

Since the inception of T.O.A.D., we have initiated nearly 6,000 individuals into this sacred practice, serving many on multiple occasions. We have conducted well over 1,500 ceremonies over that period. However, it's not about the quantity of how many we have served, but about the quality of the duty of care and service provided to them, that is so vital in this endeavor of planetary cultural awakening. Really caring about the person that has entrusted their body, mind, spirit and lives into our care is what is truly important in this individual and collective process. Cultivating real community and connection is what this has always really been about and is what we have always aspired to manifest.

We have worked tirelessly to enhance and refine our approach to this Work in the spirit of "Scientific Illuminism"; defined as the "Methods of Science & the Aim of Religion" inspired by the religious/spiritual system of Thelema. Codified by British author, occultist and mystic, Aleister Crowley, whose important early contributions in the field served to inspire and influence such psychedelic luminaries as Aldous Huxley and Timothy Leary, among others. We have opened our approach and the individual experiences of many of our community members to the realms of academia and science by actively participating in anonymous survey studies, the results of which have been featured in several important scientific research studies from institutions such as Johns Hopkins, and more recently, Columbia University. We continue to offer our insights and knowledge into the rapidly expanding psychedelic field through our active participation in conferences such as the Exploring Psychedelics Conference, the World Bufo Alvarius Congress (WBAC), the Los Angeles Medicinal Psychedelic Science Symposium (LAMPSS), and numerous other in-person and online events and fora.

We have aligned ourselves with a growing global collective of responsible, professional practitioners in the field, freely offering our experience and expertise to the development of best practices and ethical frameworks in directly assisting both practitioners and participants alike to gain a deeper understanding of how to effectively approach this Work in safe, consensual and responsible ways that enhance and optimize positive benefits while reducing challenging or negative outcomes. Additionally, we have established an in-depth and comprehensive training program, offering instruction, guidance and hands-on experience to acolytes committed to undertaking this important and sensitive transformational Work. And that Work continues...

Our "Methodologies & Protocols of the Temple of Awakening Divinity" document presented in this volume is an iterative, internal document of our spiritual organization. It is specifically meant to set out one framework within which our sacred

Facilitating 5-MeO-DMT

Eucharist can be safely and effectively administered to those seeking this uniquely potent and puissant communion. It is a continual work-in-progress, which we felt was important to begin to share more openly. Originally drafted in August of 2010e.v., to provide interested persons with a clearer overview of how and why we chose to approach this Great Work in the way that we do, it is one model. And this particular model, having been tried and tested over the last 15 years, has proven to be effective, repeatable, and scalable in terms of opening the portal of the initiate's consciousness, thus allowing them to commune directly with Source consciousness.

It specifically does not lay out the exact liturgy, theurgy, and thaumaturgy of our initiatory ceremonial rite, as we consider these to be private and confidential, only revealed directly to those who so chose to participate directly with us in the context of our Temple offering. This document was then clarified and further revised in December of 2017e.v. to provide an appropriate context of our specific approach to the Work, that was then presented to the scientific research team who conducted the anecdotal survey study that served as one of the data sets utilized in the research studies mentioned above. It was further revised in the Spring of 2020e.v. before being offered to our friend, Dr. Ball, for its inclusion here. He has subsequently made some further revisions for the sake of... brevity – something I have never been accused of, personally.

As we move forward in this collective endeavor of planetary awakening, I feel it is vital for each of us to maintain our clear perspective. Recognizing the importance of proceeding consciously and with great care, keeping our focus on being of the greatest service possible to humanity and to all life upon this garden planet. Part of our being physically incarnated within this world is for us to gain a clear understanding that there is a progressive arc to this process. And while Source consciousness exists everywhere, all-at-once, forever, right now – as individually incarnated aspects of this Source, we need to learn to take things one step at a time. Those of us who have been graced with this singularly unique experience, who have partaken of this Lamp of Invisible Light, now carry that light shining brightly within each of us. As we always have, for that Light is simply the purest Love. And yet, with the advent of this sacred communion, that Light within each of us, is now just as little bit more "switched on."

We encourage each of you, as you go forth into the world, to shine the light of your lamp as brightly as possible on everyone that you encounter. Because it is by You shining Your Light brightly, that You give everyone else permission to shine their light just as brightly. Thus, may we each serve as "per-missionaries" of that Light. May we each continue to shine brightly as we assist in this collective process of enlightening and re-enchanting our world.

Martin W. Ball, Ph.D., Editor

Brightest Blessings to Us All,

G∴H∴ Frater Hal Lucius Nation
Grand Hierophant / Chief Officiant
Temple of Awaking Divinity (T.O.A.D.)

Methodologies and Protocols:

The Temple of Awakening Divinity (T.O.A.D.) is a syncretic spiritual organization, established in December of 2007, which exists to provide a safe and practical context for the direct spiritual experience of the Divine for its participants through a ceremonial rite of Entheogenic Eucharistic communion.

While the T.O.A.D. could be viewed as a formal church or temple, and its practices deemed religious or spiritual in nature, the T.O.A.D. intentionally has no formalized dogma. In fact, it specifically eschews dogmatic constructs, as these tend to create division and generally serves to distance individuals from the direct spiritual experience of the Divine or Source, which we seek to foster and provide. Therefore, there are no formal requirements of specific religious/spiritual beliefs, affiliations or practices for those wishing to attend and/or participate in gatherings or "circles" of the T.O.A.D. Each individual seeking participation in the activities of the Temple is left to develop their own unique understanding of their particular spiritual nature and relationship with the Divine and are encouraged to develop their own particular spiritual praxis that suits their needs as they deem fit.

Some level of practical spiritual work, understanding, and context is generally useful for participation in the "Work" of the Temple. The "readiness" of any individual to take part in the Eucharist is generally left to the individual themselves as well as the discernment of a Temple "officiant" who will interview any new prospective participants before their attendance.

We refer to the direct personal experience of the Divine as the "Entheogenic Gnosis." This gnosis is achieved through personal Eucharistic communion and ingestion of a naturally occurring sacramental substance that exists within the human body and that we refer to as the "*Samadhi*"; an ancient Sanskrit term that literally means "Union with God."

The Samadhi is a naturally occurring neurochemical that exists in trace amounts within the brains, nervous systems, and bloodstreams of all mammals, including humans. It is also found within various visionary plants found throughout the world,

Facilitating 5-MeO-DMT

in addition to one known species of amphibian, *Bufo alvarius,* or Colorado River Toad (and also known as the Sonoran Desert Toad). It can also be produced synthetically within a laboratory environment. The technical chemical name for the Samadhi is 5-MeO-DMT (5-methoxy-N,N-dimethyltryptamine), an indole alkaloid tryptamine, which had been a non- scheduled substance within the U.S. until being designated as a Schedule 1 substance by the DEA, effective January 19, 2011. This Eucharist is a profoundly potent entheogenic agent that is utilized with great care and prudence by trained practitioners and only within the specific context of a safe and controlled ceremonial temple environment.

Over the course of the Temple's existence, we have utilized several varieties of this sacrament. Since 2011 we have utilized several different varieties of synthetically derived sacrament from a number of sources. All of these synthetically derived versions have been lab tested, in advance, via mass spectrometer and bio-assayed before being employed within our ceremonies. These generally ranged from 98%-100% in purity.

The T.O.A.D. provides this Eucharistic communion for the betterment and enrichment of all its participants. It is our profound spiritual belief and understanding that the gnosis provided by the Eucharist has many useful, dynamic and practical applications in the lives of those individuals who are prepared for the revelation that it conveys. This can include a "spiritual awakening" to our true purpose in life, as well as a deep connection and abiding understanding of our true spiritual natures and our personal relationship with, and direct experience of the Divine. Additionally, the Eucharist can, in some cases, facilitate practical healing on a variety of levels including the physical, emotional, psychological, and spiritual.

The officiants of the T.O.A.D. are considered as trusted guides and guardians, charged with the specific sacred duty of creating a safe, solid and sacred container (The Grail) within which the Eucharist can be safely and effectively administered. Some are trained healers in a variety of disciplines. Officiants are effectively responsible for overseeing the wellbeing of each "communicant" and being of service to them in whatever way may be necessary – both during and after the ceremony proper. This can include "holding space" and conscious presence, deep listening, consultations and dialog with communicants before, during and sometimes well after the ceremony has concluded. We are not "teachers or gurus," though we may provide instruction and guidance to those within our community whom we serve.

While we may be considered as a "priestcraft" as such, we do not in any way serve as intermediaries between communicants and Source. Instead, we are responsible for co-creating an effective sacred context for each communicant to experience Source directly. We are at pains to ensure that our important Work does not in any way become a cult of personality or an incestuous clique. We maintain appropriate boundaries during the Work of the ceremony and are completely responsible for all aspects of appropriate decorum and safety during these ceremonies.

Optimally, each standard celebration of the communion, which we refer to as a "Deep Dive," will consist of a maximum of between 6-8 attendees or participants. Of these a total of 5 participants or "communicants," generally, will be invited to receive the communion. The 1-3 remaining participants being the chief officiant and a healer/assistant and/or "sponsor" who will generally not communicate but assist to facilitate and hold space for those communicating. Participation in this manner is considered as an act of service, which is at the very foundation of the Work we do. All communicants prior to receiving initiation are referred to as "aspirants." After receiving the Eucharist and being duly anointed, they are considered "initiates" and members of the T.O.A.D. for life, regardless of their continued participation. Officiants generally do not partake of the sacrament in ceremony; however, if an officiant chooses to partake in the Eucharist at a given gathering, they will be the last to do so. In organizing circles of the T.O.A.D., organizers shall seek to establish an effective gender balance among those participating whenever possible.

The gnosis provided by the Eucharist generates an ontological shift in the consciousness of the communicant that can never be taken away by another. While the memory of the experience may fade over time, we hold that the shift in consciousness engendered by the Eucharist causes physical and psychic changes within the initiate that will last throughout the individual's lifetime and activates processes that the individual will either choose to integrate into their lives or ignore. The choice to proceed further in the Work of Transformation is wholly theirs.

Attendance at ceremonial "circles" of the T.O.A.D. is by invitation only. Each new aspirant is then screened for suitability and contacted directly via telephone by a Temple officiant with an introductory phone call. If they express interest in participation, they are given a verbal health screening before their attendance. Once an initial contact has been made the aspirant is provided with an "Introductory Information" e-mail including a general set of guidelines for their participation, several resources documents, and web links with a significant amount of detailed information for their review beforehand.

It is important to note that anyone who is invited to attend a gathering of the T.O.A.D. is NEVER required to take part in the communion of the Eucharist, although it is generally their intention to do so. In fact, those invited to attend are encouraged to come with an open heart and mind in order to participate in the ceremony, actively "holding space" for those who communicate. While it is generally expected that those

Facilitating 5-MeO-DMT

attending will hold the intention of communicating, it is ALWAYS left up to the individual to choose whether participation in the communion is right for them. No one is ever compelled, coerced or pressured into receiving the Eucharist as this would be fundamentally antithetical to the principles of our Work.

Before participation in our ceremonial circle, each new aspirant is required to attend one of our Orientation circles, which generally last about 2 hours. The Orientation covers a general history of the use of entheogenic sacraments within various spiritual traditions, specific information on the sacrament of 5-MeO-DMT itself, including details on: duration of the experience, sourcing of the sacrament, physical & psychological effects of the sacrament, the process of ego dissolution, dosing protocol, possible after-effects & side-effects, as well as functional instructions on dealing with "shadow" or challenging aspects of the Work. There is also significant information provided on the details of and the overall structure and contextualization of the ceremony itself.

All those attending gatherings of the T.O.A.D. will be expected to hold space and actively witness each communicant during their reception of the Eucharist as part of their participation. This generally requires quiet, focused concentration and "deep presence" on the part of all those in attendance for the duration of the gathering. This effectively involves actively witnessing each communicant's process without projecting any subconscious (egoic) content onto the communicant no matter what one may witness occurring.

This includes giving communicants who are in state plenty of physical space and not intruding in any way on their process including any unnecessary talking, movement or actions during their process. It also demands being conscious and paying close attention to any subtle instructions or cues that may be given by the officiant during communication. Often, the nature of the communion can bring up an intensely powerful reaction within the communicant. It is vitally important for those witnessing this process not to assume that they know what may be transpiring within the consciousness of the communicant and to give the officiant the necessary space and benefit of the doubt in handing whatever may arise. Often, those witnessing may feel the urge, or be directly called upon by the communicant, to provide physical touch or some form of healing modality. Witnesses are welcome, when requested, to provide such acts of service; however, they are asked to use discretion, tact and prudence in doing so and are encouraged to work closely with the officiant when the occasion arises. Physically touching a communicant during their process should only occur if specifically requested and should immediately cease when any indication that it is no longer required or desired is given.

Martin W. Ball, Ph.D., Editor

The sacred communion practiced within our Temples is one of incredible intimacy, great depth, and beauty. It can also be quite powerful and challenging for some. We therefore work diligently to create an environment of safety, comfort, and well-being where all communicants can feel held and supported within a place of great sensitivity and vulnerability. As the nature of the Divine Gnosis within the Temple is one of deep and abiding Love, creating a safe and conducive environment for the free and unrestricted expression of that Love is a high priority and of major importance. We have found that the Eucharistic experience produces what could be considered a full "Kundalini" release within many (if not most) communicants and deeply opens up the psyche in a profound way. This can manifest in an extremely sensual (sometimes sexual) manner. This can and has created a highly charged sensual atmosphere within the Temple precincts.

Therefore, appropriate conduct and decorum within such an environment demands a high level of emotional literacy and social maturity on behalf of all those participating in order to respect the personal boundaries of communicants, as well as to guard those whose sensitive psyches are opened within the process.

Each individual's experience of the Eucharist is distinctly unique and yet universal in scope. In most cases the communicant's experience manifests smoothly and without difficulty. However, the Samadhi has the dynamic ability to evoke and release long-suppressed psychic content and complexes, as well as bringing any trauma that the individual may be carrying to the surface. No matter how the experience may manifest for an individual communicant, whatever may come up for them, is always welcome and received with great presence, care and compassion. Officiants are prepared to assist individuals who may experience any challenges or difficulties, such as fear or intense emotional states, that may arise during the course of their experience. This can and often does include compassionate vocal coaching, psychic clearing, physical touch, as necessary or requested and/or other specific healing modalities as available and needed.

There are four effective stages to the process of participation in the communion of the T.O.A.D. They are as follows:

Stage 1: Preparation:

The social, spiritual, emotional, intellectual, etc., training and preparation of each individual aspirant wishing to receive communion through the T.O.A.D. is exclusively left up to the individual. The T.O.A.D. requires no particular spiritual belief(s), practice(s) or "level of spiritual attainment" for participation. Some level of practical

Facilitating 5-MeO-DMT

spiritual work and understanding is preferred and generally expected for participation in the Work of the Temple; however, one could be an agnostic or atheist and request an opportunity to participate. While participation in the rites of the Temple is invitational, we do not discriminate in any way regarding race, religion, creed, class, sexual orientation, gender identity, etc. We also do not ask those wishing to attend to "believe" anything, but to only participate in our ceremony, "receive" the Eucharist, and experience the Divine directly for themselves. They can then formulate any beliefs or understandings based on their direct spiritual experience.

Stage 2: Initiation & Communion:

The "Initiation of Communion" is the active receiving of the Eucharist itself. Communion, ultimately, is the core of the "Great Work," which we do, requiring no philosophical or dogmatic explanation. The Eucharist itself provides each communicant with the Gnosis. Each initiate is then charged with integrating that Gnosis by the "light of their own lamps" and/or with additional assistance of an officiant of the Temple if and as they so choose.

Once the temple has been opened (see below for specific list of ceremonial elements and procedures), the individuals participating self-select who will partake of the sacrament or "commune" first. The Temple is suited with a soft mattress, futon or similar padding (*The Launching Pad*). This "pad" should be as low to the floor as possible yet thick enough to provide adequate comfort, support and safety. Each communicant, in their turn, is instructed to lay down comfortably on their back with their legs slightly apart and arms wide open. We have found that this is generally the best position for going into state. They are given an opportunity to relax and begin a process of relaxed, deep breathing while the officiant prepares "*The Lamp.*" Soft music composed specifically to assist with greater relaxation is played throughout and serves as an important component of the experience as well as covering any background noise that may arise. The choice of music is critical to the process, and anything utilized should have no real melody or rhythm. Soft ambient music serves best.

The other participants array themselves around the launching pad, allowing for adequate distance; each having been instructed within the Orientation in the effective methods for *"holding space."* Once the Lamp is prepared it is ceremoniously presented to each communicant individually; each having been instructed on the appropriate methods of inhalation. Once the inhalation is complete, the communicant is gently instructed to lay back and relax, to hold the sacrament in as long as is comfortably possible, to exhale when ready and prepare to *"surrender and remember to breathe."* Their experience unfolds as it will, while space is being held for the communicant throughout the process, which generally lasts from 35-45 minutes. Close to the 35-minute mark the officiant does a simple *"check in"* with the communicant asking, *"How are you feeling?,"* in order to adequately gauge where they are at in their internal process. By this time, the communicant is generally already integrating their egoic structure quite naturally. They are assisted in this initial integration process by the offering of sacred *"Prasad"*; the Sanskrit word for a material offering of food generally offered at shrines within the Hindu tradition. This short ceremonial "welcoming" feast of sweet and savory finger foods assists in very effectively "grounding" the new initiate into their physical body and psyche.

Stage 3: Integration:

Officiants of the Temple work diligently with initiate members who may need additional assistance in their integration process. This means taking time within the ceremony itself to ensure that each participant is integrated and well "grounded" after receiving the Eucharist and before departing the Temple location. Additionally, the Temple provides regular Integration Circles to assist new and returning initiates in effectively integrating their initiation experience into their lives.

Stage 4: Evangelism:

The Entheogenic Gnosis, by its very nature, generally has a significant impact on the life of the new initiate. Many are deeply inspired by the profound beauty and magnitude of ontological shift and deep insights that this gnosis confers. Therefore, it is not uncommon for initiates to want to share their experience with those that they love. Frequently, new initiates will invite their friends and family members to participate in our activities. We recognize this enthusiasm and denote it by its appropriate term: "evangelism." While this term has come to be associated with spreading the Christian gospel, we recognize it for its etymological meaning from the original Greek, which translates as: "the messenger of good news." And, while we encourage our members to share their experience with those they know well, we specifically request and encourage them to do so with tact, prudence, and discretion to guard our Work and to keep it safe and sacred. We are also at pains never to proselytize, publicize, advertise or attempt to convince anyone that this Work is "right" for them. We work on the general principle of "attraction rather than promotion."

FACILITATING 5-MEO-DMT

While there are always some potential challenges or risks when engaging with powerful entheogenic sacraments, it is of primary importance to the officiants of the T.O.A.D. to provide a safe and protected environment and context, both during and after the ceremonial Eucharist, to ensure that the outcome of the communion is of highest benefit and greatest good to all those participating.

Every effort shall be made to ensure the safety (physical, psychological, emotional, social, etc.) of those participating in the Eucharist. This means conferring with each proposed communicant in a brief interview process or screening, generally conducted by telephone, before participation to ensure preparedness and suitability for attendance. This includes a general intake and analysis of the individual's emotional, psychological and physical well-being.

None of the specific Work within the Temple should be shared in an open, cavalier or casual manner. The privacy of those participating should be considered sacrosanct. The identities of those present, their experiences, and the location of our activities should never be shared with others. The nature of the communion is considered initiatory, so specific details of the ceremony itself should also not be shared with others.

Participants in the activities of the Temple are expected to be adults (generally viewed as at least 21 years of age in the U.S.). A particular level of social, psychological and spiritual maturity is also taken into consideration when assessing a participant's preparedness to receive the Eucharist.

Participants must be in good physical and mental health before participating in the Eucharist. This includes our screening for pre-existing cardio-vascular disease, significant high blood-pressure, respiratory disorders, stroke or other neurological conditions. We also screen for significant food allergies or other conditions that could be exacerbated by participation in the Eucharist. We also screen for any history of psychological conditions including schizophrenia, psychosis, manic-depression or bi-polar disorder, PTSD, OCD ... etc. Although some conditions such as PSTD and depression may be benefitted by participation, these considerations are made very carefully, and on a case-by-case basis. Should any concerns arise they are clearly and openly communicated with the approaching aspirant during the screening. All information provided by potential aspirants is considered completely private and confidential. On occasion officiants may informally consult with medical professionals in making their determinations.

In any event, no person taking anti-depressant medications, specifically SSRI's and MAOI's, should partake of the communion, as these medications are contraindicated with the Eucharist and could produce potentially adverse effects. This last criterion is mandatory and there are no exceptions. Those who have taken such medications should wait a minimum period of time (generally 15-60 days, depending on medication) before participating, and it is recommended that their titration process from these medicines be done under supervision of a qualified health practitioner. Also, women who are pregnant should not participate in the communion as it easily crosses the placenta into the developing fetus. Expectant mothers are honored and welcome to attend, hold space, and participate within our ceremonies without the necessity of partaking in the Eucharist.

While we have found that there are generally no contraindications or negative interactions with specific foods, alcohol, tobacco, cannabis, etc., it is generally recommended that those who will be partaking in the communion refrain from drinking alcohol or taking other substances on the day before, as well as the day of the gathering, in order to keep their consciousness as clear as possible. Regarding food consumption, there are no specific restrictions or "dietas" suggested; however, we highly recommend those attending to eat lightly on the day of the ceremony and conclude any meals at least 1 hour before their arrival. As a common courtesy, it is also requested that individuals attending refrain from smoking tobacco or other herb products for several hours prior to and for the duration of the gathering for the general benefit of all those participating.

There are no specific requirements in terms of appropriate dress for attendance at the Temple; however, it is recommended that those participating dress comfortably with minimal jewelry and nothing that is physically encumbering or restrictive. Meditation and/or yoga wear works very well. Yoga pants are recommended for woman as opposed to skirts or dresses. A good general guideline is to dress as you would for attending sacred ceremony. Also, the use of heavy perfumes, oils or other aromatics is discouraged as these may affect the sensitivities of others in the group.

The Eucharistic experience generally lasts from anywhere from 35 minutes to an hour for each individual communicant. The average duration of the experience for most is about 45 minutes. However, each individual is uniquely different; especially when it comes to the reintegration of the ego. No one is ever rushed to complete their experience and we recognize that some may need additional time to fully process their experience to conclusion. This means that, with the ceremonial opening and closing, our Temple gatherings with the maximum number of participants lasts from 6 – 7 hours (and follows the ceremonial process outlined below). Officiants are responsible for the flow and timeliness of the ceremony and may choose, when absolutely necessary, to gently move an initiate who may still be integrating to a convenient place

Facilitating 5-MeO-DMT

within or adjacent to the Temple space, with someone to hold space for them, in order for them to fully complete their integration process.

The Temple generally offers a facilitated Integration Circle at the end of each series of ceremonial circles and on a quarterly basis at our home Temple, in order to assist new initiates in their process and to ensure that they are effectively integrating their initiation. We also provide each new initiate with an "Integration & Grounding" document with specific details and additional information to assist them with their integration process post ceremony.

In some cases, individual initiates may experience spontaneous "reactivations" of the Samadhi experience. When this occurs, it is generally during sleep periods. This can be alarming for some in the instances when it does occur. An experienced officiant or senior initiate can assist in further processing with an initiate, as necessary, during this period. In our experience, these kinds of episodes may last a few days to upwards of a week or more after the communion is received. We have generally found that what is required is further dialog, reassurance, and a recommended regimen of one of more of the following: Acupuncture, bodywork, soaking & steaming, grounding foods, rigorous exercise, being held, psychotherapy, voice dialog and/or coaching, etc. This kind of follow up generally assists new initiates in effectively integrating their experience of the Eucharist.

The preparation for each ceremonial circle actually begins with the initial communications with each participant and includes all interface (personal, phone, e-mail, etc.) with the aspirant until they arrive at our Temple door. Preparation also includes appropriate Orientation and the physical set up of the Temple, further preparation of the physical environment in advance of arrivals as well as the psycho-spiritual and practical preparation of any officiants and/or assistants in advance of the ceremony.

Attendees are each welcomed warmly into the temple space by the officiant and introduced to the other attendees if they have not yet met. The introduction consists of sharing some basic background information about the Temple and it's Work with the attendees; the nature of the Eucharist experience itself, and a basic explanation of the ceremony and how the evening will flow, as well as how long participants can expect to be there. It may also include some symbolic explanations about the ritual and/or its components and any symbol sets utilized within the ritual. It also gives an opportunity for participants to ask any remaining questions they may have and/or have any last-minute concerns addressed.

The procedure at the T.O.A.D. follows a standard format that participants can expect for each communion with each of the following ritual stages: Opening

Ceremony, Banishing Ritual, Purification of the Space and Participants, Consecration, Check In, General Invocation, Communion (at this point, each participant will be offered the opportunity to partake of the scared communion of the Samadhi), Prasad (offered after each communion per participant), Concluding Invocation/Release of the Light, Check Out, Conveyance of "the Mysteries," Benediction.

Since the Temple's inception we have realized that integration is a vital and necessary aspect of our sacred Work. To that end, beginning in early 2010, we began hosting formal, facilitated "Integration Circles" in order to accommodate this process and to assist initiate members who require and request deeper participation in this process. Generally, these gatherings are offered at the end of a particular series of ceremonial circles when we travel to various major population centers where our communities exist. We also generally offer these on a quarterly basis at our home Temple location.

It is our general rule to make ourselves available to these new initiates, either in person or via telephone, to assist them in their integration process. We may also choose to enlist the new initiate's sponsor in this process or refer them to other senior initiates of the Temple who may have specific personal experience, expertise or prowess in a specific area or with a specific issue.

Standard Dosing Protocols of The Temple of Awakening Divinity:

The following represents the standard sacramental dosing protocol for inducing what we refer to as a "Full-Release" entheogenic experience and has been effectively utilized for over 5 years within the Temple and should provide a useful guideline for those working with our sacred Eucharist.

The following applies either to use of high-grade (90-100% pure) extracts or synthetically derived material, in free-base form. It should also be noted that the T.O.A.D. uses a very specifically crafted alchemical administrative device known as "The Lamp of Invisible Light" which is a custom crafted, argon gas, piston vaporizer utilized to administer highly accurate doses of this sacrament in the most efficient manner possible. While Dr. Ralph Metzner, in his book, *The Toad and the Jaguar*, speculates that an individual's body weight (milligram per kilogram) is a factor in determining effective minimal dosage (EMD), our research has shown this not to be the case. We have found that appropriate effective dosing with 5-MeO-DMT is much more dependent on the individual's physical and mental ability to process the molecule and their willingness to surrender fully into the entheogenic experience that it engenders. A solid understanding of the individual's prior history with entheogenic

FACILITATING 5-MEO-DMT

substances is a key factor in determining precise effective dose. We have also found that it is best to err on the side of providing a slightly lower dose as the ability to provide a second (or even a third) subsequent dose will generally provide the desired result and the effects are definitively cumulative.

Lower Dose Range:

For those who have little to no experience with psychoactive substances it is highly recommended to start in the lower dose ranges. This is generally between 5-7 milligrams.

Medium Dose Range:

For those who have moderate experience with psychoactive substances (perhaps some psilocybin, LSD or MDMA experience) and are generally familiar with and can navigate other psychoactives effectively, a medium dose range may prove more optimal. Somewhere between the 8-12 milligram range has proved sufficient.

Higher Dose Range:

For those who have a good deal of experience with other psychoactive substances (perhaps a regular ayahuasca practice or have experience with higher dose ranges of LSD or psilocybin) the suggested dose range is between 13-20+ milligrams. It must be noted that in higher dose ranges it is generally optimal to start on the lower end of the scale (13-15mg) and work up progressively and prudently.

Subsequent Dosing:

It will be readily apparent if a participant needs or can handle a subsequent dose. In most cases this will not be necessary if the protocol has been effectively followed. However, there are those who can effectively process large amounts of tryptamine and we have found that if the participant can indicate that they would like more sacrament (there are several approaches for doing this) that any subsequent dose should be reduced by 1/3.

Drinking tea with God and the Path to Surrender

by Magda Leszczynska

Becoming a detached observer of the inner landscape is one of the most profound lessons of all entheogens in my experience. It was never my desire to serve the medicine, and I was strongly discouraged from stepping into that role for others. My deepest wish working with medicines was to experience and heal myself, and to let go of my existential story, conditioning, and patterns of the mind.

I lived with psychosis for almost 20 years and spent another 20 years healing myself with the help of a spiritual teacher and shamanic training that gave me the tools of breathwork, extractions, illuminations, and shadow work. At that time, I practiced diligently and full-heartedly without any inclination for psychedelics, but rather deep disregard and judgement for all of them being just "drugs"!

For many years I suffered from insomnia and physical pain that could only be calmed down by a strong cocktail of opioids at the ER department. Pain and lack of sleep humbled me to become open to a prescription of cannabis. This teacher worked with me for 5 years in preparation for shifting directly into 5-MeO-DMT.

If not for fear-driven psychosis with suicidal ideation and raging anger or deep sadness as the only options for emotional self-expression, I would have not looked into medicines to later find equanimity: the state of mind of neither expressing approval or disapproval, judgement or praise, fear or love, but observing all and allowing all to exist side-by-side and having no preference for either experience. The understanding of equanimity was consciously emerging over a long period of time. The process was sped-up with psychedelics and understanding of ego transformation and shadow death. There is a strong misconception and misunderstanding of ego death which truly is a shadow death. It is by transforming and transcending our shadows that we reshape our ego. The ego is a guide and programming as one of our facets we live with here on Earth. Ego can be transformed into more a functional and practical self as we heal ourselves more and more deeply.

Deep emotional and physical pain were the means into trusting something beyond me when I said YES to 5-MeO-DMT. In letting go of control and fear I found freedom from the story, the patterns, and all the self-created obstacles I was living in. If not for letting go of all I knew, I would have not found surrender and the ability to embrace the unknown, that, in turn, embraced me with love and compassion.

The medicine, 5-MeO-DMT was introduced to me by Tantra practitioner I worked with for five months. It felt like a very natural step on my healing journey and the offer was greeted as a last chance and possibility to let go of trauma and suicidal ideation. There was no doubt in my mind that I was done with life, and a lot of speculations roamed through my head that this "medicine" was just a big hoax! The doubt about the medicine grew exponentially bigger when I was asked just before my first inhale whether I wanted to experience Tantric orgasm during my journey. I declined, offering the medicine the opportunity to introduce itself to me in its natural form.

After my first experience, I was relieved, but also very deeply disappointed. I didn't expect to walk a full circle back to my childhood to feel the infinite field of energy called love where I created butterflies and had experienced my presence in its purest state of being. What was I expecting to feel? I truly don't know, but my ego-self had me prepared to expect something that I didn't know or didn't remember already. In that journey I also experienced the infinite continuum of life in many different forms and timelines from here now to forever, as only one of endless possibilities of self-expression. The journey to go back in time was as available as the journey to move forward in the space where time doesn't exist, and everything is happening

FACILITATING 5-MEO-DMT

simultaneously within me, for me, with me, and around me. All that, simply, is an ecstatic expression of my being. At that point I was wondering what Tantric orgasm may feel like with 5-MeO-DMT and regretted declining it. Maybe I had refused to really know what I was looking for, I thought to myself minutes after returning to my body and to human consciousness. Another strong thought was the realization that there is either something very wrong with me, or that I am perfectly normal, and I just had to fight to accept the truth I knew all my life.

Karma, also known as unresolved self, cords, or simply the marvel of existence, is one of the mothers of life and the very spark of curiosity propelling existence forward. After all, we are very curious beings in need of companionship, presence of others, and being witnessed and acknowledged. Karma is simply fulfilling our dream of not being alone, and the opportunity to fall in love with ourselves over and over again presents itself in many different ways. The love we seek is seeking us to love itself back through and with us once we surrender to it.

The lesson in my first journey was simple, familiar, and annoying at the same time. I am that I am, and to move out of the mess I had created for myself, I needed to go right through it. I booked another session shortly after the first one to go deeper into the process of acceptance.

It was very apparent from my first journey that the medicine itself is the spark that ignites the knowing, the experience, the memory and realizations within. It was also very obvious that the healing process consists of infinite opportunity of choices and changes that I can make in my life based on my current level of consciousness. Without self-judgement, the level of consciousness fluctuates, changing the trajectory of my soul significantly, but never permanently, always leaving choice as an option. The 5-MeO-DMT was merciless by offering me the truth that I am the dis-ease, the healing process, and the healed version of myself, all at the same time. Remembering my childhood ability to shift my conscious presence into different dimensions and states of being, the choice of what I wanted to experience, manifest, embrace deeper, and simply experience myself as, was within my conscious ability to do so right now and always. As much as the choice was unfolding fully within, so was the temptation of resistance and doubt. "Which wolf will win within me grandpa? The white one that is loving kindness and compassion, or the black one who is always angry, frustrated, and unkind to others?" asked a young man who just discovered qualities of polar opposites within himself. "The one you feed more will grow stronger," said grandpa!

In the last three years I've had close to 40 journeys with all different psychedelic medicines, where over 25 of those journeys were with bufo or 5-MeO-DMT. There was strong interest in 5-MeO-DMT, but I didn't particularly seek this medicine or the frequency I journeyed with it, so perhaps the medicine itself was calling me ...

I will correct myself here! I was introduced in 2005 to the Quechuan language of the Inca people while studying shamanism. Inca people don't have a singular pronoun "you" in their language. The equivalent to "How are you today?" is "How is the village inside (you) doing today?" The perception of "I" perhaps was invented by modern culture and civilization to denote individuation and self-awareness in the form of separation. It seems logical to assume that according to Quechuan language, the medicine lived and is an integral part of my village I was born with and was calling me within. So therefore, the medicine and I were seeking each other as there is never one-sided seeking or interest in anything since I am also what is seeking me, and I am the result of the union, the future outcome merged within me. I got curious why this medicine was the most available for me to experience and get familiar with, or a better approach to it is: I got curious why I made this medicine the most available for myself to experience and get familiar with. Also, there is a deep knowing that my being has equipped me with all I needed on my journey on Earth.

The flavor of 5-MeO-DMT as a teacher is kind, multidimensional, and patiently persistent. Having tea with God is simply drinking God from cup-God with God and talking about the weather-God, the future-God, the healing-God, and all God-related aspects including nothing-God, silence-God, wish-God, joy-God, etc. ...

The following trip report was my first conscious experience with preparation and participation, but my third journey with 5-MeO-DMT:

> *I took a month to prepare for this encounter with the 5!*
>
> *Breathwork, meditation, fasting, prayer, awareness, and being in the moment were my daily staples. Additionally, I got a long ceremony prep list for 3 days prior, so I followed it.*
>
> *I was very nervous going in. Some of it was plain and simple fear! There was also anticipation, reluctance, negative self-talk, wounded self, healer, drama, along with perseverance, courage and curiosity. Yes, I invited all of me to partake this journey! It was a family trip!*
>
> *In a lovely space of music codes, magic tea, and getting to know each other through conversation, I felt a big YES in my whole body to simply surrender and receive.*
>
> *I was ready.*
>
> *Sipping slowly, the vape hit me really hard and I couldn't complete the inhale as explained prior. Drifting in and out of consciousness, whiteouts, visions and realizations, I had only partial awareness of what was happening, but with absolutely*

Facilitating 5-MeO-DMT

no say which way to go, the medicine took over my willpower and senses! It was the only way to proceed as I had trained myself in self-control very well over 5 decades! I would travel "horizontally" and "vertically" through time and space, and also time and space would travel to meet me where I was, with a gift of awareness. All of them presented as different consciousnesses infused with their unique purpose of function. The consciousness of the one and only WHOLE-ME would split into individualized "pockets" of intentional "meaning" to make interpretations of feelings, visuals, senses, awareness, flow, and fluidity possible for me to capture as more dissectible, manageable and translatable take-away fitting into constraints of my human brain and 3D reality, or where I am in my personal and spiritual growth. This meant slowing down to almost a stop (which is absolutely impossible!) the fluidity and constant movement of all particles, the energy that I am. This is the state of Qi I used to teach in Chinese Medicine. The Qi is constantly active, moving, and reorganizing itself within itself and within the form it was representing for familiarity and simplicity for me to understand. I taught Chinese Medicine for over 10 years with great passion for its mysterious meanings. I was called the best teacher at the Academy. I humbly admit, I understood very little! Since my first trip with the Medicine nine months ago, the Tao itself taught me about Chinese Medicine. It showed me its beginning, flow, the seed of all creation. It showed me myself as the Tao, the beginning of my Universe. As I looked at the Qi/energy in constant shift yet representing itself in a slowed-down motion for familiarity and simplicity for me to understand, I remembered how I created butterflies and birds from golden energy when I was 3 years old. It came to me that slowing down the energy to a specific frequency with a specific intention was the manifestation of particular life form. It was a concept I clearly understood in childhood but had forgotten for decades!

All those visions, memories, connections, and realizations happened within just a few short minutes.

Whiteouts and states of in-and-out-of-consciousness, as merging with One and becoming separate, I would wake up in new "environments" and awareness in different parts of experiencing myself. The sacred movie of past events in my life was playing right in front of me. I was in a super-fast forward through the past and present and through the future into the now mode. There was no confusion in that state, as I was not experiencing time and space until the very moment of recognizing it as so! It was clearly the recapitulation of my life before death.

At one point, things came to a halt! In front of me I saw my darkness (D), who's my partner (in an absolutely pure meaning of this word), my teacher, and guide. The pathfinder to the light through "stuff" called life on Earth, along with my charming, sensitive, enthusiastic, loving and curious 3-year-old light (L). As an observer I heard a conversation through feelings between the two:

D: How many lessons do I have to create for you to learn (grow up)?
L: I'm just fine, I don't feel like being different (growing up)
D: I worked so hard and I feel unappreciated!
L: What does it mean?
As the darkness chose not to say that she feels unloved... so she said:
D: I can come up with a strategy for you as my master plan to feel complete and fulfilled myself!

The light was just staring at the darkness with amusement, totally not understanding the concept and need to be complete and fulfilled!

It hit me; this is my internal daily dialogue in 3D mind structure: I don't want to grow up; there are responsibilities to carry! I don't want to create my reality; the naïveté is blissful! I don't like to surrender and become a slave... I thought to myself.

The Medicine took me through dimensions going up, seeing white light within everything and myself but knowing that where I was going was the ultimate meeting of myself in my grandest, limitless, and nondual form that exists.

Every step of the journey I would be asked to let go, to surrender deeper and deeper, over and over, into absolutely no resistance to experience of the pure magic of myself, the absolute miracle that I Am, pure pleasure through unbelievable orgasmic constant bliss into the essence of it infusing all that exists...

This is when the last struggle presented itself. I had a feeling offering to open my heart! It was torture! I rather die, I heard, and at the same time, I realized who was speaking... The tug of war, the internal conflict, the perception of control... My consciousness was flipping, from me wanting to surrender to me wanting to control. From me who originally said YES to myself stuck in individualization, the ego self who wants to create a separate universe, a better life for me and myself, that I could ever have by surrendering to the unknown... As this war was unfolding within myself, I felt physical pain in my chest while being in pure energy form. A thought, a spark of intelligence, spoke in the language of love to everything within me: we all are one! In this very moment, my heart exploded into an infinite number of particles of pure white light and the essence beyond bliss infusing all that exists...

This was the opening of my heart chakra, which I felt physically and energetically at the same time. The shift was dramatic, but integration was fluid and instantaneous, as the experience simply brought me back to what I remembered feeling and knowing.

Facilitating 5-MeO-DMT

The following encounter with 5-MeO-DMT recounted below brought deep understanding of my inner landscape. While ET abductions were an integral part of my childhood experiences, most of them happened as a feeling of an altered state of consciousness. In one instance, I was guided to enter McDonald's and ask for the largest Coke they had. When I refused, the request came through my mouth without my control of the words. It was a large 2L bucket of Coke. For someone who doesn't drink pop, this was a challenge, but when I started feeling the familiar shift in my body, I knew immediately that I was leaving 3D and drank the Coke in 30 seconds bottoms up!!! The Coke was the fuel my body needed to protect itself from disintegration. Many years later and 24 hrs after sitting with 5-MeO-DMT, I had a similar, but much longer, experience lasting 40 minutes. Here is what happened:

Next morning after the ceremony I followed with my morning routine of breath and movement. There were further realizations and releases, so I allowed this process until it felt complete. At 2 pm I left the Airbnb in the direction of the train station, which was about 50-minute walking distance.

I heard a voice inside, my usual guide, suggesting not to close myself off by listening to music on headphones, but have my sunglasses on and walk slowly on the shaded side of the street with attention to feelings inside.

I stepped into a busy and rather strangely unfamiliar flavor of the city! Once I chose major streets to maneuver through, I opened myself to presence. The very first person approaching me stopped and said in a loud and vibrant voice, "You are so beautiful." My instinct was, as usual, to keep on walking, but instead I stopped and said, "Thank you!" We both smiled and moved on. The importance in this encounter was for me to realize that I was not in control of my reactions. There was a presence, a force, inside me that guided me, and I was to fully surrender to it! It was a familiar feeling from childhood abductions; definitely a little altered, but grounded and conscious at the same time. I wanted to give myself a semi-negative thought of, "Here we go again," but the thought evaporated, leaving conscious awareness of my intention, but morphing into clear, sunny nothing! Its absence made me feel happy and aware of the process in my head! Consciously psychedelic-minded, I felt a giggle of that contradiction, so I giggled along, realizing that WE giggled together. There was more than "I" on the inside. Every word was consciously aware of its own meaning, definition, and consciously present, having discussions with other words in form of a sentence that my brain would normally understand with a limited number of translations. My brain became supple enough to let go of worry and control in a projected pretence to save ME! The mind became an observer.

I took a few steps and felt conflicting feelings of knowing where I was, the streets I was walking on, but at the same time, a notion that I hadn't been there before! Everything about the city was different. Every few steps I would turn 360 degrees to look around and absorb what I was seeing and hearing, the unfamiliarity of the surrounding that carried the street names I have walked on before! The visual and auditory information was passing through my skin rather than my sense organs. I was feeling visuals and feeling sounds. Smelling and tasting also came through every cell in my body.

I was taken to other dimensions with my physical body before, I started to wonder and even asked myself, "Where am I?" Is the 5-MeO-DMT able to prevent my body from disintegration? Is it able to change my brain chemistry and DNA structure for my human body to become elastic and a "screen door" like to move time, space, and the whole rainbow of different frequencies through me with ease?

Fear was hardly ever a part of my experience with abductions, but awareness and conscious processing without the ability to stop or change my experience was always a sure sign that I was not in 3D reality.

The streets were filled with people with mental challenges, addiction problems, prostitution, naked bodies sleeping on the grass, malnourished people sitting on benches smoking cigarettes and having blank stares in their eyes. Ghosts were roaming between the living. Looking for nothing, wanting nothing but fully surrendering to lack of ability to be conscious. These were dissolving consciousnesses! Becoming deeply unaware of existence, life would bring them back as energies without consciousness back into oneness.

Spirits were jumping out from by-passers into me and scanning my internal landscape, coming out with a word or two with their observations. "Nice," said one. "I wouldn't be able to connect here," said another spirit popping quickly out from my body.

I had no resistance or fear, I surrendered deeper and deeper into this experience I called conscious psychosis via observing and nonparticipation.

Houses and buildings looked like prisons; there was no room for people to self-express or community to build. It felt that the collective disease permeated the soul of this city. I looked at the architecture and wondered about functionality and adherence to universal laws of freedom and conscious liberation of existence for its sheer pleasure to experience itself. What surprised me was the fact that I had no pity and no judgement about it besides the observations. What's more, I had absolute admiration for life the way it was... I had indifference in my heart with at most respect for all I observed.

A feeling gentler than a whisper, more subtle than a breeze, entered my awareness and left almost silent words and an invisible note of the most profound, yet so obvious, revelation: what if this is all you, Magda? All you are and have created? All

Facilitating 5-MeO-DMT

you have experienced within yourself so deeply and profoundly... This is unity, this is oneness, nondual reality that is you...

I stood there expanding into every human I met that day, each tree and each blade of the grass, and each grain of sand, the air, the sky... I allowed tears to roll down on my face and a smile to stretch from ear to ear! I felt caressed and cared for by my mind, the "I" within my universe, the shadows, the mentally challenged, and all the unhealed ones within my psyche who waited for me to wake up! I'd lived in this city all my life, expressing myself as unhealed aspects of myself.

A feeling of profound, blissful love flooded my existence for every person I met, every soul I saw, every ghost that passed by or entered me with warmth and gentleness or pure curiosity. I loved myself infinitely in any state of existence I chose to experience myself. This was the moment I truly opened myself to love, to oneness, to nonduality... To experiencing myself as the Creatrix that I AM.

Be the change you want to see in the world, Magda! Dietary change, self-care, nourishment for my soul and body, healing comes through touch, sex, self-expression, but also by surrounding myself with beauty, daily practice of breath and movement, slowing down, and embodying stillness...

Becoming a Facilitator:

Facilitation didn't come easily, as I was deeply discouraged form stepping into this protected world by the very person who introduced me to 5-MeO-DMT. I heard strong opinions and derogatory statements directed at me when I expressed that the experience invoked something in me that at that time felt overwhelmingly big and impossible to fulfill. The strong discouragement started informing me, and in turn, I started internalizing it and finding reasons taking me away from looking into the possibility of stepping into supporting others on their journey. The knock on the door was soft, and I didn't move to open the doors being discouraged from seeing what's on the other side. I struggled with finding my core, purpose, and reasons for offering the medicine to others. The minute I let go of the doubts and thoughts of learning the art, teachers appeared, and I was invited to sacred circles, and workshops and mastery of facilitation literally came to my doorstep. I travelled outside my country to heal, learn, and study the art of facilitation. Undeniably, the biggest teacher in facilitation is Bufo himself, regardless of what substance is being used, the organic or synthetic one. His energy came down to my body during one of the ceremonies I participated in and started working within and through me.

Martin W. Ball, Ph.D., Editor

I realized that my whole life prepared me for facilitation, as I was involved in health and healing for myself and others all my life.

There was something beyond my comprehension, yet with deep familiarity of meaning when I read at the age of 12 "The Only Revolution" by J. Krishnamurti. My fascination with ancient philosophies became my lifelong journey and study.

In shamanic training, I learned to track energies, manually do extractions, and guide people on shamanic journeys of shadow work and quantum transformations. In deep work on myself for many years, my third eye and my perceptions have significantly opened and enhanced. My whole being is open to seeing, feeling, and knowing, which is a tremendous support in bufo/5-MeO-DMT facilitation.

I have been working in medicine as a Chinese Medicine Practitioner for 15 years and have seen over ten-thousand patients with all kinds of diseases and disfunctions. My fields of specialty are psycho-emotional, mental challenges, and spiritual awareness and awakening. For many of these conditions I have prescribed TCM herbal Earth medicines as single herbs and compound formulae. Working with patients taught me what the Academy of Chinese Medicine was trying to impart, but due to its nature, could be only fully understood in practice. I learned subtle differences between diseases and the influence of an individual patient's personality that gave the disease a specific expression and reason for being. While teaching Chinese Medicine for over 10 years, I was teaching the nuances of Taoist philosophy of existence, as well as ethics, in working with patients, including my own practical clinical experiences. Chinese Medicine and shamanism became inseparable as one body in diagnosis and treatments for all patients.

The philosophy of Tantra and Tantric healing introduced me more deeply to human Source Energy called in TCM Yuan Qi, the Original, Prenatal, or Source Energy. The Ida channel is Yin in TCM, the Pingala is the Yang, and Sushumna is the combination of Ida, Pingala, and Fire together. During bufo/5-MeO-DMT experiences, this is the channel where energy moves from the second chakra, lower Dan Tien in Taoism, or Earth Center in Shamanism into 7th chakra, Upper Dan Tien in Taoism, or Heaven in Shamanism.

The three philosophies work exceptionally well in explaining and understanding of the spark that ignites all energies in human beings, called bufo/5-MeO-DMT.

Facilitation:

I don't wear a lab coat or feathered headpiece to ceremonies, but I come equipped with experience and knowledge gathered along the way. The biggest surrender I can

Facilitating 5-MeO-DMT

offer to myself is to allow the spirit of Bufo to enter my Sushumna as a mirror reflection of those with whom I am working. Thoughtless presence grounded in a human body able to feel itself in others as the same and separate simultaneously for the purpose of facilitation, support, guidance, and stillness. In the unity of consciousness, I clear pathways in myself for the client to experience themselves fuller and in their highest potential.

I mostly work with the synthetic form of 5-MeO-DMT, but include Bufo's spirit, as it was requested by him. This is to respect the lifeform and presence of Toads on Earth, but also respect humans who are sensitive to organic medicine which contains more than the one ingredient we want; the 5-MeO-DMT. The medicine is intuitively measured for each person based on many factors. I take into consideration prior work with medicines, reasons for sitting with me, depth and length of personal healing journey and self-awareness, expectations versus surrender, the support system they have, all facets of their health condition, personal constitution, and emotional state in that moment. All this information creates safety and is part of consent in my interview session with all clients. All this, however, is just a knowledge that is slightly disregarded once we sit in person with Bufo's spirit.

I don't advertise and don't seek clients to sit with me, they come as they hear and feel the call within to ask questions and book a ceremony time with me. Once they contact me, we'll have a Zoom chat to see whether we are a good match to work together. The informed consent comes from both parties through discussing needs, reasons, aspirations, vulnerabilities, and the explanation of the way I serve the medicine.

The medicine is gentle, loving, and grounding if we let it work this way with our beings. The best way to understand the medicine the way it informs my being is through Corinthians 13:4-8:

> *Love is patient, love is kind.*
> *It does not envy, it does not boast, it is not proud.*
> *It does not dishonor others, it is not self-seeking,*
> *It is not easily angered, it keeps no record of wrongs*
> *Love does not delight in evil but rejoices with the truth.*
> *It always protects, always trusts, always hopes, always perseveres.*
> *Love never fails. But where there are prophecies, they will cease; where*
> *there are tongues, they will be stilled; where there is knowledge, it will pass away.*

Martin W. Ball, Ph.D., Editor

Once the client is cleared of any hazard that may result in malpractice, we invite each other to sit together. I measure the medicine intuitively, from the smallest grain of sand for some into a substantial hippy scoop for others, and I place it in a pipe. This is just a part of embodying the medicine and being one with it. This dance starts with measurement and ends with the client coming back to full presence and human self-awareness when we share tea together. What happens to me during this time may be called a surrender or stepping away and giving room to the spirit of Bufo to work its magic. The deeper I surrender, the less I am asked to take the medicine with the client. I become the medicine who tracks, sees, removes blockages, and directs with voice and words that are not really mine in sound and often straight directiveness and even commands. The knowing is clear and times when my ego steps in are also very clear. The voice that doubts, boasts in pride and wants the client to be wowed is very familiar to my being. The ego seeks opportunities to step in and "do the work" to get recognition and appreciation. The Spirit of Bufo is humble and loving, he is a masculine aspect of myself. Surrendering to Bufo energy is no different than clearing the mind of thoughts in meditation to hear only the God-self speaking inside.

I offer individual, private sessions, and group medicine circles. Serving is a little different in both scenarios. In both however, the client has control over the experience in many ways. It starts with letting me know when I can start preparing the pipe. This is a big step for many to say YES to the experience again. Even though I eyeballed intuitively the amount of medicine, I offer them the freedom of how much they are ready to inhale, gently letting them know how much they inhaled already. They hear me say, "You are quarter in, we are halfway through…" I feel their courage to inhale everything, and courage when they give themselves permission to stop before I ask them to take one big inhale and hold it in. They are self-monitoring on how long they are willing to hold the medicine in their lungs before exhaling. I may count down for them or only say, "Let go when you are ready, of the medicine first." In this very vulnerable state, it is important to give them room to consciously step beyond their own fears and limiting beliefs.

As a client sits with the medicine, I get to feel and see where the medicine ignites pockets of energy and propels it upwards and sideways beyond the human body that embraces the experience. I observe the shadows play and often witness and hear the call and plea for rescue.

We are multidimensional beings and in 10 or 20 minutes of medicine experience, we travel wide and deep in time and space to reorganize ourselves completely to come back and organize ourselves in our physical experience in more functional and practical ways. This is how we upgrade the DNA, including the multidimensional nature of our ego-self. We never transcend the ego; we transcend our shadows. These are our obstacles, limiting beliefs, and unhealed parts of ourselves that keep us in lower vibrations.

The sessions are a combination of nondual, shamanic, ceremonial, and therapeutic experiences. I personally have no particular style, preference, or reason to offer any experience to anyone besides knowing the experiences I had with the medicine and how it influenced my life.

I am a channel and a student.

"Less is more" is a known saying in prescribing and working with Chinese herbal medicines. It is never the amount of the medicine but the depth of surrender to the experience that brings us deeper into experiencing the true self. With bufo/5-MeO-DMT we can melt into a pool of love for full disintegration of the ego-self and have a nondual experience, but we can also consciously melt into oneness with everything here on Earth to release ego perception of being a separate being, and self-identification as such. In my practice, I have observed that the latter is more common and as profound for clients as the big guns that wow and blow them out of the water into nonduality.

In self-preparation for a group medicine circle I was offering, my first inhale was about 5 mg of 5-MeO-DMT. I have experienced universal awareness and clarity of existence without the concept of self, me, or I. It was consciousness in presence aware of the surroundings and my body as one of the forms I was experiencing myself as and in. The consciousness that is the one and only being that exists.

I consider myself very lucky! Over the last 3 years I have observed the work of 8 facilitators, studied with one, spoke to a few about their journey with the medicine, and have been ghosted by only a couple. I don't have a tribe of many, but a Family of a few strong supporting facilitators.

What was the lesson for me? The medicine is protected, and it is a good thing in the long run as truly this is not for spiritual tourists and wanderers. I recognise in all of us self-taught skill and relationship with the medicine developed to the best of our abilities and understanding. For me personally, it was a very valuable lesson on cultivating deep connection, inner healing, inner knowing, surrender and trust. I trust completely in this journey now with the presence of Bufo's Spirit. I feel enveloped in his arms like dancing with my lover. The nuances of work we do together, his trust in me, patience as I take time to allow him to work through and with me, his humility, self-realization, and grounded, vulnerable confidence and surrender are teachings for me like dance steps... We are mirrors of each other where I am the student but also the vehicle through which he can be present on Earth. It is always in the humility and courage to see myself in others, whether greater or smaller, that I become whole and healed more and deeply. There was a scene in the movie *Avatar* where the adoptee was training his dragon but was unable to control and fly it safely. He got only one advice: control your mind!

Integration:

I had no expectations going to my first experience with 5-MeO-DMT, but it was clear to me that this was my last resource at giving life a chance. I wanted to turn over all the stones before checking out, and this one was the last one on my journey, it seemed. The integration period lasted over a month and taught me a lot about myself. It became life-changing when I introduced a small amount of cannabis in the evening to gain as much of this experience as possible. During that time, I had one meal a day, slept maybe 4 hours a night, and was able to function without problems. I felt different and tender inside, new to myself, reborn. There were states of being in soft and constantly moving energy within, but had no reactivations, or negative and fearful experiences. In the contrary, it was a constant deep learning and shifting. The changes and experiences were stunning and lasting, and there was no more hope for recovery from suicidal depression but evidence of betterment and coming out from the grave that held me in since I was 5 years old.

This was the only time out of all my trips where integration was a process; all other times it felt like an instant upgrade where I only needed to shake off the old programing for a day or two, hence the number of trips within a very short period of time.

This experience taught me two things: there is an integration period which may require guidance, and that sometimes it is an instant upgrade in consciousness which doesn't need to be profoundly felt for long.

What I offer to my clients is an invitation to contact me as needed, access to Facebook support groups, and 30 minutes post-trip Zoom chats, preferably within a week. I also send motivational quotes, supportive and related to the experience, articles, YouTube clips, suggestions, and now, monthly integration group meetings on Zoom. When issues are more difficult, we may schedule one-on-one integration session or breathwork. I have prepared a rescue kit with suggestions for electrolytes intake, daily body movement, walks in nature, and self-acupressure treatments. The acupressure is a key in gaining balance and grounding, and to move energies to balance the body. Often a simple suggestion involving the client is most valuable and appreciated.

FACILITATING 5-MEO-DMT

One of the difficulties with integration is with clients going into a fear zone even on a very small dose of the medicine. Sometimes it happens in shamanic healing or acupuncture where we see people coming out of the session in a state we would call a "bad trip." They feel worse before feeling better. It is always a very difficult time for the practitioner to observe someone regressing after a session, especially those going into PTSD and trauma afterwards.

I am trained and have years of clinical experience in trauma-informed approach, ethics, and client care. Compassion is the most delicate and powerful approach to care for the experience of another human.

Since I am still very new in facilitating 5-MeO-DMT, I have reached out to other practitioners asking them to share their stories and experience in cases of heavier energies, PTSD, and trauma-related sessions with clients.

There is a tendency to support assumptions and expectation that the temporary freedom after experience with 5-MeO-DMT from a lifetime of accumulation should stay forever. Clients are chasing that feeling instead of using the window of opportunity the medicine has offered to establish better life habits and allow changes in patterns and behaviors. Education is a big part of the integration process, even if that comes with a disappointment like bad news.

Hindrances in the Experience:

Many people who've had a difficult first experience with 5-MeO-DMT will negatively influence and discourage those who want to sit with the medicine. In my observation, the most common factor is purely lack in preparing the client to embark on the journey. When there is no basic clarity in understanding the process and no prior psychedelic experience, the trip can be rough and even brutal. The second most common factor in my observation is lack of preparation and giving clients too big a dose as their first experience, followed by insufficient support and integration. The common Western mind perception that more is better feeds the mind and may not serve in any other way. Often the biggest shifts may come like a feeling of a warm summer drizzle without the drizzle or feeling of breath without breathing. That is how love moves and stillness is the path to feel it.

Clients who've had prior psychedelic experiences may have expectations of visions, time to "be with it and in it," instead of experience it in its entirety as it unfolds by holding on to nothing. Some catch on to a feeling to expand and dwell in it. This is often done for safety reasons out of fear and inability to surrender. Once we realise that we are no longer in the driver's seat, we may want to hold on to a familiar story, feeling, memory, and scenario to survive the experience. The only way out is through! We are like a screen door: the wind will come and rattle it a bit and pass through leaving the doors intact. Sometimes the wind is stronger, the blockages are bigger, and this is reflective of the depth of surrender we need to allow so the door will not be damaged at all. This is the art of allowing the discomfort to pass, flowing with the energy, and giving up control, over and over again, until we will be spit out from a cosmic washing machine back into our bodies. I call 5-MeO-DMT a truth serum. It will clearly show our blockages, resistances, and fears.

Some clients say: "this is what I want" to experience or have an answer on. Both young and older, men and women, from different backgrounds, ethnicities, upbringings, and religious backgrounds are setting traps for themselves. It amplifies the misconception of psychedelics, especially 5-MeO-DMT, with fortune telling, psychic readings, and the use of other divinity tools.

Outcomes:

There is never a predicted outcome of any psychedelic medicine, but what people get out of the experience with 5-MeO-DMT is beyond their words and expectations. It is surreal but familiar, ineffable but real, complex yet very simple in nature. Some come out from the journey laughing and calling it a cosmic joke, others feel bliss for the first time and free their sexuality, and some experience oneness and the nondual state of being. In the journeys, major issues and problems in life get exposed and conscious healing can begin. Suicidal people find peace and love for life and living, like I did. Others find purpose in life as it changes their trajectory and understanding of the self and the healing process, or the experience will advance them on their healing or spiritual path.

Our most powerful tool is intention, a thought that creates and changes our reality. Conscious intention replaces all the intentions our shadows may have with all the unfulfilled desires that are hiding in the darkness that may be triggered and come up to the surface. An intention is different than a want or expectation. I've often heard: my intention is to experience love, or experience who I am, or see the universe, God, energy, or feel fully free. Some people want to practice letting go, others to have near death experience as letting go of fear of death and dying. The truth is, the smaller the intention, the bigger might be the experience with the medicine. Who knows how many layers we buried love under, or how many walls of fear we have built to protect trust? To experience love or trust all layers and walls will be unearthed within …

FACILITATING 5-MEO-DMT

The majority of people come in with trust that the "medicine with show them, tell them, direct them" to what they need to know, see, feel, and experience. This medicine is a powerful truth serum, and it doesn't want or need to take anyone's power. With the help of 5-MeO-DMT we are showing ourselves what we normally don't want to feel or see or don't have access to on daily basis.

Regardless of difficulties, it is a privilege to know our inner landscape and to understand the intricacies of the lessons we wanted to teach ourselves this lifetime or maybe through many lifetimes altogether. The major individual outcome of working with 5-MeO-DMT is an ongoing and stronger curiosity and love for life and all living forms. It is the journey that brings us home to discover who we are experientially, not intellectually.

Conclusion:

As the medicine becomes more popular around the globe, it is my wish for heart-centered and practical training programs to be offered to those who are serious about facilitation as it is not for everyone, just like being a surgeon is not for everyone. Learning facilitation is like going to a medical school for the body and the soul and using Earth Medicine to deal with the problem.

A few years ago, the FDA banned in the USA use of the Chinese herb *Ma Huang*, also known as Ephedra, due to safety concerns. This is one of the most powerful herbs to treat lung conditions such as asthma and bronchitis. It also treats muscle pain and arthritis issues and is used as a weight loss agent. Some athletes used it as a performance enhancement drug to increase lung capacity and decrease muscular fatigue, and as a weight loss supplement. Unfortunately, they didn't know much about the herb in terms of safety in prescribing dosage, frequency, precautions, and contraindications, which resulted in deaths. 5-MeO-DMT has a challenging legal status in many countries, there is a very little research done on it, and it is just entering into clinical studies. Protecting the medicine means offering safety to those who are ready to sit with it and be supported by practitioners with training. When it comes to personal preparation, knowledge, experience and training, there is no difference in approach to serving 5-MeO-DMT and all other psychedelic medicines. The difference is in the personal relationship with the medicine, oneself, and the self-realization/healing journey of each practitioner.

One of the biggest responsibilities all facilitators have is to educate the client. This is a well-known fact in all healing arts. We can offer them to sit with the medicine, but the choices, changes, and realisations that happen in day-to-day life make the biggest and most lasting impact on everyone's life. It is the ceremony of life after the ceremony with medicine ends that we celebrate our breakthroughs and retrieve our power to become consciously present in our own journey through life.

Experience as the True Teacher

by Juan David Alvarius

- *How were you introduced to 5-MeO-DMT/Toad? What was your experience?*

I was introduced by a real estate agent selling a retreat center that was up for sale in Costa Rica. My wife at that time was interested in buying a retreat center, but I was not really interested. To pacify her interest, I agreed to go take a look. Upon arrival at the center, it was obvious it was a yoga/ayahuasca retreat center. In our discussions about the center, the real estate agent mentioned there was going to be a shaman coming from Mexico who would be serving something called *Bufo alvarius* the following day. I asked him, "What is the ceremony of this 'Bufo'?" "Have you ever heard of it?" he asked. Me: nope. "Well, you smoke it and then you just literally explode into the universe," he said. I thought that sounded awesome, so I agreed and reserved our space for the next day.

The following morning, we arrived at the ceremony. My wife and I had an arrangement; she could go first, and I'd take care of her, and then I would go after she

FACILITATING 5-MEO-DMT

had returned from her journey. But this nice young couple, one of them was from Canada, had two little children with her and she was breastfeeding. She asked politely if she could go first so that she would have time for the medicine to dissipate so she could feed her children in a couple of hours. Of course, we said yes, but we didn't know she'd had a kambo ceremony just a few days earlier. When the shaman served her the medicine, she smoked it and she sat there with a beautiful sitting pose, just slightly rotating with her eyes closed. That continued for approximately 15 minutes, and then she got up saying she felt incredible.

So my wife decided to go next, thinking she would have a similar experience, so the little shaman guy from Mexico sat down in front of my wife and told her to just smoke as much as she could because there's a zone where if you don't smoke enough, it's very uncomfortable, so just keep smoking and smoking and smoking until you can't smoke anymore and hold it. That was his instructions to her. She did follow his instructions, and then she fell backwards in a very energetic cringing body and rigid pose. She tried to put her hands in her mouth, and they had to hold her hands. Then she would grab onto the grass in the dirt and try and put it into her mouth. In addition, she actually did cut the inside of her mouth with her fingernails, but after she relaxed into the journey. And then the gentleman asked me if I was ready to go.

The Shaman was this little man, much smaller than myself, and he was with an American lady in her 40s, I'm guessing. At the time I thought she was also a participant; later I realized she was training with him. So she got behind me and he proceeded to tell me to smoke as much as I could, the same instructions that were given to my wife, Raquel. I remember smoking and smoking and smoking, holding, holding, holding, then BOOM, like a rocket ship, I just launched right into the universe in a burst of bright white, golden light. I remember passing through dimensions, seeing some type of golden machine elf world, going right past it, just right into what I would consider creation. It was pure energy. When coming back, there was a thunderstorm with a lot of lightning and thunder. It was very powerful. The bufo magnified the sounds of thunder, making me feel like I was lightning.

We were right next to a river, and I remember the lightning strikes and when the thunder came, I could literally feel them pulsating through my body. The lady-in-training came by, checking in on me, and in the blur of all that was going on, I was just beginning to put myself back together. She sprayed me with this a little bit of Flower Water. I could smell it and I realized I was OK; I'm coming back. I'm not completely gone into the universe! I started pushing on my face and arms and hands and realizing that I was back. I looked over to see my wife and she was still in her process. She had probably close to an hour-long journey, whereas mine was more like maybe 15 to 20 minutes. That was my first experience with 5-MeO-DMT / *Bufo alvarius*.

- *How did you become a facilitator, and why?*

My first experience of *Bufo alvarius* was so paradigm-shifting, it literally did more for me in 15 to 20 minutes than the past eight or nine years of somewhere between 30 and 40 ayahuasca ceremonies. Ayahuasca is a beautiful medicine and it's very helpful. It allowed me to stop drinking alcohol and consuming substances. It allowed me to see that I had just been looking to fill myself up with things from outside me. What I really needed was not from the outside, but had been with me all along. I was just not able to understand it. It was just simply unconditional love for myself, from myself: in other words, loving myself.

But my life continued on and was relatively normal. I stopped drinking, stop using drugs, and became much more loving and not so ego-driven. But my first bufo experience shattered my ego completely. It literally it took me a few days to really understand what had happened, but it gave me the "God perspective": I'm not a physical body; I am eternal energy, soul, entity – however you would like to phrase it. From that point, I wanted to know more about *Bufo alvarius*, and we started our journey being in service to others without ever realizing what we were getting into.

My wife and I booked a flight to Cancun and arranged to meet with the facilitator for more bufo sessions. After a few ceremonies, he told me that I had the mind that will allow me to control the medicine in a way that very few do, and was I interested in serving? Of course I thought, "Sure!" I was a naïve person, not realizing all the implications and responsibilities of being a facilitator.

The facilitator said that if I was interested, he would be happy to help me and show me how to serve. Of course, being very excited about my shift, I wanted to help others also experience a similar transformation. So we acquired a couple of instruments, just a little bit of bufo, and he told me to go home and just experiment with myself using a little bit at a time so that I can learn the different stages that a person goes through. That way I could understand how to help others and what they're going through at these different levels. And it was to ensure I could stay conscious wile under the influence of bufo. Basically, just proactively developing my brain to manage the sessions.

My desire to be in service to others led me to come back to Mexico many times over the next 6 months. We spent several months in Mexico training with a many different people and attending the ceremonies of others, observing and helping. It

Facilitating 5-MeO-DMT

takes time to see how, what, and why people react the way they do, and many ceremonies and experiences were needed to become a responsible medicine man.

There were many trips, many experiences, and then with a friend in Cancun, we served together and shared experiences together. Each day we communicate with one another, so we have a mutual support system. This is very important, especially in the beginning, because all experiences are new to you. You are changing. The more bufo you consume, the more you can see and manage energy. It's a cycle of almost becoming insane at times, and unless you have someone to express your daily concerns and feelings with about what's happing to you, personally, and then on to the people who you serve, then you can become ungrounded. You need support, and the more, the better, especially in the beginning. A mentor is good to get advice from when you are unsure. Even today I have moments when I reach out to more experienced facilitators on specific issues that I don't normally deal with to ensure I am on the right track.

- *What, if any, training did you receive?*

I would consider my training to be primarily informal. Mostly it was just attending ceremonies, consuming bufo, and other psychedelics, seeing many different experiences, helping other servers or providers, etc. Each has their own unique technique, and I'd be helping in ceremonies and participating myself. You cannot get enough experience prior, but in the end, all you've experienced will help you when you begin the process of serving others.

Most of my real personal training has come from trial and error and serving – learning by doing. You can read, watch videos, listen to podcasts, etc., but that is all theory until you actually do it yourself; then it becomes knowledge.

Before serving I read many books which gave me a great insight into what was going to happen, plus all the ceremonies I attended and experienced helped me immensely. I think personally this was one of the best tools that I had had in the beginning. And I read your books, such as *Being Human,* and *Entheogenic Liberation.* I always tell people who are interested in serving medicine to read your books. I believe they are the most comprehensive that I have read, and they are the closest to my own personal experience to being factual, at least from my perspective. I am not into the shamanism side as much as the energetic vibration side, which is where I think there is the maximum truth. Everything is energy, everything vibrates, and bufo increases this vibration.

Martin W. Ball, Ph.D., Editor

To me, most of the shamans, or self-proclaimed shamans, are a lot about the show or the performance. I don't really believe this serves much purpose, except for possibly the spectators and the ego of the shaman. This is just my perspective. I do not consider myself a shaman but rather a medicine man. I serve medicine and tell people they are the lock and the key. It's their choice how much they want to unlock. They are, in truth, the medicine. For me, it's about them regaining their personal power and being responsible for themselves.

I have discovered in my journeys that everything is just vibration or energy. The universe is unconditional love, but that unconditional love is just pure energy, both "positive" and "negative": it's all energy. Being just energy makes everything so malleable or possible. The concept that everything comes from the darkness is very clear now. All is manifestation from ourselves, our culture, our ethnic consciousness, society, etc. This is just my perspective. A shaman may have a different perspective, and it's totally valid for their perspective as seeing into other worlds, fighting with entities, etc. In the end, for me, it's 100% vibration or energy. The higher your vibration or energy, the more you will overcome the limits of lower energy or vibration. So, in the end, for my training I would say 30% came from other shamans or facilitators, a good 10% came from books that I read, and the 60% came from personal experience in simply serving people, going through the experiences, learning what happens, what to do, or not to do, when to do it, or not to do it.

I also personally smoke quite a bit of medicine with my clients so that I can go in energetically with them on their journey. I often get criticized for this, but it is how I have learned to be of the most help to the person I am serving, as this allows me to become part of the experience rather than just observing it and interacting not from a logic-based system but from a dynamic on-the-go direct connection to the person we are serving. When you reach that energetic state, there is a connection energetically and you can see where energy is trapped. Those are typically emotions, traumas, but everything in the end is just energy. I can see specific colors or places where energy is stored, and sometimes just a simple touch or squeeze will allow the person to release that energy. Often you can also purge or vomit on behalf of that person, and then the person will just feel so much better. You can see the relief on their face, and their body will relax and help their journey. Sometimes a message to say "forgive him" or her, or mom, or dad, or whomever. It's always different for each person, but when you get the person to forgive themselves, for me, that is all that is needed.

So, what was my formal training? I guess it's been a little bit of everything. You'll learn the most by doing it yourself. Just be aware of the legal ramifications of the country you serve in and be prepared for worst case scenarios. It's not just smoking

Facilitating 5-MeO-DMT

toad and good luck. It comes with immense responsibility for yourself and for the recipient.

- *How do you conduct sessions?*

I conduct my ceremonies a little bit differently than most providers or shamans. Often, I will use sage, smoke, or copal to cleanse the area and people. I will also do a lesser banishing ritual enabling the angles, and I also invoke Anubis. This way we have the angels, and we have the underworld, so if any entity comes into play or negative energy emerges, it is quickly dealt with. There are "entities" some might call demons, or negative beings. They are in some people, or attached to them, but again, that is still at an energetic level. It's just energy, or a connection to an energy. Bufo, if used correctly, can eliminate attached negative entities, but it is not for the faint of heart, I assure you, and ultimately, very uncommon in my experience.

I normally have the person sit down read a healing prayer that has been given to me by the first person who first served me. It has been adjusted many times to improve it and translate it into various different languages. We ask the recipient to read the prayer out loud as this helps them release tension and begin focusing on their journey. Typically, we have a little bit of very light medicine music playing in the background. Then I tell the person to take some really deep breaths, releasing the tension and getting a lots of oxygen into their body. Then I begin heating the toad secretions, and when the smoke begins boiling up, I tell the person to exhale completely and then to inhale gently while raising their arms above their head, as if they were diving into the universe. Keep going, keep going, keep going, keep going, keep going, more, more, more, until they can consume no more. Then hold, hold, hold it, and then within a matter of a few seconds, BOOM, they're gone.

Typically, I will have a minimum of four people sitting beside us to assist us to ensure that the person is safe if they start moving or shaking or pulling their arms or their hair or anything that could be physically damaging to themselves. We're also there to ensure that nothing harmful can happen, because when the ego is breaking down, there is a fight for life sometimes. The ego really believes that it is dying, so the body is struggling to stay alive, and sometimes that can be very violent. On the flip side of such reactions, the person can sit and or lay back and just flow and look like they are in blissful sleep, and it can be very peaceful.

It is important that you have good helpers with you to avoid physical harm to yourself, your helpers, or the person who is receiving the medicine. Someone there should be CPR trained. We are very fortunate in that we often have medical personnel who are helpers, but if you intend to serve you should at the least have CPR training. I have never needed it but there is always a first time. Be prepared as it could save yourself and the person being served and you from a long prison sentence.

Once the person calms down, that's typically when the ego has broken down and the person has gone off into their journey, this is the letting go and just relaxing into your journey. For some it is hard, for others it is easy. I smoke enough medicine with most, so that I can go into the journey with them, not only from a visual, but also from an energetic vibrational level. I can start finding energy points that need to be released. Everybody is different. Every person is unique, and there is never a process that is identical. I try to allow the person to do all the work personally possible without me helping, but at times it's required to interject yourself into their journey for the best outcome.

Once the person begins to come back, sometimes the energy can be too strong and their ego is trying to put itself back together and there can be a fight once again, so it is very important for you to have people around you that can help you and help them calm themselves down to keep them safe until they're completely back in their ego and their mind has restructured them and they're safe.

I personally instruct them before the ceremony. I'll let them know they're going to have and ego death. Sometimes that scares them. Sometimes people leave, and that's OK because it is the truth: they're going to go through a type of death. It is not a physical death – it's an ego or mental death. It's all in the mind and the body is perfectly fine, but I've discovered that if you don't tell people, sometimes they can become very angry at you afterwards. But if you tell them this and are straight forward and honest with them, and you allow them to make their decision, then it's OK. The medicine is shattering their ego and it can be painful or it can be blissful. In my perspective, it's the closest thing you could ever get to a near-death experience.

It can take from 20 min to 2 hours for a person to feel like they're completely back from the experience. I always recommend people to take their time. There is no rush to try to put words around their experience. The most typical recall is, "I just remember a flash of light . . ." We hit nonduality there, so I am happy. That is where a reset will happen, if it is going to happen. Often these changes happen weeks after the ceremony.

When they come back, we instruct them with simple instructions to pay attention to your body, what smells good ,what tastes good. Often you can eliminate bad habits at this point just by paying attention to what your body is telling you, not what your mind is addicted too. Some people stop eating sugar, meat, others gluten, others begin eating animal proteins, so I think it's just the body's way of resetting. Alcohol, tabaco, many harmful drugs often go away as the body does not want or need it any longer. I

Facilitating 5-MeO-DMT

tell them to get lots of exercise, ground if you can walk in nature with your shoes off, go to the beach if it's close by, get their feet into the sand and salt water, hug a tree, eat fresh fruits, vegies, etc. Pay attention to what feels good and what does not, energetically, emotionally, etc. This is a guide to what is or is not good for them, and it's their own body expressing it so it might be good to pay attention to what it has to express. I usually give them a card with my website on integration and a WhatsApp number to contact if they have any questions or need help. I always let them know they are not alone in the process. I think that can be the scariest part for a participant – the feeling of being alone and unable to communicate what is happing to them post-medicine.

- *How would you describe your approach: nondual, shamanic, ceremonial, therapeutic…?*

I'd describe my practice as primarily focused on the nondual, taking people to complete nondual experience and allowing them to experience the infinite for just a split second. It is enough to shut down the person's brain and allow for a reset, which can lead to a therapeutic outcome. I normally only repeat a few basic things to the person at this level of experience such as, "Love yourself," "Forgive yourself," "You are God: if you do not exist nothing exists," "It's your life: make the decisions with love, forgiveness, compassion, acceptance to all," "This is a one way ticket you are not coming back again as you are in this lifetime, so enjoy your life while you have it to enjoy." Sometimes a flash of something happens and I will ask the person to forgive me, or male energy, or female energy. I have felt harsh physical traumas, sexual traumas, lots of military horrors for ex-military personnel, things we could never imagine seeing people have had to live through and sometimes they just need a shift in perspective to let it all go, which is the last thing I typically say: "Let go of what does not serve you – everything's like the water in the river, it constantly flows – just let it go, let it flow – it's just energy – let it go and something new will come in its place." It just depends on what my understanding of the person's needs are at that time, so using all these techniques may lead to the best therapeutic outcome.

- *Do you work one-on-one, in groups, in retreats, at a center, with a team…?*

I work with one-on-one on occasion, though not as much as I would prefer. I live in a 3rd world country, and cost is not favorable to one-on-one experiences. Pricing limits the amount of people I can personally work with. For some, $50 is maybe their food for the week. We have developed a way to help people in small groups of 5 to 8, and this is our preference. We have also been doing this out of our backyard, thereby keeping costs to a minimum, which brings its own issues.

Some recipients of 5-MeO-DMT are not quiet and scream, "Save me! Help me!" or just a hair-raising scream that anybody hearing would think someone is dying, so it's delicate to do in a condominium environment where we live. Hard-core drug users we won't serve at my home, as they are typically the loudest, or violent rape victims also are quite loud and people could misconstrue what is happening as the recipient often relives the traumatic experience. It's not good for your next-door neighbor to be thinking, "What the hell is going on over there?" The extreme cases, we prefer at a retreat setting where the space is safe and they can yell, scream, cry, or do whatever they need to do to release.

I do also serve in retreats. We have some local hotels like El Sabanero where the owner just charges for the rooms and the medicine is on a minimum-donation basis. We have a few retreat centers also that we serve at for locals, and for tourists coming in, we typically direct them to these centers. I never work alone with 5-MeO-DMT, and I always try to have my wife or another woman who is preset to balance the energy of masculine and feminine. Our helpers are locals and expats from all over the world who do it all out of the goodness of their hearts. It is beautiful to see people show up to help others they do not even know through this explosive experience.

- *What do you see as the purpose of working with 5?*

The purpose of 5-MeO-DMT is allowing the person to feel at ease, to know there is something else out there when we die. To allow the person to reset their life's potential or to now be able to look back and laugh instead of lamenting their past, to see their life as an adventure of the greatest kind, so unique it can never be repeated or replicated. I want them to really realize they are here to enjoy and experience life. Not the Western concept of more, more, more, or the Eastern concept that less is more, but just simply realize they hit the galactic jack pot when they were born on planet Earth to have a dualistic experience of being. Most people go through life thinking it is too hard, always looking for something outside them to be at fault, never realizing they are the center of their universe, and they have the ability to change whatever they want. Realizing they are literally on the journey of their lives, and it all has no beginning and no end. When they die, it's a door closing and another opening and while here in duality enjoying each moment (the present moment) becomes so spectacular, even in the difficult times, there are things to be grateful for.

FACILITATING 5-MEO-DMT

- *If you use unconventional or controversial methods, what is the rationale? In your own view, how does it serve your practice?*

A controversial method I guess would be consuming 5-MeO-DMT at the same time with the client, allowing for a deeper connection. I think I have expressed this above, but doing so allows me to connect energetically with the person's journey leading to a much more complete experience.

I do not like to use micro dosage, the famous "handshake-dose." I prefer a full-on experience, a white-out nondual experience. I have had clients tell me, "Oh I have already experienced bufo, but I am ready for another," and when they sit with me the most common response is, "Wow! That was a real bufo experience?" because they'd only previously received a "handshake" micro-dose and haven't really experienced the medicine's full nondual potential. That's the real potential – not a Barbie dose to make you feel good, but a dosage that actually has the power to allow you to shift, if you so desire, to a nondual experience.

I have seen how with low-doses people remember the feeling vaguely, so they did not shut down the mind. This only allows for a positive, euphoric experience, or even a negative experience, but not allowing for true energetic healing or the releasing of deep trauma. It's an easy play for many providers. It is cheaper to do so and it produces more income. Potentially a single gram could serve up to 15 people, where I am lucky to get 5 or 6 people from the same amount of medicine.

I also let people know I work at the energic level, so I may need to serve them more medicine as we go and to please accept it. It's not for me. It is for them in that moment. It is the opportunity to leave them as energetically clean as possible; i.e., removing most blocks. I do not stop serving the person unless I think they cannot handle more or physically they need to stop. I have gone as far as 5 full white-out doses on a single person in one session. But this person was able to return to her life happy and free of what previously held her back.

- *How do you handle issues of informed consent?*

I have a non-disclosure contract that is signed also ensuring they have disclosed all medications or physical issues they have. I personally speak to them expressing what will happen before, and after, before they ever receive the medicine.

- *What do people get out of their sessions/experiences?*

This is a huge topic. It can be something simple as a change in habits, a change in character, becoming less angry, on and on. I have seen illnesses such as cancer disappear from patients who were to go under the knife and now there is no need. The actual reason is unknown. It is my belief that most illness are emotional-based and the mind controls the emotions, which sends commands to the body to obey. If your brain says it is dying, it sends messages to body to die. If it wants to live, it can change the message. I have seen people who were in deep, deep addictions resolve them, but again, this all is dependent upon the person receiving the medicine and the experience; it's not a silver bullet. It's powerful, but only as much as you allow it to be. Remember, the true medicine is you the person. You already have the answers and cures to all that ails you. It's simply a matter of remembering or allowing, forgiving, loving yourself unconditionally, accepting all and letting go of what you don't need, etc.

- *Do you provide pre-session information, screening, prep? If so, what?*

Yes. In most cases, clients have been to my website, or reached out to my wife or center prior to ceremony. They have been screened for their medical condition and medications, their state of health, blood pressure, any accidents, and if they have had any implants, etc.

- *What are some of the best results you've seen?*

Cancer gone, depression gone, people getting off the cocktail of drugs they are on that are preventing them from really living. I have seen a stage-4 lung cancer patient still with me 4 years later. The most rewarding was a woman in her late 70s with dementia and Alzheimer's. Her husband is older also, and she was unable to function and was becoming very angry. She had a single full white-out experience that left her happy and her husband was able to keep her home. It was not a "cure," but a good way to extend a better life where she is here for herself and her husband. I have so many similar stories, but honestly, all are spectacular, even if it is just modifying how they see their lives for the better.

FACILITATING 5-MEO-DMT

- *What are some of the difficulties you've encountered with patients/clients?*

I've had a few people who've needed another dose of bufo to ground back. I think it has something to do with their brain and how serotonin receptors are engaging or disengaging – it seems like a biochemical inability to disconnect. The solution is more 5-MeO-DMT, in my experience, from a few days after to a long-term issue. I have helped a lady who was disconnected, or overconnected, rather, for 3 + years. I convinced her to try bufo again and it worked. It was not easy to get her to retake bufo, but she was very grateful she did afterwards. In truth, any client can become difficult if you are not following up with them.

I have had people express how low they have dropped to come for a visit with someone like me. This is typical in religious fanaticism. I have had every bad word in most languages of this earth and outside said to me. 99% come back in a few weeks or months to apologize and thank me. Clients who do not follow instructions and go drink alcohol or use other substances, and then they have a bad experience, simply expect bufo to be their magic bullet, not needing to put out any effort afterward and no responsibility for their own actions. They only want an easy solution. These clients are the most difficult for me. They do not want to meditate, it is still all outside, they do not yet grasp their responsibilities, but a few more sessions with bufo might help them understand. Not everything is solved in a single session, and that needs be made clear from the outset; this is not always a quick fix, but then again, it can be just one, and that is enough.

- *What are your recommendations for integration and post-experience processing?*

I have an integration page on my website which covers integration, but in general, I tell people to pay attention to their bodies and likes and dislikes after their experience. Drink lots of coconut water or electrolytes, eat good food, fresh vegies, fruits etc., avoid processed foods, no alcohol. If they're wanting to let go of habits, it's a good time to start. For at least 2 weeks, no alcohol, get good sleep. If they need to use melatonin, or a bit of marijuana before sleeping, it's ok for a few days. And if they need help, ask for it. About 1 in 300 needs to have another dose, but it's highly unusual. Clients should make sure to let me know if they are having issues. We are here for them.

- *What resources do you use or recommend to clients?*

We use our website and are also available before people commit to having the experience. Most people will want to hear your voice on a phone call, ask questions, and get solid answers. Or in retreats, we show up and answer questions the day before and will have a lunch or dinner and happily explain bufo and its effects to allow the person the chance to ask and be informed.

- *How many people have you served, and what kinds of people have you worked with? (Drug addicts, spiritual seekers, vets, ages, genders, occupations, interests, nationalities/ethnicities)*

I have now served into the thousands of people and have stopped trying to keep track. For more than 3 years I have served close to 50 to 80 per month. We are approaching 4 years, so that's a minimum of 2,500 to 3,000 people.

I have worked with drug addicts & alcoholics, vets, individuals with PTSD. Spiritual seekers are the easiest in general to deal with, such as yogis and those who meditate – not necessarily people seeking relief or healing – just an opportunity to deepen their self-knowledge.

I won't serve anyone under 18 and the oldest I have served is an 83-year-old man.

Genders: trans, gay, lesbian, unknown. And of course, men and women – gender is not considered at all. These are just labels and all are humans. I know my personal preferences may not be the same as another, but we can accept one another at a human level and it's all ok. All is acceptable if coming from love. Every person is unique, and I am no different. To some I may seem a hero, and to another I might seem strange or even evil – I have been told this from religious fanatics a few times, but it's just words and ignorance is at play. My point is that not everyone will fit into your specific category of acceptable and not acceptable. It's easiest to simply accept people as they are. I have no issue with serving any person as long as their physical condition is not something that could lead to a negative outcome.

Some examples are someone with herpes (cold sore) or other communicable disease. We are careful to keep pipes sanitized for each person. HIV is a concern also, as some people can bleed or scratch etc., so you also must be conscious of these issues, have anti-bacterial soap, alcohol, etc. I have been bitten many times, vomited on, spit on, etc. So, body fluids are being transferred, mostly unknown to the person you are serving, but it's frequent and a danger to you as a server of bufo. Make sure to keep yourself in good physical shape, and also your auto-immune system. Do not become

FACILITATING 5-MEO-DMT

part of the problem of spreading diseases to your clients. On the flip side, you, as a recipient of bufo, might want to pay close attention to the person serving you: do they have any notable issues? Maybe you might want to know if they have anything that could be transferred to you? I know a few people who serve who do have AIDS. I have had many surgeries due to a spinal injury and been tested many times. I easily tell them no I do not have any known communicable diseases. You as a client should feel totally comfortable in asking questions of the person who will be serving you, or the helpers that will be handling you, etc. It is your life and your decision; do not just leave it up to chance. ASK.

- *Do you see different issues between serving men and women, old and young, healthy and those will medical issues?*

Most women, in general, are more sensitive than men. Most women have had some sort of physiological or physical abuse somewhere in their life from the opposite sex. Men, in general, have more ego, so it's harder for them to let go, or are less in touch with their feelings.

Young people typically have an easier time, as they have much less traumas in general. This isn't always true, because you will find youths that have had lots of traumas, but in general, the youth have less baggage to deal with due to simply not having the experiences yet.

Older people can have more difficult processes. It seems to me that people from their 30s to 60s typically have the most difficult time. This is the "average" person still in their EGO, very full of who they think or thought they are. Most people think they are what they do: their value as a person is tied to their profession or ability to produce or not produce.

From around 65 to being in their 80s, they are now on the other side, realizing life is about over and the journey is coming to an end. They seem more at peace with it, or they are afraid of what will happen when they pass, or perhaps have many regrets. It is such a relief when someone of any age lets go of regrets, past mistakes, etc. Each moment is a chance to turn it all around. An entire life of negative outcomes can be shifted in a second and the remaining life can be full of positivity. I have seen bufo blow that away, and just see the glow in the face and the realization the person has knowing now every second of what is left is a true gift. AMAZING!

- *What do you feel are the responsibilities of those serving 5?*

Primarily ensuring the person is safe physically and mentally, and being available after for weeks, if needed. Being there not just to light a pipe, but really *be there* if they need you. Not all clients have issues. 99.5% are OK. It's that 0.5% that require more dedication and time. Normally it's reassuring them, making sure they are OK, helping with supplements to eliminate sleeping or other issues that can arise.

- *Do you have an opinion on synthetic vs. "natural"?*

To date, I have not served, or have personally used synthetic. I do know there are differences between female and male bufo, but between bufo and synthetic, I have no personal experience.

- *If you choose to work with Toad, what's your take on sustainable harvesting, toad protections, and related ethical questions?*

I only purchase from a certified source regarding bufo. If you go to the black market and buy anything that is cheap, you are promoting the destruction of the toad.

Sustainability at this time is not an issue, but I can see it could become so in the future as bufo becomes more popular. Protection of the species at some point may be required. I constantly get people asking me why I don't just bring back some toads. To me this is the most dangerous to the species: taking it out of its environment. Please leave them there.

Most of the toads are in the Sonoran Desert of Mexico and parts of the southwestern USA. Within the USA, it's a protected species. In Mexico, the Sonoran Desert is basically inhabited by the narco traffickers. I don't recommend anyone go messing around in Mexico in the desert as you might not reappear. To quote from Wikipedia: *Bufo alvarius* has been designated as "endangered" and possession of this toad is illegal. It is unlawful to capture, collect, intentionally kill or injure, possess, purchase, propagate, sell, transport, import or export any native reptile or amphibian, or part thereof…

I personally will try synthetic 5-MeO-DMT when an opportunity arises and see if it's as effective. If so, then obviously this will be the best to use for sustainability. I also would like to test synthetic verses toad on specific types of issues to see if one is more effective than the other. To me it will be interesting to see. Does synthetic have spirit? The toad secretions come from an animal and has hundreds of other compounds

Facilitating 5-MeO-DMT

within it other than just 5-MeO-DMT, so are these other compounds responsible for different outcomes verses the synthetic? This is unknow to me personally and is something worthwhile to be investigated.

- *How do you feel 5 works with other entheogenic medicines? What are their relationships?*

Kambo is often used prior to bufo, to help cleanse a person out prior to bufo, but never use bufo within 2 hours of kambo as the mix can be very dangerous. There are a few known deaths from this experimental process, but also realize bufo is new to the world as we know it now, so a lot of experimentation must happen for all of us to know what is appropriate and what is dangerous, and this is only going to happen with experimentation. This makes it even more important to have some sort of common data-base or info on what is OK for beginners to not repeat the mistakes of others.

- *Who should take 5? Who shouldn't?*

Anyone who wants to have a near-death experience, a nondual experience, or wants to strengthen their ability to meditate could benefit from 5-MeO-DMT. Anyone wanting to release emotions of past traumatic events, those who are terminally ill, those with cancer and most other illnesses (with exception of those listed below in the next paragraph). I honestly believe every person on the planet that could take it without risk to their health, should at least try a full-on white-out once in their life. The sooner, the better. It will allow them to then go forward in their lives with a much different perspective. Our world would be a much better place if they did.

I won't serve anyone with the following: schizophrenia or sever bipolar disorder, brain damage, stroke, super high blood pressure, heart transplant, or any other organ transplant. You don't want to have a death on your hands. So be prudent and realize not all people are apt for 5-MeO-DMT. Also make sure to get a complete list of meds people are consuming. Many within these groups take massive amounts of antidepressants, antipsychotics, mood stabilizers, etc.

Some of these medications actually block the effects of 5-MeO-DMT, and not nearly enough public info on the effects between these meds and 5-MeO-DMT are available for servers or participants. Autistic people are extremely sensitive to exterior stimuli, and it's also a bad idea to serve them. I have tried and a few were positive, a few negative. I have tried working with these groups with little success with 5-MeO-DMT and it potentially could make their condition worse. On the flip side, we have worked with this same group of people using mushrooms with a much better success rate and know no danger to date. So not all people fit into the same box; there are different issues and different remedies.

Anyone taking MAOI anti-depressants should not use bufo. I did a simple experiment on myself to test this: I personally consumed some Syrian Rue (an MAOI) and bufo. I am very experienced in bufo, but when I consumed the Syrian Rue and then proceeded to bufo, my experience was much stronger, and it took me a few days to recover and feel and think like myself again. I used a minimum amount of Syrian Rue and the effect was huge, so just imagine a pharmaceutical MAOI that is much stronger! Bad idea! Don't do it to the poor person. You could really mess them up.

- *What role do you see for 5 in the global community?*

I see 5-MeO-DMT as being a perfect tool for therapist who have a short window to interact with patients or clients as it's typically less than an 1hr process in total, so that would allow for more professional usage of the medicine. Of course, I also see this as a spiritual awakening tool, which is not a mainstream concept, but it's very effective. Many addictions can be removed also. Illness can disappear – it's really a mystery, but it is all about energy or vibration and the higher vibration always wins. Anyone who has been told they have a terminal illness should have the experience; it just might shift them from terminal to living out their life that is left to be lived, or potentially going into spontaneous remission.

I have seen it happen in cancer patients; one example I had was a pediatrician who had been scheduled to have her uterus removed. Two weeks later there on her doctor visit, the tumor was gone and there was nothing there that needed to be removed. I've also had women with breast cancer resolve itself. I have an *Alzheimer's* patient that has dramatically improved the quality of life for herself and husband. It's a beautiful medicine, but it all comes back to the person, and the exact outcome is always an unknown. But 99.9% of the time I have seen some sort of positive outcome; maybe not what the person expected, but nonetheless a positive result.

- *What are the lessons you've learned from serving 5?*

Stay humble. Not everyone is apt for 5-MeO-DMT or bufo, and the ceremony is for the client, not the servers. Our job is to keep them safe physically and energetically. Always ask the client about their health. Get an overall understanding of their mental and physical health to ensure the best possible outcome.

Facilitating 5-MeO-DMT

I see so many get wrapped up in the rattles and feathers and drums – it's just ego. Do your best to use grass or very soft surfaces. I have served in many temples where the floor is hard, and in that case, you need 4 to 6 helpers to ensure safety for the client. You never know what is going to happen and what the outcome will be. It is imperative that we as providers allow the people have their experience without injecting ourselves or beliefs into their experience.

SSRI anti-depressants are OK. I was told, "No, it will do great harm!" I have not found this to be true. It might make them a bit more resistant to bufo is what I have seen. I have served hundreds of clients with SSRIs now without issue: full white-outs doses, not micro-doses.

Many people see this as a path of spiritual growth and being in service to others. I have seen people claiming to be a shaman with a certificate. How do you get a shaman certificate in 3 days to serve bufo and kambo for the fee of $4,000? Do not go into a bufo ceremony unless you did your research on the person serving. There are wolves in sheep's clothing!

The biggest lesson is *the lesson just begins when you serve.* Then you have people that need help for weeks integrating. Integration is, for some, the hardest part, and most people will not reach out to you as they feel like they are imposing, or they are embarrassed. But the truth is, if you serve them, make sure they can reach you in the event they just need a few kind words or a meditation or any other reason. Be there for them after, even when there is no economic benefit for you.

- *Do you see serving 5 as being different from serving other entheogenic medicines? How? Why?*

Yes. 5-MeO-DMT is, for me, always a one-on-one experience, as opposed to a group ceremony or context. Ayahuasca, mushrooms, San Pedro – all these can be served well in groups, but 5-MeO-DMT is more intense and requires more individual attention and care – as I've said, it might take 5-6 people to really manage just one person's experience at a time.

- *What concerns, if any, do you have about the surging interest in 5 globally, and the sharp increase in demand for the experience (and its possible negative impacts on toads)?*

At some point it will not be sustainable to serve everyone who wants bufo. I think synthetic might be the answer, but I have not experienced yet so I have no real experience to base a valid opinion upon.

- *What hopes do you have with 5 and the experiences it makes possible for people?*

Simply put, it allows people to be the best version of themselves possible and to live their lives with the knowledge that they are infinite.

- *Have you been public about your work with 5? (ie, presented at conferences, WBAC, given interviews, etc.) If so, how do you navigate being public?*

I was invited to speak at WBAC (the World Bufo Alvarius Congress) in 2020, but the pandemic hit and it was a very busy time for me serving. I was asked to do a video virtual version and I decided to not do this as this was simply not my preference. The only interview I've done is with you on The Entheogenic Evolution Podcast.

Less is More for Working One-On-One

by Oliver "Olli" Martin

"If the doors of perception were cleansed, everything would appear to man as it is, Infinite."
-- William Blake

When I first read that famous quote from Blake around 1995, I wasn't aware of its true deeper meaning. By "infinite," what he means here is another word for consciousness, love, or God. However, I went another 15 years down the road of being Olli (only) until I finally realized that we indeed are truly infinite.

So why has it come to be that we limit ourselves to the form we inhabit in the first place? Looking at how society is built, and who it benefits, you might come to the conclusion that this is all not an accident. But looking at these times of change we are in, it seems there is an awakening of consciousness happening for humanity: trusting the intuitive heart and releasing the attachments to the form with fear (of death) being at the center of them. And part of that change, which is already coming about, though

Facilitating 5-MeO-DMT

slowly for about 10-15 years, is the new-found interest in psychedelic drugs. One that stands out, 5-MeO-DMT, appears to be the most potent known to humanity.

So let me introduce you to how I work with this molecule, what I experienced about its miraculous abilities, and what I find most important: how to fully embrace and integrate the experience.

When I was 20, I experienced my first true psychedelic; self-gathered *Psilocybe Semilanceata* mushrooms. I was blown away at how different this was compared to smoking cannabis, or even having hash cacao (which was my first cannabis experience three years prior). From then, I got sucked into the world of psychedelics through that first mushroom experience. And I wasn't coming down for months, trying to find and learn all I could about it. This was not that easy, since it was a time before psychedelic information was easily available on the Internet. I had to go to bookstores, libraries, and so-called "head shops." They were not only selling everything about cannabis, but also books and even, in those days, mushroom grow kits.

It was that same year that I first heard about psychedelic toads – namely, *Bufo alvarius*. A friend of mine was the owner of a pet shop and had them in one of the little glass terrariums in his shop. He heard from his supplier that these toads were known to contain a psychedelic drug in their glands. That was all we knew about them, and I never asked him to "milk" one or allow me to "milk" them myself ("milking" is the process of squeezing the toads' glands and collecting the excretions to be dried and later smoked or vaporized). And buying a toad to trip was a no-go for me. I felt that nothing good would come out of it. So, I opted to start growing mushrooms, and quite successfully from early on, despite having to deal with the lowest quality and cheapest equipment. But it was my thing. And it still is my greatest passion. Even though I don't grow as many species now as I have throughout the years (almost 30 different varieties), it is still around a dozen different *Psilocybe* species I am working on every week in my little amateur lab.

Over the course of the next several years, I would experiment with mostly Psilocin. It was in 2004 that I tried "psilohuasca," the intense combination of *Peganum Harmala* and *Psilocybe* Mushrooms, for the first time. That first time brought me to a state of total dissolution; what I today call a nondual experience. However, there wasn't the realization that I am more than my thinking mind, so there was no awakening to a higher consciousness happening. I learned a lot from that night, though, and my love and trust in mushrooms was the reason that my friend and I went through this physically and mentally unharmed. Years later, in 2010, I finally went above that initial psilohuasca dose and also my wife added *Peganum* for the first time. So, in that night we not only both experienced that nondual state, but coming back realized that we are

IT, and the personal self of the individuated ego is more like a suit we wear, but not the fullness of who or what we are.

At the same time, I discovered how to extract DMT from Mimosa root bark. In the following months, I extracted a lot and recrystallized the pure molecules in many different shapes, with the purest quality always ending up in a diamond, crystalline structure. I had many experiences vaporizing it, and also researching different results from different crystal structures. Many people say that DMT is rather weak compared to 5-MeO-DMT, and that it can't get you to a nondual state. From my experience, this is not the case. The challenge here is to inhale enough of the vaporized molecule in one take, since tolerance sets in fast, and with tripping already started, inhaling more becomes impossible.

What I would call a "full-release" dose of DMT is around 50 mg of pure freebase. I use a self-built device ("the machine") to vaporize it, and with that, it is easily possible to inhale 50 mg in one breath. Taking even more than this is possible, but I have not found it to be necessary for the nondual experience.

After months of tripping almost daily with full DMT dosages, I came back from an experience knowing that this had to stop. I found myself abusing the psychedelic to become "more enlightened" in the process. As I've noticed with many people over the years, this is a very common trap of the mind. Being spiritual or becoming more spiritual becomes the new "get rich and famous scheme" for the mind. The core idea surely always is that the mind wants to be loved. The little child in us just wants unconditional love from mum and dad.

Then, after a few months break and what felt like a come-down, I slowly started experimenting again. But now I was back into "full-length" psychedelics (as opposed to the relatively brief experience of vaporized DMT). I had numerous very high doses of LSD, DMT (taken orally), psilohuasca, and ayahuasca trips, always coming to the same conclusion: there is no "letting go" needed. All *doing* is not *being*, including "letting go," which is still a form of *doing*.

So, when I finally encountered 5-MeO-DMT, it was more of a reaffirmation of what I already had experienced multiple times than something decidedly new or different: we ARE all one consciousness, energy, love, ether, GOD...

Maybe this is the reason why I am not totally going crazy and promoting the idea of there being one way only for the abilities of 5-MeO-DMT. Instead, I just experience it detached from the romantic view of it being the "magic pill" to "enlightenment."

Yes, when I finally obtained some crystalline 5-MeO-DMT from a Polish research chemical vendor in 2012 and tried it, I was thrilled at how potent and different it is compared to DMT. The way it comes on is best described as a total dissolution in

Facilitating 5-MeO-DMT

pure liquid sunshine. However, I also immediately felt an intense dopaminergic rush on the come down from it. There was a feeling of intense personal power, pretty similar to how cocaine is active in the brain, especially when smoked in freebase form (which I have tried few times, but luckily was never really interested in, though).

I have always been thrilled by natural science. I helped toads and frogs cross the streets when I was a child and hunted lizards and snakes to just hold and study them. And later went all in-depth with the mushroom grows and extractions. So for me drugs are not attached to any kind of shamanistic views calling them "medicine" to "heal" the self. I just study them. I am neutral, yet ambitious and curious.

My childhood interest in amphibians and reptiles was also the core drive to finally get interested in caring for the gorgeous *Bufo alvarius* toads. Since I, at the time, already had a way to get crystalline 5-MeO-DMT freebase, I didn't need them to obtain the molecule. In 2012 though, there were still only wild toads for sale, which was another "no-go" for me. A year and a half later, though, I finally got four of them from a breeder in Germany who was very successful in breeding them. In November 2014 those four were joined by five small 2-month-old toadlets to complete the bunch. When they then later reached maturity, I would milk them for a while to support myself supplementally at that time, while as I was already running psilohuasca weekends for clients. But eventually I needed to stop this since it never was pleasant for any of us (the toads and myself). But let's go back and let me tell you how I started working with clients, first facilitating group weekends for almost five years.

In the end of 2012, I took part in an ayahuasca retreat for the first and only time. I went there with my friend J, who later assisted me on the psilohuasca weekend retreats. There were two Shipibo shamans from Peru present at the ayahuasca retreat. The only reason for me to go there was to experience the authentic Shipibo *icaros* and their ayahuasca without needing to leave Europe and travel to South America. But I was blown away by the love the Shipibo would give the participants, totally without condition. This really changed how I see other people. And it made it clear to me that I would need to finally share my mushrooms and serve others with the same unconditional Love. I also wanted to do my best to have a nondual experience available through the sessions. So, it became clear that it would be psilohuasca that I wanted to offer. A lot of people I met throughout the years that were into psychedelics still had a dual view on it. It was always about the "me" having an experience.

In summer 2013, the first psilohuasca weekend took place. We did two more that year, and then later up to ten per year. Since the weekend would include two evenings, I needed to have a kind of introductory experience for the Friday night. My wish would have been to just be together and share personal stories and open up as a group by sharing with vulnerability and being honest. However, this wasn't really what people were expecting. So, the sharing was minimized to an hour; just a basic introductions of the guests. This was then followed by a session with vaporized DMT at a medium dose around 30mgs. This way people would go deep, but not cross the line into a nondual experience. Still, some personally got a lot from these sessions. And for the group, this was a way to open up energetically and bond as a group, though not always, or not for everyone.

Later in 2014 I started to replace the (illegal in the Netherlands) DMT with the legal (in the Netherlands) 5-MeO-DMT. And this is where things got interesting. The DMT sessions did teach me how to facilitate these small-scale experiences within a group. With around 30 minutes for each participant, with 12-15 people to serve, it was quite exhausting. We were only two people facilitating, and often I needed to help out when things would get difficult while my partner was the sitter. The way DMT works is far more calm and gentle, also physically less reactive. 5-MeO-DMT, on the other hand, is highly energetic, and if the experimenter is not letting go into the experience, the reaction can be one of intense physical resistance. 5-MeO-DMT does release energies with everyone. If a person already rests in love and gratitude, this release is gentle and giving. If one lacks love and gratitude and has a huge amount of suppressed energy, then it can release quite explosively. Screaming from the top of the lungs for up to five minutes, kicking in all directions with arms and legs, rolling around, trying to stand up and all similar manner of physical and energetic reactions take place, which we tend not to see with DMT. Purging also takes place, which was difficult to prevent since people would have had food before the sessions. Today, I have people stay sober during the week before the session, and fast the day of, except for some water.

When it became clear that too much "unwanted stuff" was happening with the guests on the Friday nights, and the idea of an introduction to the mushroom-MAOI combination of psilohuasca experience wasn't in demand anymore, I started to lower dosages from 12-14mgs to 8-10mgs of pure freebase 5-MeO-DMT. With this range, the people who would naturally be able to fully release would have enough, but those who resisted wouldn't drown in a total psychotic or chaotic experience and would come out far less disturbed. This is what happens with people who are not yet naturally "ripe" to realize God within in nondual unity. I know this might sound arrogant, but this is not meant in a judgmental way, but simply as feedback from a witness and facilitator. Not everyone is ready for that full dissolution experience and unity with God as there is resistance and unprocessed energies within them that lead to challenging experiences.

FACILITATING 5-MEO-DMT

I have received multiple emails from people who ended up with a type of PTSD from a 5-MeO-DMT experience they had with other facilitators, with anxiety and panic attacks haunting them. Some ended up in mental institutions. Over the years, I've worked with groups on weekends where I had guests that I couldn't "screen" sufficiently, and I, too, had guests whose 5-MeO-DMT experiences became very traumatic and disturbing. These people typically then stayed with the group and, with personal support, they were able to find peace with what they experienced. The bond within the group also helped them to come down enough to then enter a small dose, non-MAOI, mushroom experience on Saturday after their 5-MeO-DMT experience. And miraculously, this, compared to what the others would have (small amount of Psilocin: 10-12mgs) would allow them to close all violently-opened "channels" in themselves from the 5-MeO-DMT experience with love and acceptance.

Still, this was a lot of extra energy invested on my side, and also created disturbances inside the group. And when considering how gentle and loving the mushroom experience is, compared to the 5-10-minute space rocket ride without a proper release time (only 30 seconds compared to 1-2 hours), I realized that I had to start putting more effort in deciding to whom I'd offer 5-MeO-DMT. This wasn't easy, taking into account that people come to such a weekend with expectations. And with all the hype around the "one and only drug," 5-MeO-DMT, it wasn't easy to swallow for some to then not have the opportunity to experience it. And it didn't really help that I offered them DMT instead. Overall, this turned out to be much better than the "everyone gets it" approach and mostly people would follow my advice to take things easy and wait for the "real deal," the psilohuasca, seeing the Friday night experience as the introduction it was always supposed to be, and not the main event, which was the psilohuasca.

I surely always screened the guests for medical or psychological issues prior to the weekends, but besides that, I didn't ask too many questions on their background. On one hand, this was just way too much work with 10 retreats a year, each with up to 15 guests, at least for me alone. And to be honest, I was just happy to have so many interested people coming and didn't want to pull the brakes on their enthusiasm of coming to one of my "famous psilohuasca weekends" they heard me speaking enthusiastically about on numerous podcasts. Over time, I learned though to look at people a bit more closely and see what their intentions were for coming and what their experiences in life had been, prior.

To measure the dosages for the psilohuasca night, I always would have an individual conversation with everyone in the afternoon prior to the Saturday night session, typically when we had the two-hour walk outside. To meet the perfect dose range, especially with MAOI-enhanced mushrooms, it is important to know more than just the physical details of a person. And in the end, I always wanted to meet expectations and let everyone have a word about their dose, too (though expectations are typically in the way of a release into "What is"). With all that said, for the 5-MeO-DMT session on Friday, though, there was simply not enough time for this. Sometimes people were arriving at the venue when we had already started the ceremony at 7pm, even though I tried everything to not have this happen and planned with everyone to be there on time at 5pm.

At the same time this all developed (around 2015), I got more and more requests to facilitate private one-on-one sessions with people who simply did not like the group approach, or some simply didn't have the time for three days off. Even though I had my hands full from my main job being a househusband with children, plus the monthly group retreats, I started to then have private sessions. In the beginning, I was offering both 5-MeO-DMT and psilohuasca in one event (over two days). But then learning to keep them separate, to fully embrace each psychedelic, a way that was wiser and a more spiritual approach than the "I want it all!" mindset. I always followed the learning-by-doing way of life, all my life. And with all that the group weekends taught me, it was clear to me that the single sessions would give me a chance to work as perfectly and productively with the substances as possible. Still, even there, I had so much to learn, and while this still is something which never ends in life, I am proud to say that I found the best way for me to conduct a 5-MeO-DMT session that is both safe and beneficial for the client. Which finally brings me to the format in which I am currently offering 5-MeO-DMT.

How I work with 5-MeO-DMT:

All the above leads us to how I grew into working with this substance currently after my first experience with it in 2012 and having started offering it in sessions to people in 2013. I meanwhile wouldn't do sessions with more than two people in one session and over the course of the past six years of doing private sessions, I learned that even if the format is a one-on-two, the actual 5-MeO-DMT experience itself always needs the one-on-one format. This means only one client and I are in the room as the session is facilitated. The reason is simple yet of the utmost importance. Any additional person, especially when connected personally (via their relationship) to the person who takes the drug, is interfering with the energy in the room. I have experienced this with couples and friends, regardless how hard they tried to not interact in any way and be a neutral presence. My role is always to be the safety net, the reality-check, and part

FACILITATING 5-MEO-DMT

of the environment the experience takes place in, but nothing more. Yet the fact that we live in a dual world makes the one-on-one approach, the two becoming one, so important. Which is also the reason why I carefully tune in with the energy of the person writing me requesting a session, and these days, only follow my gut feeling, my intuition, when deciding if I will enter a session with someone or not. It is decided by the ONE, there is no *someone* involved. The moment my mind wants to help, or do good, already denies this higher wisdom of God. Interestingly, it isn't rare that people I then refuse, and who initially came across as all loving, end up swearing at me out of their disappointment for not having been accepted to have the experience they eagerly want to have. They were advertised into having it, if we look at the almost insane hype around this drug, interestingly, often by people who feed their ego with the popularity they get from their crowd of followers instead of sharing the true unconditional love this experience can engender. Like I said before, I have the feeling that 5-MeO-DMT stimulates the dopamine system which is responsible for this "all-powerful" rush people seem to have from it, feeding their mind.

For me, it is really important that I keep my mind "out of this," and this is why I follow my intuitive feeling rather than rationally trying to decide who goes and who doesn't from some kind of pre-determined criteria. The way I try to get this feeling, via tuning in, is through letting people tell me their story, openly, honestly, and out of the flow. By simply writing a letter to themselves where they share their "history," those who follow this realize quickly that this is already part of the session, and the outcome will stay with them, regardless of if the actual 5-MeO-DMT experience will then take place, or not. They can feel how beneficial it is to write down how it all started and look back on all the developments, all the progress they have made throughout the years being on this trip as a human being. We all are so obsessed – and again this is not a coincidence – with thinking about projected results and outcomes, not on the now, and only focusing on the future. The future where we will be healed and better, perfect, and happy. Yet, only by looking back does the true progress we've made become apparent. And this progress is an evolutionary one. This is how life itself grows, naturally: making mistakes, then taking another route.

But back to the 5-MeO-DMT sessions.

The format is always one-on-one, and the place I do this needs to be one where all outer input is controlled and safe. Thus, I serve in my home. Our living room is the ceremonial place. There is a documentary out, *The 5MEOMOVIE* (.com) where you can see what this environment looks like. (I did a one-on-three *only* for them, which took place a day before the footage shown in the film. The footage featured in the film shows a low-dose DMT session, as I would not allow them to film an actual 5-MeO-

DMT session. Frank's and Boris's [two individuals featured in the film] reactions were intense to this small (10 mg) amount of DMT, since it triggered a 5-MeO-DMT flashback.)

What this room offers in my sessions is darkness (very dim candlelight), a comfortable place to lie on (Thai massage mat), unobtrusive sound (Brian Eno, "Discreet Music," A1), little Palo Santo scent, and that is all. Anything else distracts the mind, and I see the essence of a psychedelic session overall as reduction of sensory input to the absolute minimum to have a release from the form as easily as possible. It is also very important that the client lies down flat, so only a very small cushion below the head to lift it to the height of the torso is used. But any pressure in the neck is to be avoided. Also, so too with any pressure anywhere else in the body. Arms and legs should not be crossed to stay energetically open, and overall, clothes should be as comfy as possible. No jewelry, watches, belt, or anything else which could be dangerous, in the case the person moves around uncontrolled while under the influence. I always have a bucket on hand, though it is very rarely needed. In fact, I haven't had a client going into resistance and/or purging for 2-3 years now, since I invest so much effort in trying to tune in to whether a person is genuinely "ready" for the intense, overwhelming death of the mind. As mentioned before, gratitude, as well as the amount of suffering in life that one has already had, is taken into account, and finally, the ability to trust and follow the intuitive heart. All of these are signs of this readiness. Searching for healing, improvement, killing the ego, or any other form of denial of the present moment is not what I support with my sessions. I've learned that it is all about acceptance, gratitude, and giving the self the love that it always looked for on the outside, conditionally. Yet, only from inside, this love is detached from all conditions.

If a person is not yet ready for the release, the realization of God within, then they could enter into a release, but come back with no memory of it via a white-out. So even if there is no resistance, it is not the guarantee that the session will unfold to its true potential. If the physical reaction is peaceful, though, it is always a sign that there are no severe blockages within the person. Often these people just became too obsessed with the idea of "becoming enlightened," or being "more spiritual," overlooking that only the seeking is in the way of finding, and that they already are sitting on the golden throne while searching for it around or outside of themselves.

To increase the dose wouldn't change any of this outcome. In the past, I offered clients the chance to repeat the experience and to have another round following the first. Since I now solely work with pure crystalline 5-MeO-DMT (I recrystallize it myself), I can precisely measure dosages, and with the special vaporization device, can

FACILITATING 5-MEO-DMT

assure the full inhalation of the desired dose, which is between 12-15 mg. Women, in my experience/perception, are typically "closer to God," and therefore need less of the substance. People with less, or no, psychedelic experience, also need a lower dose. And then finally, weight/body mass, also plays a role in dosage. I also did offer rectal application in the past, where dosages are around 20-25 mg. I do not offer this anymore since it is very difficult to reach "full-release-dosages" through this route. Typically, the ego stays present, and therefore, the core idea of my sessions, the nondual experience, is not delivered via rectal administration.

The "container" for a session comes in three parts, and if you look at testimonials of my former clients, this is highly appreciated, and I therefore recommended it. Part one is a 1-2 hour walk in our nearby gorgeous forest, a forest that is kept natural and wild. It houses massive fruitings of a rare and special European *Psilocybe* species every year. This walk is essential for "grounding," for releasing tension, and for bonding and developing trust between my guest and myself. After that walk it's always as if hours have passed and though it's quite a walk with 5 kilometers, it leaves one with a fresh and clean state of being. Following that with part two, people are introduced to my home, where it's all about making sure they feel safe, at home, and relaxed. Slowly, the session then is prepared with all the needed information delivered. I show guests the 5-MeO-DMT crystals, explain the recrystallization process, and also how the device works that they will be using to vaporize the substance. We go through the stages of the actual experience and what I will do to assist them. For example, letting them know that I will throw a blanket over the clients upon "landing" (often around the eighth minute in), since it helps with feedback of the body and the sensation of cold (which can be typical with psychedelic sessions where temperatures can fluctuate wildly, and one might feel exceptionally cold). Once the person is safe, around 15-20 minutes after starting, I leave the room to give the client the chance to be with themselves, though I'm sure to stay close by in the open next room just in case I am needed.

Part three then is another essential part where we have lunch together of warm vegetarian food and fresh salad, which I prepare before the session. It is essential to then address all things that want addressing, but nothing is forced. Talking too much can destroy the experience by pinning it down to form/words. I do make clear what to expect within the next few days, or weeks, and assure the client that I will be available at any time, should they need to reach out. I also prepare them about what to do about the not uncommon flashback sensations/reactivations they might experience. Typically, this happens around the fourth night. Depending on the actual 5-MeO-DMT experience, and if the person tries to force it the days following the session, the reactivation can be very intense, and it is crucial to not enter into fear or meet it with resistance. The reactivation gives a chance to fully integrate the experience, and if one is prepared, (including the people around them) nothing bad can come out of it. I've never had a person having a flashback during the daytime or while functioning in "reality." Reports of reactivations while driving or elsewise, I can't verify. Once the client is all sober and settled, they are free to leave or have a visit with the toads downstairs (in my home) that finishes our time together, typically after five to six hours of sharing.

I know that what I wrote here might offend some of you and might seem to be totally different or opposite to what the common belief is about this drug and why it is seen as a medicine. From all that I learned in the 46 years of being human, I came to the conclusion that I do not believe that the mind needs to be crushed, purged, or fixed. I believe in gratitude for what is, and for the fact that all creation is not an accident, but a way to express, explore, and experience the divine consciousness that is All That Is, and which we are a part of. Not like a piece of a puzzle, but with every tiny bit containing the whole, like with a fractal. I do not think that more of some-thing will help to release into no-thing. The need to improve, the constant obsession to look to the future seeking the better self, while always denying and fighting what is, is always the same, regardless of the method used. 5-MeO-DMT can be a tool, just like most of the other natural psychedelics can, but it is in no way the ultimate pill to enlightenment. People saying this are only seeking applause for themselves, since these quotes are only there to draw attention, just like with any other newspaper headline. It's like insects following the light; our mind follows anything promising more than what we already have. And while this might be fame, money, possession in the past, it will easily shift to enlightenment, spirituality, and death of the ego. Only the mind wants/needs to separate. God is every-*thing*. Love does not exclude any-thing.

Thank you very much for reading and again let me say that all written is solely my opinion from my experience and nothing was meant to attack or deny any other position about 5-MeO-DMT and how to work with this substance. The only thing I really wish for is that everyone receiving this substance will be safe and unharmed, just like I hope the toads will be in the future. Like I've written on my homepage: how spiritual is it to have such an experience on the back of the suffering of another being?

On the Responsibilities of Those Serving 5-MeO-DMT

by Victoria Wueschner

5-MeO-DMT, in the form of toad secretions or pure molecule, is a relatively new medicine with no specific lineage or history. It does not belong to anyone, nor can any one single spiritual culture or tradition claim it as their own. It naturally follows the ancient Hermetic law of Correspondence, "As Above, So Below." On the macrocosmic level, a peak experience with 5-MeO-DMT can result in the total liberation of the self. As this principle reflects through on our microcosmic physical level, we can recognize that 5-MeO-DMT too is liberated. It can never be apprehended, and it never will. While the truth of this subject matter brings with it a hope for the unification of humanity, it also brings with it a spiritual teething process with far-reaching consequences. As we are now being afforded an opportunity to work in unison to shepherd in this powerful medicine, a substantial amount of responsibility needs to be accepted by all those involved in working with 5-MeO-DMT.

Facilitating 5-MeO-DMT

We are now witnessing the aftermath of what can happen if this responsibility is ignored. Due to a lack in education and accountability in facilitation, seekers of this medicine are falling victim to physical harm, crippling anxiety, paranoia, suicidal ideation, PTSD, death and more. A simple investigation into these issues reveal a much more complex series of obstacles, stemming from a wide variety of root problems. Ultimately, they can be summarized by an importance in cultivating a deeper sense of safety, ethics, and practitioner integrity. As a real understanding of these key topics are both integrated and supported by a genuine application, facilitators will have the ability to begin rewriting the skewed narrative of 5-MeO-DMT as being a dangerous compound.

So where do we begin then?

As it always should be, as facilitators, we must first bring our focus to the needs of the participants. At the center of their necessities lies the gem amidst it all, which is their ability to fully surrender to their own experience. On the surface this sounds simple. However, this is not necessarily the case, as there is a wide variety of external factors to be considered, almost all of which are the responsibility of the facilitator. As participants prepare for the most powerful experience a human being can embark on, a presumptuous trust on their end must be reached in order to proceed to the experience. This hope rests on the possibly misleading assumption that their facilitator possesses all the necessary knowledge needed to focus on covering all these many factors. If we slip into a participant's perspective for a moment, it's easy to understand why they might perceive a facilitator, who is sharing the world's most powerful entheogenic compound, as having been through an extensive training and arduous process to become qualified as a facilitator.

Unfortunately, as stated earlier, there are no past wisdom traditions with ancient roots with 5-MeO-DMT to pass tried and true knowledge on from teacher to student. Naturally, this has led to the creation of many first-generation 5-MeO-DMT trainings by students as self-proclaimed teachers of this medicine. One consequence of constructing these trainings in the absence of proper guidance, mentors, or elders to hold students accountable, has resulted in a shockingly large portion 5-MeO-DMT trainings that are incomplete. I can speak for myself here in my own personal experience of having to go through 3 separate trainings with 3 different facilitators over the period of a year to feel complete enough to serve this medicine safely, effectively, and with full integrity. To take things a step further, we are now beginning to witness the spiritual trap of Ego-Superiority within facilitators.

This occurs when facilitators unconsciously bypass their own personal work and integration while having no one to hold them accountable in their medicine practice or to their personal actions. Completely unaware of it, they begin to over-identify with *their* practice, and suddenly the work of serving medicine becomes about the facilitator and not the individual coming for healing. In addition to an already challenging situation, those under the spell of Ego-Superiority often don't have the ability to access the perspective needed to get a handle on it. This is where the support of an elder or guide is imperatively needed to support facilitators through the challenges of the path, rather than egos getting left unchecked to run rampant.

The paradox of 5-MeO-DMT is philosophically intriguing. While it's a medicine that gifts facilitators a key to higher realms of consciousness, and ultimately spiritual alchemy, it simultaneously offers to facilitators access to the deepest dangers and traps of the ego. As facilitators navigate the path, they carry with them the very medicine which, in its peak experience, deals more directly with the ego, than any other psychedelic medicine. Is it possible that perhaps these facilitators are also some of the most susceptible to learning the deepest complexities and teachings of the ego? To further explore this, the alchemical law of polarity, which is expressed above, states that everything has two poles or two opposites. In the case of 5-MeO-DMT, the particular polarity experienced by the facilitator is largely determined by the facilitator's own personal choices and decisions along their own unique spiritual path. This is what can end up being extremely dangerous to participants, as many facilitators choose to walk the path without the need for any guidance or support.

A brief and insightful glimpse into the wide variety of different spiritual teachings and scriptures point to the path of a spiritual seeker being a tedious and destructive process. Its terrain is littered with countless challenges, battles, and traps along the way. It is arduous, no doubt, but miraculously enough, as long as there has been a spiritual path to walk, there has always been a spiritual guide to help those walking it. These guides have acted as the ancient wisdom keepers shepherding both students and initiates through the darkness and towards their own inner truth. Spanning back to the beginning, through different cultures and lineages, these guides have worn different names, though all working towards the same common principle. Hindus have called them *gurus*, while Buddhist (in China) call them the *laoshi*, Tibetans have *lamas*, and Hebrews have *rabbis*. Even the sacred indigenous medicine traditions reveal ayahuasca, iboga, peyote and San Pedro, to name just a few, as also having these guides, being referred to as *shamans* or *curanderos*. Without easily slipping into an entire paper dedicated to the history of spiritual guides, we can see the level of importance our ancestors have placed on spiritual guides as one seriously enters into their own spiritual work.

Facilitating 5-MeO-DMT

Applying this understanding, let us turn our awareness to 5-MeO-DMT facilitators. They are not only carrying the world's most powerful entheogen, but also ushering others through the biggest experience a human being can have. Clearly, it would be a significant understatement to convey the magnitude of this responsibility. So grandiose, that the very action of serving a participant without proper guidance in one's practice, both before beginning one's practice, and consistently during one's entire practice, can result in little-to-no results for participants, and possibly even dire consequences.

For many initiates of this powerful molecule, by default, the facilitator becomes a type of pseudo-spiritual guide, or lack thereof. As participants encounter their many bumps, difficulties, and challenges of the process, they rightfully reach out to their facilitators for support. This is beautiful, but what if this facilitator has chosen to facilitate this experience with little-to-no guidance on their own path? Maybe it is a facilitator who took a weeklong training and was left to run on their own, or maybe it was a facilitator who found themselves access to sourcing the medicine and decided to start serving with no training or oversight, or possibly even a facilitator who became so overly-identified with their practice as a facilitator that they refuse any outside guidance from others in their community. These scenarios are a not only real, but much more prominent within the 5-MeO-DMT community than we may like to admit, and is frankly responsible for where the narrative of this medicine is currently.

So how do we get out of this mess? Well, this takes us back to the original question at hand. What are the responsibilities of a facilitator? In short, the answer to this question is *integrity*. Integrity would be reflected by the facilitator having enough insight to determine if their container, protocol, and practices are complete. This can only ring true with the proper and continued guidance along the way. A facilitator should always have a team in their community helping to hold them accountable as they too hold themselves accountable. Accountability does not need to be seen as a judgmental regiment from higher-ups rather than a community working together to build a strong and ethical container conducive for participants truly getting the most out of their experiences.

In conclusion, it is indeed true that no one can lay claim to this medicine and perhaps it has been divinely orchestrated that way. Perhaps we are being gifted the unique opportunity as human beings to find a way past our perceived separation in working together to support the evolution of this beautiful medicine in the world. One thing is for certain though: as facilitators working with the crown jewel of unity, we can no longer continue operating in anything but unity. We must learn to work together by accepting guidance from others in the form of teachers, mentors, and peers for the good of all humanity. This medicine is much bigger than ourselves as facilitators. It is not about us, and never will be about us. It is about those coming for healing. Let us all step into the true definition of what it means to be in service.

IN EVOLUTIONARY SYNC

by Joël Brierre

- *What hopes do you have with 5 and the experiences it makes possible for people?*

We're often asked in our work at Tandava Retreats here in Mexico, why do we work with this particular medicine? What is our drive behind working with this powerful molecule?

I can only speak for myself, but what really does it for me is the look of peace on a participant's face during the tail end of their journey. After working for weeks of preparation with a person and knowing what kind of traumas or suffering they're bringing to the table, it's something special to see them feeling truly whole. When I see this look of peace that is so visible you can feel it, I can't help but wonder what this world would be like if we all felt whole, what it would be like if we all actually LIVED, rather than simply experiencing life as a day-to-day, perpetual trauma response.

Facilitating 5-MeO-DMT

I feel that 5-MeO-DMT is right in sync with our evolution. It is a powerful tool to help bring us into right relationship not only with each other, but with ourselves. The fact that it is unattached to a past that can be claimed by one culture or group of people makes me think of an open road ahead, unbound by the grips of yesterday.

There are no elders to point out the perilous traps. We will have to learn to work together, drawing from the collective wisdom and learning from one another's mistakes.

This is a medicine that breaks through all mind, dissolves away the sense of individual self, and allows us temporary freedom from the whirlpool of chaos that is human existence. Now while this of course can be a blissful and liberating experience, this can also be extremely confrontational to the sense of self. Are we truly ready to give up our suffering? Are we really ready to give up the numerous identities we've created around our own agony?

Our suffering is such a large part of personal identity, much of our personality has been created from trauma responses or defense mechanisms, and we, by nature, attach to our own perceived identity. Sometimes the patterns that we know are harmful to ourselves and others are the hardest to let go. The ego will fight the process at all costs. This is because the ego feels it is a part of us and we will not be the same if we let it go. The ego enjoys familiarity, as the familiar is based around the aspects that support our projected identity, if we were to let go of part of that identity, it would shift us into the unfamiliar, a landscape that requires learning new navigation. We don't want to let part of ourselves go, because subconsciously we fear the death process. We naturally have an aversion to impermanence.

The Yogis maintain that *dvesha* (aversions) and *abhinivesha* (fear of death) are direct causes of suffering, as they keep us complacent and trapped within our own emotional patterning. We can learn to understand that leaving the known, and facing the death process, is the gate that separates us from realizing our true and boundless nature. But first, we must take the blind leap into the unknown. Some may find this exciting, while others will be simply terrified by the concept, but the chance is here.

We have been invited to let it all go and evolve into something completely new, and we seem to be knee-deep in the process.

How will we, as humanity fare in this process of death and rebirth? What aspects of our whole will resist the coming change? What parts of ourselves will attempt to grasp onto and maintain control? What must fall away before we can surrender and deliquesce from the shackles of our own suffering?

The Logos Portal

by Arthur

- *How were you introduced to 5/Toad? What was your experience?*

My first connection with the toad was at an ayahuasca retreat on the Spanish island of Tenerife. On the second day of the retreat, we took the toad. I went into a beautiful, but dark, place where there was a deep, dark voice of "God" telling me that I was one of the main creators of this experience, and that we were creating and experiencing our dream life. I got the distinct feeling that I could, at any time, wake up and open something similar to a tanning bed control center and high five my fellow main co-creator group and say something like, "We are killing it! This lifetime experience is awesome! Yay!"

When I came back to my body and open my eyes, I realized that I was in the middle of a wrestling match with the facilitator who served me. Immediately, I told him, "I am here again!" and to myself, "Relax, trust yourself." His panicked face softened, and we smiled towards each other. It turned out that when my soul/consciousness left my body, I started rotating on the ground, bumping into another 5-MeO-DMT traveler, and needed to be restrained. When the facilitator was trying to hold me, I apparently started screaming, "You are not me!" and wrestling started, to the distress of the facilitator. I am a former Swedish champion in wrestling, and even though my consciousness was not there, it seems like my body and reptilian brain were doing well at grappling.

*Editor's Note: This account above is a good example of how the subjective experience of one under the influence of 5-MeO-DMT can be quite different from what is taking place at the physical level, where there may be no awareness of what the physical body is doing. This is particularly common in early experiences and often involves a flight-or-fight acting out.

- How did you become a facilitator and why?

The first time I connected with toad facilitating myself, was only my third time connecting with the medicine. It was a very small dose, and during the experience, the only topic that came up was that I should do the toad medicine together with MDMA, because it would integrate the experience in the most efficient way. A name came to the instructions of, "The Logos Portal."

- What, if any, training did you receive?

I received no training. I formed a private group of two other consciousness expanders and explorers. We started connecting with the medicine monthly, and later, bi-weekly through the "Logos Portal Method" with MDMA. We also shifted from using the toad, to using pure 5-MeO-DMT. There was a small difference, but the main objective of achieving expansion and heightened awareness, and harmonizing with our higher selves, was very well achieved with the pure 5-MeO-DMT substance. It was also easier to dose more exactly.

After a year and a half of working in this small, private group amongst ourselves, I got the calling that it was time to share with others what we felt was beneficial and was working for ourselves

- How do you conduct sessions?

We are usually a group of around 10 people. We usually start with connecting with each other through 80-160mg of MDMA, or 1 to 2 seeds of Hawaiian Baby Woodrose

Facilitating 5-MeO-DMT

seeds (which contain LSA). My experience is that these can relax the person so that we have had almost no challenging out-of-body experiences. In 95% of the cases, it is a very calm experience for the soul to leave the body and enter back. Our experience is that there is a very efficient integration happening with these mixes. It seems the energetic field of the body is more open and harmonizes the energies and experience very fast and efficiently. My personal feeling is that my body can feel "overcharged" from the 5-MeO-DMT experience if I don't do it with LSA or MDMA, whereas, in combination, my energies go into harmony almost immediately.

Also, after-effects, like reactivations, seem to be non-existent with the mix. My belief is that the main part of integration is energetic, and that is greatly helped out by the mix of substances/sacraments. Usually, we connect with the first medicines for 2-3 hours to get that experience first, and then we connect with the 5-MeO-DMT.

- *How would you describe your approach: nondual, shamanic, ceremonial, therapeutic…?*

I would call it ceremonial-light, therapeutic, and nondual, done in a physically safer way (no panic, or bodily and heart stress, or cramps), and with more efficient integration than the ceremonies I have participated in or seen on YouTube with only 5-MeO-DMT (as opposed to using MDMA or LSA prior).

- *Do you work one-on-one, in groups, in retreats, at a center, with a team…?*

I work in a group of 10, usually. Sessions are held every 2 weeks, outdoors in nature.

- *What do you see as the purpose of working with 5?*

I believe that 5-MeO-DMT is the most efficient way of achieving left and right brain coherence to expand our consciousness and harmonize our energetic fields from all disharmony (stress, fear, anger, mental illness, and maybe even physical illness). I believe that 5-MeO-DMT might be the magic pill that we have to take many times to elevate our consciousness to a higher level. 5-MeO-DMT is not the only way to do so, but I believe it might be the most efficient.

- *What do people get out of their sessions/experiences?*

Results vary, with everything from life-changing experiences to a nice experience, but maybe not life-changing. Very few have had a challenging experience. Some people get information about their life purpose and highest potential in this lifetime. Many individuals unite with unity consciousness and come back and say, "We are one."

- *Do you provide pre-session information, screening, prep? If so, what?*

I check on previous heart/health conditions, and if they take other medications that might be dangerous or interfere with the experience.

- *What are some of the best results you've seen?*

I encounter very good results for depressed people, and also people that feel lost and without purpose. I also had good results with a bi-polar woman, but the sample size is only one person, so I can't expand beyond that.

- *What are some of the difficulties you've encountered with patients/clients?*

There can be a short period of confusion for the patients when they come back, but no bigger problems. The biggest problems are the ones I have encountered myself while exploring the medicine.

I had a period of exploration to understand the limits of the medicine and myself. I could connect with the medicine up to 10 times in a day/ceremony. It led to moments of confusion. When I am connecting with the medicine at the same time as the client, I feel like their disharmony is being channeled and harmonized through me. Sometimes that could lead to strong sexual arousal, or other intense emotions and urges for actions. I have been blessed to be able to control these emotions, energies, and drives, but I can see how this can lead to actions and behavior that is not perceived as normal, logical, or acceptable from a normal consciousness state point of view.

Also, I have encountered a short state of confusion where I thought I solved the puzzle of life and it was time to go back home again by ending my life. But then I remembered my wife and child and realized that is not the right thing to do. Also, I felt that 5-MeO-DMT was becoming highly addictive for me at some point. It felt like the answer and solution to everything, and I started to drift off into a state of detachment from "real," "normal" life. After coming through this period of great challenges for

Facilitating 5-MeO-DMT

myself, I had to set up strict rules for myself, based on my experience on how I can use and serve 5-MeO-DMT in a productive and balanced way.

I am careful with how many times per ceremony I connect with 5-MeO-DMT myself, if at all. I'm also careful with whom and when I connect with clients at the same time. My conclusion became that its more important to make sure that I am in control of what I do and how I act, than giving the client the absolute most beneficial experience every time. Its more beneficial to serve 80% of maximum benefit servings, than serving at 100% efficiency but risking that something will happen so that I cannot continue serving and regretting doing something while not at my full senses.

This might also be a circumstance of the fact that I am serving bigger groups at the same time. I am usually very comfortable connecting 3-4 times in a ceremony with 5-MeO-DMT. But I have also become very challenged at times with the energies being channeled through me on my first connection of the ceremony. Spirit works in mysterious ways.

I also have a friend who took 5-MeO-DMT by himself, and he left his body and his jacket caught fire from his lighter or a candle nearby, and he is now recovering from 40% burns on his body. One simple safety rule to give is to never do this by yourself. I have also experienced that I plan to connect one time, but immediately when coming back, that whole narrative is changed, and in a state of confusion I keep on connecting more than was good to do at that point. So don't do it alone, I would say.

But even though this medicine is very powerful and tricky to manage, maybe more challenging than any other sacrament, I believe it might also be the most beneficial when used in the right way. I think it's very important to share this information, so that we don't get people hurt and in trouble from using or working with 5-MeO-DMT. And the biggest challenge is to keep the facilitator balanced and sane in his or her service.

- *What are your recommendations for integration and post-experience processing?*

My best advice is to use the mix of MDMA or LSA that I have described for ease of integration. Also, I believe that it's more beneficial to serve in amounts of 10-15 mg per serving of 5-MeO-DMT, rather than 20-25 mg +. It gives the most beneficial effect, without the worst side effects of reactivations and cramps, or confusion. Since I served a combination of the medicines and a smaller amount of 5-MeO-DMT than I think most do, I cannot distinguish exactly what the part of my practices is that gives the most benefits. I just know that the sweet spot for a safe, pleasurable, awesome, easily-integrated 5-MeO-DMT experience is MDMA/LSA + 10-15 mg of 5-MeO-DMT.

Sometimes, for people that have a hard time taking a deep enough breath, or if they are very large individuals, they might need 20-25 mg, but I always start with the smaller dose and work up from there, as necessary.

- *How many people have you served, and what kinds of people have you worked with? (Drug addicts, spiritual seekers, vets, ages, genders, occupations, interests, nationalities/ethnicities)*

I have facilitated around 500 servings, and connected myself probably 200 times with 5-MeO-DMT. I think I have served around 200 different people by now. It has been women and men from 20 years old to 50 years old. They have been mostly spiritual seekers, but also depressed people and those with other mental conditions.

- *Do you see different issues between serving men and women, old and young, healthy and those will medical issues?*

In general, 5-MeO-DMT is a very positive experience for all my clients so far, except for one small woman that I served 25 mg 2 weeks after each other, and after the second serving, she was struggling to integrate the experience for a week before she could make sense of it all and harmonize it into her life. After that I started serving smaller doses, as described above. Also, the ones with depression and mental conditions are usually having a harder time in general with their life, so even though the 5-MeO-DMT experience helps them a lot, it usually takes more servings over a longer time-period for them to find full balance and strength in their lives.

- *What do you feel are the responsibilities of those serving 5?*

I feel the responsibility is to serve the medicine in the most beneficial and safe way possible. You need to inform the client about the process and follow-up with them after about how they are doing. It's also important to be informed about the client so that you can determine if serving them is safe or not. In general, I have found that my described way of serving seems very safe from a physical and mental standpoint. There is very little strain on the heart and body as far as I can tell, compared to other ceremonies I have observed or seen on YouTube. I would still not risk doing it on people with heart conditions or too old or weak individuals.

FACILITATING 5-MEO-DMT

- *Do you have an opinion on synthetic vs. "natural"?*

My opinion is that they are 95% the same thing, and the 5% difference does not make it worth the problems it causes for the toads to use bufo. Furthermore, it's harder to dose bufo, so even if there were no problems with the toads, I would choose the synthetic 5-MeO-DMT to serve the clients in the most safe and beneficial way every time.

- *Who should take 5? Who shouldn't?*

Everyone that feels the calling to do so, and who can do it in a safe way from a physical and mental standpoint.

- *What role do you see for 5 in the global community?*

I see it as the single most beneficial sacrament in evolving and expanding human consciousness. It might also be the most mentally healing compound, and my intuition tells me that it might also heal physical illness and sickness by harmonizing the whole energetic bodily system, though the latter is something that I have no evidence of, but I am very keen to explore further.

- *What are the lessons you've learned from serving 5?*

That it is hard to be the facilitator, and that the medicine, like everything else, can accelerate problems as fast as it can heal, depending on how it is used.

- *Do you see serving 5 as being different from serving other entheogenic medicines? How? Why?*

I see 5 more potentially psychologically addictive to the facilitator than other compounds I would imagine, as the experience can be so compelling, but I don't know myself.

- *What concerns, if any, do you have about the surging interest in 5 globally, and the sharp increase in demand for the experience (and its possible negative impacts on toads)?*

My concern is that there is no tradition or lineage as a facilitator, and it is very hard to be and become one. So, there are no sources of wisdom or safety nets. While the facilitators are learning and growing, many mistakes can be made.

- *What hopes do you have with 5 and the experiences it makes possible for people?*

I believe the 5-MeO-DMT experience can be life-changing for many. I believe the connection with 5-MeO-DMT, in most cases, proves (to the one experiencing it) that there is life after our physical death, and that we are spirits in a human experience. That is huge.

The Entheogenic Suchness of Being

by Ingo

How I Came to 5-MeO-DMT:

I am now 45 and was born in Germany near the Dutch border. I was very unhappy with the culture in the place in my youth and I wanted to get out of there as soon as possible. In Germany, alcohol has a high social value, but I was rather repelled by it, and I was lucky enough to be able to avoid it with friends at the time with the coffee shop culture in the Netherlands where marijuana was available. So Dutch grass became a strong companion at that time, and a little later, mushrooms were added, which you could also buy in Holland. The trips with mushrooms at that time were always very strong and deep for me. I had much stronger trips than my friends, despite taking a normal dosage and a good access to the experiences. I was very impressed by the power of mushrooms at that time, but was also still very young and clueless in dealing with them.

After about 10 years of daily grass consumption, the phase stopped and I concentrated on education, jobs, etc. I also stopped taking mushrooms, which had been a phase now and then in my younger years, as well as occasionally experimenting

Facilitating 5-MeO-DMT

with MDMA at raves/techno parties. I can't remember dates and years very well, but I think between 2002 and 2008 I was pretty much without psychedelic substances.

This changed when, with the help of an online forum, I started to learn about growing mushrooms, which I started doing, and then I was back into psychedelics again. Likewise, there was a popularity wave with "research chemicals" (psychedelic substances that are purely lab-created and don't have organic analogs in nature) where I then later mixed the mushrooms with MXE. With this phase, I then took higher doses of mushrooms and did an "introspective setting" each time. So I often did that alone, with an eye mask and sometimes with music, sometimes without. At this time, I was also drawn to Zen, so I learned Zen meditation, participated in *zazen* groups and *sesshins* (meditation retreats) to process these sometimes super-deep mushroom experiences. I felt that with meditation training I was able to have more productive and useful psychedelic trips.

This Zen + Mushroom phase over several years resulted at that time in a kind of "enlightenment," of which I remembered the date very well, on 3/14/2015. I had a very clear insight into the nature of being and then I was "done" at one point. DMT was also added around this date. I learned to make it myself (via extraction), and then had quite good success and deep experiences with it. This also ended my "Buddhist phase" and I was then no longer a Buddhist. The DMT experience summed up these experiences from before and I had no more new insights, but the "presentation" was again another level as I knew it from mushrooms. The reality shift experience was another level, but it actually only confirmed to me that I was still "done" and I am not in a self-deception or "spiritual bypassing" or something like that. Everything was absolutely clear and I felt complete.

I knew about 5-MeO-DMT at this point from publications for quite some time, but never really felt ready for it before. But now I did. Bring it on, was my thought. It then "fell into place" all by itself. A friend knew that I was now "looking for" this and gave me the information where I could get some in the form of pure laboratory molecule in the HCL form.

Editor's Note: Pure, lab-made 5-MeO-DMT is often available in the two different forms of freebase or HCL "salt" form. Freebase is more potent, but less stable and degrades more quickly. Because of its higher stability, chemical companies often produce the HCL form for sale on "research chemical" websites.

Everything came together at just the right time for me to experience 5-MeO-DMT. Do you know this experience? When you have it, you become aware of how everything led up to this point right now to get this insight into existence, where all the threads, coincidences, or causal connections come together and condense to *this*.

I had them after many years of intense mushroom experiences, where I thought much more is not really possible, and then DMT appeared and put another level on top of my prior experience. I can remember this decisive experience where I was no longer a Buddhist and could only laugh about my previous religious attempts and views and about my ego, which thought to have understood something special.

So, then I felt ready for 5-MeO-DMT, where I then also had access, but still took a while until I finally tried it.

The first time was a smaller dosage with a special glass bulb pipe (for vaporizing), and the first "full-release dose" was then shortly thereafter. I think there were about 12 mg in this glass bulb, and since I was doing it alone, I didn't manage to put the rolling bulb down safely, and at the same moment that the bulb shattered on the floor, I shattered too.

Just the memory of it gives me a queasy feeling in my stomach right now as I'm recounting it here. Everything totally dissolved into emptiness, the complete absence of *anything*. Then it became a birth into *everything, being* everything without a clue of being anyone or anything in particular. There was only oneness, pure oneness. And it felt divine, not for *anyone* at that moment, but there was God exclusively, without a separate self. At some point the astonishment how there can be something at all and not nothing overwhelmed me. And then this slow remembrance to understand what has just happened dawned on me. A person inhaled a molecule to experience this. It didn't really make sense, but it was a joyful coming back into myself and my personal perspective. Instead of nothing at all, it is possible to experience *this*: myself as a human in reality. How wonderful!

Descriptions are never enough, though I am writing this now to someone who has experienced it himself. I write to myself in the form of Martin. If you haven't had the experience I've described above, then you don't really know what it is because words and descriptions can't really express it properly.

Then I think I was like many who've had this experience the first time. I had this experience all by myself, and immediately wanted to share it with those close to me, wishing that everyone should have this experience and that we would create a new society, a kind of paradise on earth, if only more people could have this experience themselves and know this perspective on the nature of being.

Today, as I write this, I have taken 5-MeO-DMT myself about 20 times at the full-release dose level.

FACILITATING 5-MEO-DMT

I had already broken away from Buddhism and found my worldview more and more in nonduality, but rather the new, radical direction of people like Tony Parsons, Richard Sylvester, Jim Newman, Andreas Müller (a native language German, like myself) and the teachings of life without a personal "doership" from Ramesh Balsekar.

This "Pure 5" experience completely confirmed this direction I'd taken in shifting my worldview away from traditional Buddhism to more non-doctrinal and contemporary nonduality. It focuses on the fact that there is no separate self and only oneness. And it is talked about in different words and descriptions in books or speeches, but in this molecule, nondual experience is apprehended directly, without literal thoughts. It just presents itself as *what is*.

So, I talked about this experience with others. Seeing nonduality so clearly is very difficult for most people, and I thought maybe you just had to experience it. But for some, this separate self just falls away without a molecule. So, the way, if and when, someone awakens from his separateness is also not in his power or discretion or themselves. It just happens, and if some have to pull on a Pure 5 pipe for this, then it just happens so, and always without a separate "doership." You can't *make* it happen, even with 5-MeO-DMT.

With my wife, the application of 5-MeO-DMT for a nondual experience did not work at all, and I could not get her to try it again, which is unfortunately a pity, but that is also how it is. Some friends found it interesting, but few really dared. The whole thing took off when I explained this experience to a good acquaintance during a mushroom collecting hike and she was interested (while we were hunting for *Psilocybe Semilanceata* on cow meadows in the black forest).

For me, the "release" was very easy. I was ready to die, so to speak, and I knew very well that the best way to do it was with full dedication. I thought it must be like that for everyone with a full dose, but I also knew from literature and the exchange of information on the Internet, or from you and your podcast and books, that many do not have it so easy.

So, this person was my first companion, and I had a good feeling about her. She was also experienced with other substances and was very open to these experiences. I made every effort to prepare her for the 5. I also took your advice with the symmetry, which I also observed in my own applications and found it very helpful to have this open, symmetrical attitude at the start, and also to maintain it throughout the experience, if possible. I already knew from Zen how important posture is.

Editor's Note: In my own work with 5-MeO-DMT, I've identified the fact that the ego is most commonly energetically embodied with various degrees of asymmetry and imbalance between the left and right sides of the body. However, when people enter into full nondual energetic states on 5-MeO-DMT, their bodies always spontaneously exhibit mirrored, bilateral symmetry. Given this, I've encouraged those working with 5-MeO-DMT to employ symmetrical body postures to help avoid the asymmetrical energetic structures of the ego and more easily enter into, and maintain, nondual awareness and states of being, and this is what Ingo is referring to here. Similar to what Ingo shares, I've heard from people around the world that working in symmetry has profoundly shifted and accelerated their entheogenic practice, whether it be with 5-MeO-DMT or other psychedelic medicines.

And this application worked wonderfully with her. She "released" fully and was absolutely thrilled what this molecule did with her. She also experienced a kind of energetic healing and told me how much blocked energies were released. She was very grateful that I'd showed it to her. This gratitude is of course fun, and I found it very beautiful and intense to accompany individual people through such a process. Even if I did not take anything myself, I always found this accompaniment energetically very intense.

She felt the same way I did and wanted to pass it on, so we then did a few sessions with different acquaintances who were interested and took the chance to do it in a protected setting with careful companions.

I found this constellation quite successful. We both always had a feeling or an intuition whether it was okay to do this with someone, and I was also right every time. So, with people who felt good, it worked very easily, went well, harmoniously, and was releasing. With some where I had a strange feeling, it was bumpier, but we never had a real problem case.

So most went very well and the gratitude was very big. With two people it was a bit more difficult, and I had to add another session with one and then he was "released."

Your preliminary work was also there because I instructed everyone to keep an open, symmetrical posture, and I'm sure that also had very good effects. And of course, other tips from you as well.

Likewise, I think it was good that we were male and female, so sometimes I was more in the background and sometimes she, and depending on the needs, female intuition, or my male clarity and Zen focus, could contribute something. But yes, sometimes I thought, "Can't you trip like I do?" or I found my Zen and nonduality view would put it all in so easily, so why can't this work for others as well?

So, it struck me that the experience at a "release" is probably almost the same for everyone, when they get there, but what the returned ego or person then makes of it and can process and categorize, that can be very different. But in the end, it also doesn't

Facilitating 5-MeO-DMT

matter, because it was just as clear to me that everything happens as it does by itself, freely.

So no, I don't have to save the world. Actually, there is no one to save but only the game of unity and if it perceives itself separately, then that is perfectly in harmony and I do not have to infuse it with a molecule to be one again, which it always is and was anyway. I also don't believe that there is an inauthentic self that needs to become authentic again. I believe that "the one" is even authentic in being inauthentic. But of course, it's also perfectly okay if something recognizes itself as inauthentic and wants to resolve that and then maybe manages to do so. But that is simply the course of being, nothing more. Nobody does that separately.

Back to the sessions: so we gained with some the experience of what it is like to accompany others, to be present in this liberating process of the molecule as an obstetrician. For me it was also always highly intense and beautiful to see someone really released and to look into those amazed, happy and grateful eyes. They look back knowing that I know exactly what they have just experienced.

We still had an additional monthly meeting for those who were "psychedelically interested," just to talk and share experiences. I still had my own podcast at the time and, somehow, I was the driving force for these events. The podcast was called in German: Gespräche mit Psychonauten (Talks with Psychonauts). I also talked with Olli there for 2 shows about this substance and about his work and sessions with it. We've kept regular contact with each other since then.

I was planning with my wife to emigrate to a country where we could afford life in a cliché "house in the countryside" and live with the moderate income that we have with a little vegetable garden and pets. I had already emigrated once and therefore was not so rooted, so we did that, and I then also had my last application of 5-MeO-DMT for myself at the end of 2019 with a group of people I also accompanied once.

Since already before this phase of searching ended, my religious applications, my "psychedelic phase" also ended here. Also the podcast, these sessions with others ended, and I have not taken my beloved tryptamines since then.

However, there was recently a small 2CB + MDMA session and it has sparked my interest to go to a mushroom session again. I like this heightened perspective of mushrooms and looking at one's self. Also, my "assistant" doesn't do any more sessions as she thinks the experiences are too strong and impactful, and the work is very exhausting if you do it very responsibly.

- *What do you see as the purpose of working with 5?*

In the beginning, I saw the purpose as for healing and liberation, but later I found this motivation no longer so important or true.

- *How do you handle issues of informed consent?*

According to my wish, we did the procedure without too many rituals and discussed the procedure quite precisely with potential clients. We made it clear that we would rather stay in the background and only watch and only "touch" when it is necessary, for example if someone moves too much, in order not to hurt themselves. Later hugging was possible if desired by the client. With women, I preferred to leave that to my assistant so that there would be no misunderstandings later. We never had any disagreements.

- *What do people get out of their sessions/experiences?*

I think that is too individual, where someone is on the journey and the interpretations were very different. Of course, we were always available for later conversations, and our clients were not complete strangers, so it was mostly a certain acquaintance and we were available afterwards.

- *Do you provide pre-session information, screening, prep? If so, what?*

Much of the good information is only available in English, but depending on the case, I also recommended your PDF where you had a summary of the molecule, or this article was also available in German:
https://lightofexistence.com/5-meo-dmt-an-educational-overview/
I know the author, and I am in contact with many people via the internet on this topic, but mainly in German.

- *What are some of the best results you've seen?*

It's hard to say as it was always very individual. But I think all the people I served got an unforgettable insight into existence in one way or another, and some also had something like healings. Some had their worldview changed. I can't classify it as better or worse.

FACILITATING 5-MEO-DMT

- *How many people have you served, and what kinds of people have you worked with? (Drug addicts, spiritual seekers, vets, ages, genders, occupations, interests, nationalities/ethnicities)*

There were about 10 people where I actively served. They were more "spiritual seekers" or simply psychedelically-interested. They were German people, and both women and men. They were of very different ages, but not too young. Very interesting was also a man around 70. He had a special session and was able to conclude with many old stories.

- *Do you see different issues between serving men and women, old and young, healthy and those will medical issues?*

I think this experience is more for people who are already a bit further in life and if they are too young, they are in other processes and this experience will not necessarily always be helpful for them. My experience is that the older and more experienced, the better, but I wouldn't make it a hard rule that when someone is "ready," they can still be very young.

- *Do you see different issues between serving men and women, old and young, healthy and those will medical issues?*

We had hardly any with health problems, though there was one case of an individual with schizophrenia that I did not agree to work with, and one case of someone with mild and recent use of antidepressants. I asked him to have them completely stopped 2 weeks prior. This case was also someone who could not release so easily. So, if someone is taking antidepressants or SSRIs, I would already see that as a warning signal and a normal dose is not enough, or the drugs are already blocking the effect of tryptamines. So, we paid attention to health, but had hardly any problematic cases. But, we also did not have so many people, and I often wonder how the people do that, who handle so many clients in a short time. I think some first aid knowledge is also helpful, but I found the risks relatively acceptable for healthy people.

- *What do you feel are the responsibilities of those serving 5?*

I felt it was a great responsibility, but I thought it was important to do as little as possible in the session. The experience speaks for itself, and everybody has to make the experience for themselves, and I didn't see myself as an active part. Of course, we give the framework and a few rules and determine the process from our experience, but everyone must go their own way for themselves. We even had a vape device where everyone had to push the button and determine the starting point themselves and we just sat in the background and watched how it turned out.

I also believe that there is a kind of imprint when you come back from the dissolution and if the first thing is a rattling, touching, or singing from the facilitator, and this can be very invasive. I tried to interfere as little as possible in the experience of the other, and also did not see myself as being in a position to make special energetic interventions, as you describe, for example. I find your descriptions of how you did it very exciting and interesting, but for me that was out of the question as a facilitator.

Otherwise, I found myself responsible to always be there afterwards if desired, so I was then available for conversations and follow-up work.

- *Do you have an opinion on synthetic vs. "natural"?*

Synthetic has a negative connotation for spiritual people. I find "Pure 5" quite appropriate and I think it's wonderful to have a pure molecule that also occurs naturally in the body, so it's not a foreign molecule at all. And if you have it in absolutely pure form, for me there is no difference if it was transformed in the lab from similar substances or extracted from plants or toads.

But I can't speak from experience with toad, because I never actively sought the experience with toad secretions. I can imagine that mixing it with bufotenine and other trace compounds can give a different feel, but I don't think the essential, absolute experience of 5-MeO-DMT becomes more absolute because it came from a toad.

I found the appearance of Hamilton Morris at WBAC (the World Bufo Alvarius Congress) significant, and the visible rejection of the spiritual people to synthetic material.

This leads me to a "problem," or an observation, I often notice with both spiritual and psychedelic people. There is such a feeling of superiority, and one has the feeling of being in possession of a secret truth, and with that, one calls, for example, the people who don't have that "muggles," or a normal person, and one is somehow superior to that.

This gives a sublime feeling by belittling others. Or to see nature as better than something where man was involved, as if he is not nature.

FACILITATING 5-MEO-DMT

If the unity and the divinity was clearly seen, how can one still hold onto such thoughts of separation?

This surprises me again and again with spiritual people, and also with psychedelic people.

Did they have a different experience than me despite it being 5-MeO-DMT? How do they still manage to get caught up in such dualistic thought constructs? Is this just typical human behavior?

But yes, of course, that is also the game of unity to surrender then again in habits and oblivion and in the belief in a personal doership.

- *How do you feel 5 works with other entheogenic medicines? What are their relationships?*

I have always treated it completely separately. Whereas with other substances, which I like to mix, here I don't think it's necessary. But I know someone who claimed it to be even better when inhaled with a nitrous oxide balloon, though I have never tried it that way.

- *Who should take 5? Who shouldn't?*

I think there is no "should." There's just what comes naturally. Any people who find themselves in the situation with a smoking device on their mouth where this molecule is in it – that's who should have it. That's all.

- *What role do you see for 5 in the global community?*

I actually find the idea appealing of seemingly saving the world from destructive human egos. When I sometimes see what people then make out of this absolute, nondual experience, I am not so optimistic whether this could really work.

Rak Razam said the timing is striking, so the more we destroy ourselves, the more these substances come out that can heal us. But maybe we also need this experience of self-destruction to then evolve in a much longer-term and become a truly more awakened species. In the short-term, I am rather pessimistic. But also, this tension or dissonance dissolves in nonduality, all this may be, nevertheless, and it does not drive me into despair. I rather feel gratitude to be able to experience all this and have a peace of mind with it.

- *What are the lessons you've learned from serving 5?*

No one needs to be saved.

- *Do you see serving 5 as being different from serving other entheogenic medicines? How? Why?*

I think the unity, divinity, absoluteness stands for itself. Other things like mushrooms or ayahuasca, for example, go into "other" spaces. So yes, 5-MeO-DMT has a unique "selling point" from the perspective of the nondual and unitary experience.

- *What concerns, if any, do you have about the surging interest in 5 globally, and the sharp increase in demand for the experience (and its possible negative impacts on toads)?*

I have concerns that there might be a backlash against 5-MeO-DMT, like with LSD in the seventies. And I think the toads are being exploited unnecessarily.
I watch the other effects on global consciousness with curiosity and interest.

- *Have you been public about your work with 5? (ie, presented at conferences, WBAC, given interviews, etc.) If so, how do you navigate being public?*

I included my own perspectives in my podcast, but never talked so clearly about how much I worked with 5-MeO-DMT. This substance was only a topic with the conversations with Olli, and otherwise, I talked about all other relevant tryptamines, research chemicals, iboga, ayahuasca, and so on, publicly, but with a pseudonym. I set that in 2019.

Ingo's YouTube podcast, "Talks with Psychonauts," can be found here:

https://www.youtube.com/channel/UCW1WF99O09B9zWE3MZi4uTw

From Trauma to Self-Realization

by Nyx Ingen

My name is Nyx Ingen and I started working as a psychedelic therapist 6 years ago with MDMA, and 4 years ago with DMT, and 6 months ago (as of the time of writing this in the summer of 2021) with 5-MeO-DMT in Iceland, where I've managed to make a full living out of it.

- *How did you become a facilitator and why?*

I remember when I was 7 years old, I had a dream in which I discovered, looking at my computer screen, the designs of each person I knew, and then I remembered that everything that existed was my own creation, and that there was no one real, because I had programmed everyone and everything . . . I remember understanding perfectly how this had happened and why; but when I realized it, I felt a devastating and unbearable loneliness . . . And I went to bed telling myself that I didn't want to know, I didn't care if it was a dream or not; I wanted to believe with all my strength that I was

Facilitating 5-MeO-DMT

not alone and to put away the slightest doubt about whether the life I was living was real.

I come from a very traumatized family, where my father tried to kill me multiple times. In addition to the physical and verbal abuse I received from him and my mother, I received physical and verbal bullying at school by students and teachers since I entered at age 4 until I left at age 18. I had a suicide attempt at the age of 12, and I almost died from an involuntary poisoning at that age. I was never diagnosed with autism, but I am pretty sure I am on the autism spectrum. Furthermore, I am intersex and a transgender woman, and I had gender dysphoria for most of my life until I started taking hormones when I was 24 years old (I am currently 28 years old).

From a very young age I always knew that my fears were my cage, and I was always trying to overcome them in one way or another. This led me to keep trying to find my own way, even though I felt that my life was hell. I ran away from home at 17 years old and lived with what I earned doing small jobs online. It was at that age when I fell in love for the first time in my life, and I managed for a week to transmute that love into unconditional love for everything around me. It was incredible to embrace that feeling towards a life that seemed to go against me.

But at that time, I was very damaged, and in the process, I ruined the relationship I had with this person. That opened my eyes to the possibility of finding this unconditional love for everything when it exists within me without needing anyone, and so it was that, on the recommendation of a friend, I did my first Dhamma vipassana retreat at the age of 21. I did not find what I was looking for, but instead I came across a very valuable technique to cleanse myself, and I also realized the enormous work that lay ahead to heal myself.

Following this path, another friend recommended that I use MDMA. At that time, I felt a considerable rejection to drugs because of the fear I felt about the possibility of addiction, as I had seen a lot of suffering around drug use in my family, and I had decided not to try a drop of alcohol or tobacco in my life. But, reading about MAPS and its therapy with MDMA, I decided to give it a try. MDMA opened my eyes to a new way of understanding and feeling myself. I was able, in that session, to rearrange in many ways my head and face some fears that I thought impossible to overcome, like letting myself flow and dance to the music in front of people and realizing that I had confused (for a long time) the expectations of society with what I really wanted for myself. It was very liberating.

Shortly after this, I had my first psychedelic experience with LSD (200ug) with my girlfriend where I was considerably traumatized as it became obvious during the trip that I was God, because I had absolute access to understand everything around me and manifest whatever I wanted. Not being able to accept and integrate it when I came back, it became a nightmare and a chronic anxiety that lasted for half a year until finally, in my second vipassana, at the age of 22, I managed to process, integrate and accept this duality of being human and God at the same time. There in that retreat I had the clear vision that I could considerably support the growth of my little sister of 20 years following the guidance of MAPS working with her with MDMA. The session was a resounding success in many ways, and an inspiration to support the transformation of other family members and friends with this tool. I overcame my fear of psychedelics and began to introduce them to friends and family as well. And at the age of 23, in my third vipassana retreat, I had an existential crisis when I realized that my self-esteem was based entirely on what I felt I contributed to others. I realized that I was not able to love myself for simply being myself (At that time, I was making a living creating mega projects with startups and NGOs in order to change the world, and therapy with people was a hobby and I did not charge for it). This existential hole became so big that I went into a severe depression.

- *How were you introduced to 5/Toad? What was your experience?*

And it was then when I learned about bufo through my sister. She showed me a video of Nacho Vidal, a well-known bufo practitioner in Spain. I looked for more information and thought that bufo and DMT were the same thing. The same friend who recommended that I work with MDMA offered me DMT. Because of this misunderstanding, I thought the experience was going to be the same as taking bufo. I thought I would "die" if I did it, as many people describe their bufo experience, and finally I surrendered and did it, accepting my own death. In doing so, the DMT worked on me by completely resetting my ego.

The person that inhabited my body vanished. I had to relearn everything, even to speak (when I came back, I only had in my vocabulary another language that I could not describe where it came from). All my attachments and tastes were reset. I did not recognize anyone as acquaintances, not even my parents. I slowly relearned everything during the following months, generating new attachments and tastes. I completely left the job I had/the life I had (I also started hormonal transition at this time). When my family wanted to understand what happened, I offered a shot of DMT to my uncle, who was, at that time, the head of my family. His life changed radically, and through him, my family started asking me for this medicine. I also had a super therapeutic MDMA session with my mother, in which she was able to accept me as a trans person

Facilitating 5-MeO-DMT

and respect and understand my decision to transition. (Today my uncle is building a healing center in Spain where he owned the third-largest law firm in Spain).

Later, I understood that DMT and bufo are different substances. A friend offered me bufo in his house without any experience. I had just returned from my first experience with 200mg rectal DMT, in which I managed to deeply heal several wounds I did not even know I had (and it was probably one of the strongest experiences I have had in my life).

When I took bufo (a considerable amount), it made me feel exactly the same as when I was dying about to go into a coma from poisoning when I was 12 years old (I was in the hospital for a week connected to a life-support machine). I felt nauseous and scared, so I started breathing very, very hard, resisting the whole experience. And for some strange reason the light bulb in the ceiling of the room exploded into pieces at the same time I managed to get out of this state.

Much later, in a very deep meditation, accepting all that was coming, including my own death, I plunged into it until there was something that took me completely out of meditation when it came to my mind: the fear of loneliness.

I thought I had overcome all my fears (from a very young age I have sought to throw myself again and again into what I fear; and that is precisely how I learned so much with DMT, as I sought for it to show me what I feared the most). Seeing this fear, I decided to do a strong intake of DMT to ask how to resolve this fear, and its answer was: take bufo. (I want to clarify that at that time the relationship I had with DMT was basically one of guidance, as it allowed me to ask as much as I wanted and receive advice and cleansing. This effect lasted until I managed to incarnate this entity/God/my soul for 3 days, and after that I started to be able to communicate with it without taking DMT.)

I knew that bufo meant to accept my death, and I sensed that I could reset my ego completely again, I felt a lot of fear, but finally I accepted my death, and soon after accepting it without doing anything, a friend contacted me to offer me a bufo shaman practitioner in Iceland who spoke Spanish (I was born in Spain). I talked to him and within a week I had an appointment. But I felt that I had to prepare myself. Looking for information, I found your interview with Leo Gura (on actualized.org), and from there I found your book, *Entheogenic Liberation*. This was a tremendous help, because this shaman who would be serving me bufo had no interest in your knowledge, and the rituals and ways he had of conducting the session made me feel very uncomfortable long before starting.

I did 4 takes of bufo. In the 3rd one I understood that I had to stop fighting, understanding that this also meant letting me ask for what I felt I needed. So I told the shaman that I wanted to take it on my own, and adapt the space to my needs. He agreed, and I FINALLY had the physical experience of union. I screamed, laughed, had an infinite orgasm, kicked and cried; I went through expressing all my emotions, and I stayed as much as I could in connection with the source. So it went on for almost 3 months where every time I lay down, no matter where I was, I had spontaneous orgasms. I also finally started to sing without restrictions channeling what came to me in front of the public. And my trust in my intuition and in letting myself be was absolute – until a friend told me that my trust was arrogance (and that it made him feel bad, and he didn't want to be with me), and I received threats. Then my fears returned, and I understood that I still had work to do.

I got some 5-MeO-DMT of my own, and I started to experiment combining it with DMT. Without a doubt, the most incredible hit I did was in front of the active volcano of Iceland, because it hypnotized me while I let myself "die." I became light, and I was nothing more than that: absolute light, acceptance, love. That experience changed my feeling. I started to try to give 5-MeO-DMT to close friends who had had strong experiences (previously), and I started to see very good results. So seeing the valuable tool that is 5-MeO-DMT, I started to use it with clients and not just friends. I could see how, when I entered in that state, taking 5-MeO-DMT with my clients, and letting myself go with the energy to whatever they asked me without restrictions, I achieved even better results. But still, I had clients who were not able to surrender completely to finish the job, so I decided to find a way to give it more safely, where my clients could surrender. And so it was that by testing different combinations on myself that I found that the combination of MDMA with 5-MeO-DMT (with or without DMT) was tremendously effective for cleansing. To make an analogy, I see MDMA as a love anesthesia that allows the ego to rest peacefully conscious while undergoing "surgery" with 5-MeO-DMT. I started applying this combination with clients and began to have truly spectacular results.

- *What, if any, training did you receive?*

I completed, at the time of developing my techniques, in addition to learning from a shaman in Mexico, and to the various Dhamma Vipassana retreats I did, the Colloquium on Psychedelic Psychiatry 2018 in Sweden.

Facilitating 5-MeO-DMT

- *How do you conduct sessions?*

It depends entirely on the needs of my clients. I have many modalities, but without a doubt at this moment the most popular is MDMA + 5-MeO-DMT, and this is how I work with most of my clients.

- *How would you describe your approach: nondual, shamanic, ceremonial, therapeutic …?*

I consider it to be therapeutic, and as I stated above, liken it to a form of "surgery."

- *Do you work one-on-one, in groups, in retreats, at a center, with a team … ?*

I prefer to work one-on-one in a private setting.

- *What do you see as the purpose of working with 5?*

From a therapeutic standpoint, it is mainly to achieve the emotional unblocking of my client, and to give the opportunity for my clients to perceive the difference between their ego and who they really are; in that sense, to undo the illusion (of the egoic/individuated self and its self-created limitations) and help them to let themselves be in every moment.

- *If you use unconventional or controversial methods, what is the rationale? In your own view, how does it serve your practice?*

Basically, there are times when my body asks me to sing, to vomit, to put my hands on certain areas of the body, which can even be the genitals. There are times when I can change my role, cry, have spasms on top of my client, etc. I feel that all of these things are necessary for my client's energy to be processed properly. It's not just about what the client is experiencing by themselves, but how we're interacting and processing energy together as a unit.

- *How do you handle issues of informed consent?*

I have prospective clients digitally sign a document that covers what our session will involve so that they are informed and have expressed their consent in signing.

- *What do people get out of their sessions/experiences?*

It is usually a profound change in their life, in the understanding of who they are, how they feel about the world, and the realization of what they want to do.

- *Do you provide pre-session information, screening, prep? If so, what?*

Yes, when in doubt, I have a pre-session where I sometimes give the client a small amount of DMT or 5-MeO-DMT, ask them questions about their past, and the reason they've come to me.

- *What are some of the best results you've seen?*

When I gave DMT to my uncle, he completely changed his life, his profession, his relationship with himself and his family, etc. He is very happy now and I believe these changes came about because of his experience, though this was with DMT and not 5-MeO-DMT, yet it stands out as extremely transformational with dramatic results.

The work I did with my mother with MDMA completely changed my relationship with her, and it improved exponentially. Before we did this, she was afraid of me, and now she understands and supports me.

I had a case of a girl who wanted to commit suicide. I told her that if she wanted to do it, she should do "it" with me using DMT (rather than actually attempting suicide). She agreed, and after that, she was never the same person again. She left the addictions she had, toxic relationships, and she started meditating and having a very healthy life. Because she allowed herself to "die" in this way, she was able to radically change her life for the better.

- *What are some of the difficulties you've encountered with patients/clients?*

I had a client who decided to jump out of the window and climb a tree from which he fell. Luckily, nothing serious happened. I remained calm at all times and got us back home (he had only consumed MDMA).

FACILITATING 5-MEO-DMT

I had another client who fell in love with me and wanted to have sex with me during the 5-MeO-DMT session. Instead of working with the medicine, he kept exposing himself to me, and we were not able to finish the process. (I'd note that this was before I started using MDMA in my sessions).

- *What are your recommendations for integration and post-experience processing?*

I usually recommend reading *Entheogenic Liberation,* and book a space in a Vipassana retreat. I usually have meetings with my clients after the sessions to be able to talk and integrate.

- *What resources do you use or recommend to clients?*

Your books and vipassana.

- *How many people have you served, and what kinds of people have you worked with? (Drug addicts, spiritual seekers, vets, ages, genders, occupations, interests, nationalities/ethnicities)*

About 80 people (at the time of writing this in August of 2021). I have worked with drug addicts, homeless people, hippies, transgender, ADHD, autistic, schizophrenic, spiritual people, family members, from 18 years old to 65 years old, company directors, programmers, therapists, teachers, scientists, Europeans, Americans, and South Americans. It's been pretty diverse.

- *Do you see different issues between serving men and women, old and young, healthy and those will medical issues?*

Yes, of course. Men tend to put up more resistance, whereas women tend to give in more easily to the experience. Those with autism or schizophrenia tend to be more difficult. I have worked with people with borderline personality disorders, and honestly, I am not able to work with this problem.

- *What do you feel are the responsibilities of those serving 5?*

That the client stays alive, maintains his or her mental sanity, and is able to have a healthy integration.

- *Do you have an opinion on synthetic vs. "natural"?*

I prefer synthetic because it is more concentrated and easier to use.

- *If you choose to work with Toad, what's your take on sustainable harvesting, toad protections, and related ethical questions?*

I don't work with the toad, but if I did, I would make sure it was in the best possible condition.

- *How do you feel 5 works with other entheogenic medicines? What are their relationships?*

5-MeO-DMT + MDMA = Ability to go very deep with no problem in healing.
5-MeO-DMT + DMT = Allows to go in with less resistance because the ego is busy looking at the DMT (which tends to be vastly more visual in nature than 5-MeO-DMT, which is more energetic and felt than seen).

- *Who should take 5? Who shouldn't?*

Those physically fit enough not to die in the process and who are willing to work on their ego.

- *What role do you see for 5 in the global community?*

Freeing ourselves from the fear of being 100%.

- *What are the lessons you've learned from serving 5?*

I've learned that each experience and client is unique. I learn with each session about myself, because in some way, my clients serve as my reflection. I learn more and more about the importance of letting myself be, and how to take this further and further, and the enormous importance of intention and predisposition.

FACILITATING 5-MEO-DMT

- *Do you see serving 5 as being different from serving other entheogenic medicines? How? Why?*

Yes, completely. The 5-MeO-DMT works the emotional body first and from there you can go to the mental one, while most psychedelics work from the mental side, and from there you can access the emotional one.

- *What concerns, if any, do you have about the surging interest in 5 globally, and the sharp increase in demand for the experience (and its possible negative impacts on toads)?*

I think we should stop using toads; they are not necessary at all. Synthetic 5-MeO-DMT is perfectly effective, so there's no particular need to use toad secretions.

On the other hand, I think it is very important for the world to have access to this tool, but this demand may cause many people to go and take it from people who are not prepared to manage their awakening. The context in which one is served and the skills of the facilitator are very important for producing good outcomes.

- *What hopes do you have with 5 and the experiences it makes possible for people?*

I would love for it to be legalized and for centers to be created where therapists are properly trained in its use.

- *Have you been public about your work with 5? (ie, presented at conferences, WBAC, given interviews, etc.) If so, how do you navigate being public?*

Yes, I did a conference in Iceland and spoke publicly on Facebook about my profession. I think it is very important to make it public and make it known. And, I've also been featured on your podcast recently.

Fractal Expressions of The One

by Patrick S.

Lessons on Being from 5-MeO-DMT/Bufo:

With the assistance of 5-MeO-DMT/bufo, we can dissolve the boundaries of the egoic mind and realize our true nature as One unified consciousness. There are many words that people use to describe this One unified consciousness: God, Source, Ultimate reality, Christ consciousness, Samadhi, the unified quantum field. I feel these are all words used to describe the infinite, mystical, omniscient energy we experience in a state of nonduality. There is fundamentally only one universal consciousness, and our human experience of duality is this One consciousness exploring itself through the illusion of separation. To experience nonduality is to know the unity and interconnectedness of everything. Every being that I encounter is a mirror of me, a fractal of the One consciousness. We are all this unified consciousness choosing to play in the illusion of separateness so that we can learn and create and grow. We are not just the limited accumulation of thoughts and identities of the ego. 5-MeO/bufo can help us transcend the illusion of separation and realize any duality is a temporary creation of the one divine mind.

All things are created and return to this source of energy.

This unified field of energy is infinite and allows infinite possibilities. We are connected to this infinite energetic field and our frequency and resonance greatly affects how we subjectively perceive and experience reality. Every thought resonates through the unified field and affects our subjective reality. As soon as a thought is generated, our ego starts constructing reality around it and creating a narrative about it. Reality is built upon stories, and if we continue to carry old narratives, then these stories will play out in our lives. If we choose to change the narrative, then we can change our reality.

After inhaling 5-MeO/bufo, all ego constructs and identities and thoughts dissolve and we are present in the eternal Now. The illusions of duality, such as physicality and time, dissolve, and we can see how there really is only Now. Time and form are ever-changing illusions played over the eternal stillness of Now. The ego tends to project and worry about the future or ruminate over the past; however, the past and present are just constructs of the egoic mind. With 5-MeO/bufo, we can expand our consciousness beyond the confines of the current ego to a higher awareness. With this higher awareness we can clearly identify thoughts coming from our ego that are based on fear or lack and we can let them pass and then consciously focus our awareness on what we want to create and manifest.

One of the many lessons from 5-MeO/bufo is that we realize we truly are pure energy and that everything, at its essence, is energy and frequency and vibration. Our thoughts, emotions, physical bodies are all composed of energy. Our entire being is a system of energetic exchanges and 5-MeO/bufo can bring a deeper awareness to how and where we are focusing our energy. We can begin to see where we may be unnecessarily focusing our energy on thoughts or actions or relationships that may no longer serve us. We can observe where we may have energetic blockages in ourselves or an uneven exchange of energy in certain relationships. This greater awareness of our "energy economy" can greatly impact how we consciously choose to focus our energy and attention.

After experiencing Unity consciousness, there is a clarity and *knowing* that all is interconnected, and every Being is an extension of the One consciousness. This experience and knowing that "all-is-One" changes the way we treat, interact with, and love others. I feel it makes us more compassionate and more aware of how our actions may affect everyone else, because harming someone else is essentially just harming yourself because that person is literally the same consciousness as you. We are all

Facilitating 5-MeO-DMT

aspects of the One unified consciousness, and we are all at various stages of awareness of this unified Self. Some people have the awareness that they are a fractal of the One Consciousness and that everything is a mirror of themselves, and then there are other people that identify with the ego and with separation and they don't know they are energetically and spiritually interconnected. So, in reality, there is not really "good and evil"; it is more that there is "knowledge of the Unified Self" or "ignorance of the Unified Self."

It is due to the ego dissolution that many of the profound insights and revelations are realized. Especially in a society where most people strongly identify with their ego and the material world, experiencing a loss of ego can be a very transformative and humbling experience. With the assistance of 5-MeO/bufo, we can expand our consciousness beyond the confines of the current ego and bring awareness to aspects of consciousness outside the ego. Then the ego assimilates and integrates these aspects of our new expanded awareness.

The transformation that happens after an ego dissolution is profound on many levels. The instant dissolution of physical reality while maintaining conscious-awareness can be very transformative, especially for those with a materialist mindset, in proving that consciousness exists beyond the physical body. For me, I could see how easy it is to let go of any attachments. Even our egos, the accumulation of thoughts and identities and beliefs that we attach to, can all be released and let go of instantly. Any thought or form, even the ego, is temporary and will pass. Once we trust and surrender and let it all go, it clears space for new and greater things to come. We can shed any former ego constructs and start to reprogram ourselves consciously with intention. Our behavioral patterns are rooted deep in our subconscious programming outside the awareness of the ego, and when the ego is removed our higher awareness can observe and integrate the causal roots of these behaviors and we can begin to consciously reprogram ourselves.

The dissolution of the ego allows much of what is in the subconscious to surface to our awareness. One of the functions of the ego is to protect our conscious mind from information and emotions that it judges as too painful or uncomfortable. When the ego's control and boundaries dissolve, all the emotions and traumas and information that the ego has suppressed can now be brought to our awareness to be acknowledged and processed. The ego is usually worrying and projecting about the future, or replaying events from the past, and 5-MeO-DMT quiets the ego, which directs us into the present moment. When the ego is offline, we are left with the raw, unfiltered, infinite Now. This is very helpful in showing us what it's like without the ego trying to control and project its doubt. We can see how much more peaceful and expansive the present moment is. After experiencing what "no ego" is like, we can better observe how ego tries to operate in our daily lives and how ego constructs its stories of reality.

In Ultimate reality, everything is perfect and it's the ego that distorts our perception of reality and convinces us that things need to be a certain way or have to be fixed. An ego-dissolution can reveal indescribable clarity and a knowing that everything is perfect in the present moment, and it is the ego that projects doubt and fear by living outside of the present moment. The ego tends to worry about the future and project possible worst-case-scenarios and focus and ruminate over the past. However, when the ego is quieted and we are fully in the present Now, we realize that everything is perfect as it is. The ego is the cause of suffering and discomfort. There is clarity and peace and stillness in the present moment. This clarity and knowing that everything is ultimately perfect in the present moment allows us to catch the ego when it is trying to convince us otherwise. When the voice of the ego comes into our mind to second-guess or judge, we can observe the workings of the ego from a broader perspective with a higher consciousness.

The experience of egolessness also gives us sort of a "goal" to aim for in meditation. With 5-MeO/bufo, we can experience pure awareness and what it's like without the ego in control. To remember that unity and peacefulness is much more comfortable than the insecure ramblings of the ego. The experience of dissolving the ego gives us an opportunity to see how the ego constructs and operates and tries to control our perceptions and reality. Especially when we start integrating this expanded awareness into our daily lives, we can begin to distinguish between what ego wants and what is intuition/Higher Self. We can observe distinctions between what is "ego" second-guessing and trying to control the narrative, or what is our true unfiltered intuition.

In realty, everything exists and "just is," and our ego filters and projects perceptions over this neutral ultimate reality. After an ego dissolution, we can also come to realize that our identity is not the ego, and that the ego is limited compared to our infinite, true selves. When we fully experience nonduality, we fully experience "nonattachment" and "nonexistence." With this higher awareness, it's easier to release limiting ego constructs and identities we may attach to.

Once we experience the full surrender of egolessness, it can heal any fear-based programming. The ego tends to judge things as good/bad, and label and categorize what it experiences. And we constantly live with these judgements and projections, and people can maintain these mindsets and beliefs for decades. However, during a 5-MeO/bufo session, the traumatic events that our ego labels as painful and wrong can be viewed with higher awareness through a lens of neutrality and unconditional Love,

Facilitating 5-MeO-DMT

unfiltered or suppressed by the ego. We can then come to a fuller acceptance of these traumatic events and acknowledge and forgive. When the ego relinquishes control, any emotions or traumas or information that the ego has deemed too painful or uncomfortable, or even too confusing, can now come fully into our awareness so we can integrate these shadow aspects from our subconscious. Then the ego assimilates and integrates these aspects, and we can have a fuller realization of the Self.

5-MeO/bufo is the most effective treatment I've seen for releasing trauma. A lot of people bottle-up and suppress emotions or traumatic events which the ego labels as too painful, too embarrassing, too uncomfortable, too confusing, and blocks them out of our awareness. It really takes the removal of the ego to release the tension and emotions and trauma the ego has been attaching to. Once the control of the ego is relinquished, all the emotions it has suppressed and traumas it has identified with can be let go of. The emotions and trauma trapped in the body can release once the body is fully relaxed and surrendered. When people bottle up emotions or suppress traumatic events, it can cause energetic blockages and dis-ease in the body. Fear, resentment, shame, and regret are all burdens that block us from infinite Source energy. 5-MeO/bufo helps release these blockages and allows Source energy to flow more clearly. Once the boundaries and limitations of the ego are dissolved, and the mind is cleared, we can feel a deeper, clearer connection to ourselves, our emotions, our physical bodies, our loved ones, and a Higher power. The empathic connection we have with others is deepened and enhanced and we are more sensitive to the subtler energies of our environment. Experiencing 5-MeO/bufo feels very much like a rebirth, like a total reset, like a clean slate. In addition to a neurological reset, it feels like a whole energetic reset of our entire being.

I feel that after experiencing Unity consciousness, it empowers us to take sovereignty over our own thoughts and reality. Every human being is a part of this infinite unified Source, and therefore, has access to unlimited energy and infinite possibilities. This unified field is the supreme waveform/superimposition of prime consciousness. We are this supreme waveform in individual "particle" form with unlimited access to the infinite information of the supreme consciousness. Ultimate reality is this field of energy, and our intentions and thoughts have a huge effect on this unified field, and therefore, on our reality. We can learn to focus our energy and intention on what is most important and fulfilling and channel that energy into what we want to manifest.

Every human being *is* and has access to this unlimited energy and these infinite possibilities. Our "perfect being" already exists and already is here in the Now: it's really a matter of releasing these limited beliefs and boundaries in our mind to allow this infinite source energy to flow, unrestricted by the ego.

With the loss of ego and any subjective identity, it's possible to see how any duality is inherently nonexistent, and there is only one primary consciousness exploring itself through the illusion of duality and separation. Everything and nothing exists all at once in this mystical superimposition. The void of nothing and everything paradoxically existing together in an infinite mysterious Whole. Knowing that everything is an illusion and essentially nonexistent makes it easier to not get caught up in petty or unfulfilling things. It helps us take the dramas of life less seriously and laugh more at the cosmic joke. For me, I could see how easy it is to instantly let go of any attachments. Any thought or form is just temporary, and it will pass once I trust and surrender and let it all go. It then clears space for new and greater things to come.

5-MeO/bufo can be very healing in processing the grieving of a lost loved one, or in helping relieve fear around death in general. Aside from bufo being helpful with the grieving process, because it can help access and release suppressed emotions, the total ego-dissolution can also take us through the death process to help us come to terms with accepting death as something not to fear. I feel the "ego death" experienced after inhaling 5-MeO/bufo is what we experience when our consciousness or spirit leaves our physical body. So, bufo can be very helpful in "practicing" for the dying process. Terence McKenna said, "The purpose of life is to familiarize oneself with this after-death body so that the act of dying will not create confusion in the psyche." I feel 5-MeO/bufo is the perfect practice for navigating one's consciousness through transcending the physical body. The ego-dissolution mirrors the death process in that they both force the removal and letting go of all attachments and identities. During an ego-dissolution, we also transcend our corporeal bodies or any physicality while maintaining conscious awareness. 5-MeO/bufo can teach us how to fully surrender without fear or resistance and practice "nonattachment." The dissolution of the ego can help demystify death and be a sort of "practice for death" and navigating the non-physical realms.

Facilitating:

Serving bufo is a great blessing and responsibility. I feel the main role of a 5-MeO/bufo facilitator is to provide a safe and nonjudgmental space for the participant to explore whatever level of consciousness they are ready to experience. Just as the participant experiences a loss of ego, I feel it's best for the facilitator to not involve their own ego. Therefore, as a facilitator, it's important to keep a clear mind and stay present

FACILITATING 5-MEO-DMT

and mostly just observe the participant to keep them safe. Allow the participant to express themselves and release any emotions without judging or analyzing them. It's easy for the facilitator to project their own judgments and ego constructs on the participant, and many facilitators are quick to give their interpretation of what happened in a session. Other facilitators may be quick to play therapist and offer advice or project their own ideas on the person.

During the session, I feel it's best to interfere as little as possible. Afterwards, it may be helpful for some people to work with integration counselors; however, I feel during the session is not the time to start analyzing and interpreting what someone may have experienced during the session. The facilitator's role is to keep the person safe and guide them safely through the ego-dissolution. It's sometimes necessary to remind a person to surrender and relax and let go, and it sometimes may be necessary to physically restrain or protect a participant that may be volatile and dynamic. Other than instances where a facilitator needs to intervene to keep a participant safe, I feel it's best to allow the participant to go through the experience undisturbed. I also don't feel it's necessary for the facilitator to interpret the experience for the participant. I really encourage the participant to look inward and they will find the answers themselves.

One of my main intentions serving bufo is for people to realize their own sovereignty and internal power to transform themselves. Most people look externally for solutions that at their root can only be transformed internally from deep inner work. Therefore, I encourage people to feel into the experience and allow their own interpretations to form. Bufo is very helpful in assisting us in accessing deeper levels of consciousness, and I feel it's best to let each person form their own unique understanding. One of the blessings of serving bufo is witnessing each person's unique response and interpretation of the indescribable and mystical experience of nonduality. So, I allow each person to discover their own truths from the nondual experience.

The security and feeling of nonjudgement is one of the most important aspects of a safe 5-MeO/bufo container. During the session, people can be at their most vulnerable or reliving traumatic events, so it is important to remain in a state of nonjudgement and maintain a calm and compassionate presence. People can be in very delicate mental and emotional states during the session, so it's important to maintain a safe space and, as a facilitator, remain compassionate and of integrity. Also, since we empathically share the unified energy field during the session, it is important for the facilitator to reserve any judgments and projections. Any judgmental thoughts or feelings can be shared and felt across the "collective conscious" of the unified field, so it is important to maintain this clear, safe space for the participant and allow them to express any emotions that need to be expressed.

Some people can get very dynamic during their experience and, as long as they are safe and not in danger of hurting themselves, I feel it's best to let their bodies move how they want to move. It's recommended for the participant to stay as symmetrical as possible, as this is most conducive to the flow of energy; however, sometimes participants move in a way that is more conducive for them to release and express their energy. During the session, a participant's body may be releasing energy or trauma or suppressed emotions and as long as they are safe, I allow the body to move uninterrupted. Some people's bodies may shake, or thrash around, or "log-roll." Some people start doing yoga poses or mudras with their hands. Some people want to pound their fists and scream, and I just protect them with pillows and allow them to release. The participant's body will move in the way that best facilitates their own release of energy.

Since everyone is at a unique stage in their life, I feel it's also important to consider the dosage for each person. Some people require a higher dose to really break through the boundaries the ego has put up. Or they may have strong addictions, or deeply engrained ego constructs, or strongly suppressed emotions or traumas. These are examples that might require a higher initial dose to break through the resistance of the ego. Some people are more sensitive, and it may be better to start with a lower dose, or rather to ease them into the ego dissolution with a few doses, or even across a few sessions.

Integration:

The integration process after 5-MeO/bufo is very unique for each person. I find that most people will integrate the experience naturally over the subsequent weeks following the ceremony. As the integration process unfolds, many people observe a deeper awareness of thought and behavioral patterns, gain more clarity on their relationships, and realize new insights into the nature of the Self and reality. If possible after a session, I recommend taking a few days off from work or any busy routines to take time for rest and introspection. Dedicating time to rest after a bufo session allows us the opportunity to maintain our expanded awareness and begin to gain meaning from the nondual experience and how we can apply our new lessons and insights into our life. Most people will start observing their thoughts and behaviors with this broader awareness and can start to realize preconditioned patterns and programming. By being the Awareness or the observer beyond the ego, we can see how our ego

Facilitating 5-MeO-DMT

operates from this higher perspective and start focusing our awareness and taking action in a way that we can make changes in our daily lives.

I feel one of the helpful things to focus on after a session is what kind of actionable intelligence can be gained from the 5-MeO/bufo experience. After experiencing Unity consciousness, and knowing that we are infinite energetic beings with unlimited possibilities, how are we going to bring that awareness and energy into our daily lives? The session also may have revealed behavioral patterns that aren't serving us anymore, so we can acknowledge those patterns and begin to reprogram ourselves with more conscious intention. We can learn to focus our intention on what is most important and fulfilling and channel that energy into what we want to manifest.

As the process continues to unfold after the session, I recommend to keep the ego quieted as much as possible. Stay present and keep the mind clear and try not to analyze the experience too much. After a 5-MeO/bufo session, our ego tends to want to try and analyze and rationalize the nondual experience. However, experiencing nonduality and the infinite is incomprehensible to the rational mind, and I feel it's best to not overanalyze or get logical thinking too involved in the integration process. It may sound counterintuitive; however, the less we try to analyze and make logical sense of the experience, the more clarity and insights and revelations come from the experience. When the ego is less involved, it clears our mind and more *feeling* and *knowing* occurs. Therefore, during integration, I encourage people to go inward and just observe what comes up without judgement or defaulting to their programmed reactions. Also, many people may leave a 5-MeO/bufo session and not know what happened at all, or feel like there is too much information to process. In my experience, as time progresses, much more clarity comes, and things start to make more sense in the next few days.

Most people experience immense feelings of gratitude and unconditional love during and after a 5-MeO/bufo session. They feel more empathically connected to all beings and more at peace.

To sustain these feelings, it's important to continue to focus on gratitude and authenticity. Connecting with nature and with loved ones is also very nurturing after a session. Walking barefoot in nature, physical exercise, yoga and other "grounding" activities are also very helpful recommendations after 5-MeO/bufo as any grounding activities helps us feel into our bodies. Feeling into our bodies will help take us out of the mind and allow the integration process to unfold. Feeling into our bodies also helps ground the high vibrations and frequencies experienced during the session into our energy field.

Working with 5-MeO/bufo can bring up suppressed emotions or reveal aspects of our subconscious that need to be integrated. During and after a bufo session, it's important to embrace and process emotions without judgement or resisting. Just feel, and express, and release the emotions. It's normal for residual emotions to come up a few days after the session so also allow these emotions to be expressed unrestricted.

It's also normal for people to experience "reactivations" of their nondual experience for a few days or weeks after a session. During reactivations, stay calm and surrender and breathe and allow what wants to surface to your awareness to flow unrestricted. I find that once people truly trust and surrender without fear or expectations, that they come to enjoy the experience of nonduality. These reactivations can be reminders to trust and surrender to the Now.

Sometimes people can feel as if something is "wrong" or that the 5-MeO/bufo experience has altered their mind in a permanent "negative" way and I feel it is important to remind them that everything is normal, and that these phases will pass. As with most spiritual awakenings, people may feel that they are going a bit crazy or losing their mind. It's important to encourage them that everything is perfect, and these are common stages in the spiritual development process. Especially in a culture that focuses mainly on logic and rational thinking, some of the illogical and non-physical aspects of consciousness can be rather unfamiliar and disorienting for people that may have a more reductive materialist mindset. So, it's important to remind them that they are fine and they are integrating some of these more non-logical or multidimensional aspects of consciousness. I remind them it's not necessary to rationally explain everything; just trust the process.

My Ceremonies:

Each 5-MeO/bufo session is very unique and varies based on the participant. There are some people who are looking for more therapeutic and medical treatments with 5-MeO/Bufo, such as those seeking help with addictions, depression, PTSD, anxiety, or processing trauma. Other people are seeking spiritual growth and are looking to expand their consciousness, release energetic blockages, and experience unity consciousness. I always consider each person's intention in working with the medicine and realize that each session is unique and there is no standard formula for how to conduct each session. I will speak with the person beforehand and assess what their intention is. I explain to the person that 5-MeO/bufo may bring up uncomfortable feelings and thoughts from their subconscious and that in some cases it can be challenging to process through these shadow aspects of the Self. I will always

FACILITATING 5-MEO-DMT

talk with the participant before and explain the process and ask about any medications or health issues. It's also important for facilitators to explain the integration process and provide integration support for each person they serve.

In my sessions, I usually integrate shamanic elements and ritual elements of the Seri tribe in my ceremonies; however, I understand some people are not as open to those spiritual traditions. I encourage people to start the session by reading a prayer aloud that comes from the Seri tradition. When people truly speak the prayer from their heart, I feel it helps set the intention for the ceremony.

Editor's Note: The Seri tribe of indigenous people of the Sonoran Desert in northwestern Mexico have become cultural "toad ambassadors" after having toad medicine introduced to them by Octavio Rettig as a means of treating rampant drug addiction. It has since been incorporated into Seri ceremonialism and religious practice and is not exclusively used for addiction treatment. Seri practices have thus served as a model for others who have taken up the practice of serving bufo.

Usually, I will sage the person first and cleanse their energy. Then I will measure out their dose and load the medicine in the pipe and give them the pipe to hold in their hands. They then read the prayer aloud and bless the medicine. After the participant reads the prayer, I feel it is best for them to kneel with their back straight to inhale from the pipe. Once the participant is comfortably kneeling, they will take three deep breaths, and on the third, fully exhale all the air out of their lungs. Once their lungs are empty, they will slowly and gently begin inhaling from the pipe deep in their lungs as they slowly raise their arms to create more space in the lungs. After gently and slowly filling up their lungs with smoke, it's important to keep holding the smoke in the lungs as long as possible to absorb the medicine.

With the participant still holding their breath, I assist them to lay on their backs and spread their limbs in a symmetrical position. It's then up to the participant to truly surrender and let go and to release any resistance or tension and allow the ego to dissolve into nonduality. After helping the person lay back comfortably on the pillow and mat, the main role is to keep them safe. I will usually incorporate a few other shamanic elements such as drumming or rattling. I feel the vibration of the drumming helps facilitate the movement and release of energy in the body. The drumming can also help indicate if the ego fully dissolved during the session or was still slightly engaged and aware of duality. Afterwards, I expect the participant to not have heard the drumming because their ego was offline and should not be aware to hear the drumming. If they were still aware of the drumming, then their ego was still engaged on some level and didn't fully dissolve. This is an indication to me that they could use a second dose of medicine and maybe a higher initial dose for the next session.

Things I've Seen:

It's been fascinating and fulfilling to see 5-MeO/bufo provide healing in so many ways to so many different types of people. Each session is unique and it's a blessing to learn and grow with each person I serve. I serve bufo because it is one of the most transformative and healing experiences a human can have. I've seen it heal many conditions and provide instant relief from depression, anxiety, addictions, and traumas. I've seen countless people experience a love and gratitude that cannot be expressed in words. Most people report more clarity and awareness in all aspects of their lives. Most people are able to maintain a feeling of peace and tend to not be annoyed or bothered by things that may have triggered them in the past. I find most people become more authentic and more trusting in allowing their intuition to guide their lives rather than the doubts of their ego. I find most people become much more compassionate and greatly expand their current understanding of reality and the Self.

Most people find a real peace and clarity and a sense that everything is perfect, and they let their ego take more of a backseat in their lives. Most people will start to become aware of when the ego is trying to project fear and doubt and they can distinguish more between what is "ego" versus "intuition." People become aware of thought patterns and conditioning and a lot of the root causes of what is driving their behavior. People become aware that they might have been operating on a sort of "autopilot" of subconscious programming and they are then able to focus and direct their awareness and energy with more intention rather than preconditioned programming. I've had many people describe their sessions as "decades of talk therapy in an hour" because they can finally integrate into their awareness these aspects that have been suppressed by their ego in their subconscious. Once the ego is removed, they can finally process emotions or memories that have been outside their awareness.

I've seen huge transformative changes due to the neurological reset of 5-MeO-DMT. The neurological reset is helpful in clearing engrained programming and gives us a "clean slate." I've seen it help relieve negative and even suicidal thoughts and break obsessive thought patterns. 5-MeO-DMT can help reset these negative thought patterns and break repetitive behavioral cycles that aren't serving us.

I've witnessed people cease decade-long addictions after one or a few sessions. The neurological reset along with the insights and realizations of how life is a gift and blessing can be very transformative in ceasing even strong addictions. I've seen a lot of instantaneous relief from symptoms of depression and anxiety. Many people attain a great sense of peace and a feeling of fulfillment during their session and are able to sustain these feelings and uplifted mood for usually several months. I've also worked with many people that successfully discontinue pharmaceutical antidepressants that they have been on for years. I've seen bufo be very helpful in processing trauma and grief. I've worked with military veterans and people working through PTSD and bufo has been very helpful with them processing their trauma. I've worked with people who were sexually abused, and I've seen them genuinely come to a place of true forgiveness. They can view their past traumas through a lens of unconditional love and can truly forgive the people that have abused them. I've also seen a lot of people who release any attachments to a "victimization mindset" and can stop identifying with their trauma. People release old thought patterns and limiting beliefs and suppressed emotions. Once the ego is removed, any tension or energetic blockages can be released.

Most people report feeling much lighter and clearer mentally, emotionally, spiritually and physically. Bufo can be like a full energetic clearing and reset of the entire energetic body. Their awareness becomes clearer, unclouded by the ego's judgments and projections and limiting beliefs. Their meditations are much deeper, and their awareness is more expanded. People feel "connected" again . . . to their emotions, their physical bodies, a higher power, their loved ones, all of creation. Their empathic awareness and sensitivity is greatly enhanced and they feel more connected with nature and humanity and especially their loved ones.

I've witnessed countless "spiritual awakenings" which I would basically describe as people realizing and accepting the fact that they are more than their physical bodies and egoic thought patterns and that there is a higher intelligent energy beyond themselves.

After 5-MeO/bufo, I notice most people tend to take much more responsibility for their lives.

We can expand ourselves beyond the boundaries of the ego and integrate this expanded awareness and new information into ourselves, and then keep expanding and growing. 5-MeO/bufo can help empower Ourselves and take sovereignty over our own realities and thoughts and health. We can live with more intention and fulfillment and learn to not worry over trivial or unfulfilling things. We can focus more on meaningful relationships and activities and not take things so seriously, because it's all perfect, and it's all an illusion anyway, so literally lighten up!

From Initiation to Facilitation

by Matthew Schultz

- *How were you introduced to 5/Toad? What was your experience?*

I was first introduced to 5-MeO-DMT by my Mayan elders in Guatemala over a decade ago. It was not part of any paid event or retreat. I had been studying with the elders for over two years. After an extended stay for months on Lake Atitlan, and after many *temazcals,* they said, "We are going to initiate you and give you a name." This was my first sacred medicine event, and it also included a substantial amount of datura along with the 5-MeO-DMT/Toad medicine. We smoked them together. It was such a profound event that I labeled my life BG/AG (Before Guatemala/After Guatemala) now.

Martin W. Ball, Ph.D., Editor

- *How did you become a facilitator and why?*

I became a facilitator of scared medicines because I want to help others contextualize their experience. I was lucky enough to have had extensive experience with many different medicines and as a water-pourer for sweat lodges (the latter being a "medicine" practice without entheogenic medicines, which are not used in sweat lodges where the stones and steam do the work of facilitating an altered state). I traveled the world for five years working with many different sacred medicine shamans and practitioners. I was eventually hired to work as a facilitator at different ayahuasca healing centers in Peru and Brazil. More recently, I wrote my memoir on sacred medicines, *The Dark and the Light,* because I saw too many charlatans in the healing community, people without training or experience administering medicines and causing more damage than good.

- *What do you see as the purpose of working with 5?*

I feel bufo is the quickest way to obliterate the ego, obtain "The Experience," and return in a timely manner. I consider it the priestly level of medicine practice, whereas ayahuasca is a slow run where someone can contextualize their experience as they go along. I also feel people should do ayahuasca before they do the toad.

- *If you use unconventional or controversial methods, what is the rationale? In your own view, how does it serve your practice?*

I feel that we are in an era where everything and anything can be utilized for the healing of humanity. I understand the argument in regards to "cultural appropriation" or people calling methods "unconventional," but in the end, if the participants and the administrator are clear in the approach, anything goes.

- *How do you handle issues of informed consent?*

Between the practitioner and the client/patient, it has to be very clear what method and modality they are going to utilize during their event/ceremony. When it comes to informed consent in the sharing of information, I personally don't identify patients or clients. I do need to know the client/patient's mental and medical history though. Completely.

FACILITATING 5-MEO-DMT

- *What do people get out of their sessions/experiences?*

Wow! That's infinite. I wrote about many of mine in my book, not to brag or show off, but as a means to express to the agnostics that there is more out there in the universe. Initially, I hope my client/patient receives some sort of self-awareness by losing their ego. This alone can have an amazing life-changing perspective shift. More so, I hope they can experience a sense of *samadhi* or oneness with all things. I can go on and on in regards to the levels of awareness and healing I wish for people to experience while utilizing scared practices and medicines. There are the states of *nirvana, turiya,* interdimensional exploration, and many, many more. It is my job to give a potential *experience* to people and then assist in the contextualization those experiences.

- *Do you provide pre-session information, screening, prep? If so, what?*

Of course. All the above. Again, I wrote my book as a kind of warning to those new to the indigenous and medicine paths. I have found that even some of the most respected medicine shamans do not offer anything other than the experience. I find this disheartening, frustrating, and quite frankly, irresponsible and dangerous. I became a facilitator in order to counter these practitioners. I offer my services outside of even being the facilitator for the ceremony. I've had many people contact me for advice even though they did bufo or ayahuasca, etc., from other facilitators.

- *What are some of the best results you've seen?*

Personally, I've experienced the Godhead, Nirvana, Christ Consciousness, Buddha Consciousness, and much, much more. I hope that everyone gets to experience these beautiful states of consciousness. On a practical level, I hope we find the healing we need. I hope we can learn to deal with our traumas and find the means of making this world a better place for ourselves and all other beings and the planet.

- *What are some of the difficulties you've encountered with patients/clients?*

It depends on the ceremony for me. In bufo ceremonies I have seen atheists go to the most extreme version of their own hell, and I've seen devout Hindus who lived in an ashram experience nothing. It is so specific and unique that it is hard to generalize. The most blanketing statement I can make is that people should work their way up to bufo. I do consider it a priestly class medicine. Start by learning to meditate, eat right, practice yoga, do a hundred sweat lodges, try mushrooms, move to ayahuasca, and then maybe enjoy bufo. I have seen the worst reactions when patients/clients go from zero spiritual/meditative practice to bufo.

- *What are your recommendations for integration and post-experience processing?*

My job at the ayahuasca centers was to help clients contextualize their experiences. This is a very tall order considering that many people have such an enlightening experience that they cannot fathom how to engage as humans in this late-stage capitalistic society. I was there, too, when I started my practice. It takes much integration and time. I encourage my clients to regularly talk with me on a weekly basis. I also encourage a prerequisite system (diet, exercise, meditation, yoga, sweat lodges) to build their understanding and prepare themselves for the extremes they will experience.

- *What resources do you use or recommend to clients?*

This is endless as well because it depends on the client and what works for them. There are books, meditations apps, counselors, therapy, friends, the list goes on. I will discuss and assess where the client is and go from there. I created meditation mandalas and binaural beats meditation albums that my clients can utilize.

- *How many people have you served, and what kinds of people have you worked with? (Drug addicts, spiritual seekers, vets, ages, genders, occupations, interests, nationalities/ethnicities)*

I have served small groups and individuals with bufo. I have facilitated larger groups with ayahuasca and other sacred medicines. As a recovered addict, I specialize in working with addicts. My sweat lodges are great for this as they do not use literal medicine and often someone who is on recovery can't use bufo, ayahuasca, or any drug. This is very important regarding those who are schizophrenic or bipolar, etc. When it comes to medicine like bufo or ayahuasca, I feel a strict prescreening is very important to evaluate these issues. Often, 5-MeO-DMT given to a schizophrenic can do more long-term damage than good. I have worked with hundreds of people, everyone from all occupations, all interests, and many different nationalities and ethnicities. I often use the example of a couple I know who were both on different corporate boards (high-level power-players) and decided collectively to quit their jobs

Facilitating 5-MeO-DMT

after a particularly grand Experience. I had to remind them that they had kids in college and responsibilities and to take it easy and settle in with the experience. "Don't go home, get a divorce and quit your job," has been my mantra to many.

- *Do you see different issues between serving men and women, old and young, healthy and those will medical issues?*

Absolutely. Again, this is a set and setting issues that needs to be discussed with your client. Everyone is different and creating or suggesting an event should take all that into consideration. One of the biggest issues I found was this: at a certain healing retreat center that I worked at, I was told by some guests that the owner was touching the women inappropriately during ceremony and spying on them as they took jungle showers. When I confronted him, he threatened my life. You have to realize that 80% of all patients/clients who make it to the Amazon to do 5-MeO-DMT are usually suffering from childhood sexual abuse. So, this created some real new trauma for the patients/clients, as you can imagine. I had to sneak out of the center and left that job. Later, I was informed of a tragedy involving my replacement.

- *What do you feel are the responsibilities of those serving 5?*

I feel the responsibility is greater than most doctors and priests carry. After all, it has the ability to offer great healing and spiritual enlightenment. I am responsible for the individual from months before the event and kind of "forever" afterwards. It's like the myth that if you save someone's life you are responsible for it. Now, with that said, most clients and I have a limit and there are set boundaries.

- *Do you have an opinion on synthetic vs. "natural"?*

I do, but they are conflicting. I am worried about the fair treatment of the toads and the over-harvesting of the ayahuasca vine.

- *If you choose to work with Toad, what's your take on sustainable harvesting, toad protections, and related ethical questions?*

Obviously, I would prefer the toads to be cared for, etc. This is the same with kambo frogs. I appreciate that the toad can be kept in captivity whereas the kambo frog needs to be caught in the wild and (hopefully) rereleased. I've always argued for the natural over the manufactured with any medicine. For instance, I would never use LSD in a therapeutic setting. I would prefer mushrooms for therapy. I feel there is a spirit to the sacred medicines, NOT manufactured. However, the manufactured ones can still work.

- *What role do you see for 5 in the global community?*

I am a facilitator of ceremonies and an integration specialist. I wish we could change the world for the better. I want to participate in that change in any way I can.

- *What are the lessons you've learned from serving 5?*

Humility, compassion, and patience are all the foundational elements that I learned. But this is just me and others may learn different things. I have also become a much more spiritual person. Having once been a Christian, then an atheist, it was sacred indigenous practices and medicines that brought back spirituality to my life.

- *Do you see serving 5 as being different from serving other entheogenic medicines? How? Why?*

Like I said, bufo is the pinnacle of these sacred medicines. I feel it deserves the most one-on-one care and the greatest consideration, even over ayahuasca, and then psilocybin mushrooms, and San Pedro on down from there.

- *What concerns, if any, do you have about the surging interest in 5 globally, and the sharp increase in demand for the experience (and its possible negative impacts on toads)?*

We will need to see about the ethical care and treatment of the toads. But with that said, I am a strong believer that most people actually don't need sacred medicine therapy. I feel may people are seeking it out as a badge, but in actuality, do not have the preliminary foundation for working with such a powerful medicine. I mean, if you stubbed your toe, you don't shoot heroin and use a defibrillator to cure it. I think too many are too quick to jump on board with these sacred medicines. I think many need to build up their personal practice first. I truly feel may would be cured with meditations, dietary shifts, and sweat lodge.

Heart-Centered Integration and Support

A Conversation Between Robin Rivera and Martin Ball

From The Entheogenic Evolution Podcast, January 13th, 2020

This interview has been edited for clarity. My side of the conversation is presented in italics and Robin's side is in regular text.

To start, I want to give you the opportunity to go ahead and introduce yourself and whatever you would like to share about yourself, and then, if you'd like, to tell us how you got into this area, and also your focus on integration and support when it comes to 5-MeO-DMT.

Yeah awesome. That sounds exciting to me. As I'm reflecting on how I got into this, I feel a lot of nostalgia and appreciation and gratitude in this moment that was unexpected.

FACILITATING 5-MEO-DMT

I'm Robin Rivera. I would identify myself as mostly a radically healing woman in the world who just comes very raw and real with what it is to be human, because I'm someone who has suffered immensely in the confines of the hells of my own mind, not to mention the actual tangible traumas that I've lived through. I think that makes for a really interesting ability to relate to people because of the utter humility and powerlessness that I've had to learn and experience. I'm also a mother. I have three children, two of whom are very small, and I'm also engaged to a beautiful man who has two children, so I technically have five children, and I'm very much wearing a lot of hats. I wear the healing Mama hat, the entrepreneur hat, and a facilitator of ceremonial transformation hat.

What I do is I facilitate transformation primarily with the interest in building really strong integrity in leaders. The reason I'm passionate about that is because it was people who put their hand out to me and helped me learn to use my pain and suffering and the shitty things in life that I've endured to build me into a transformed leader. This kind of transformation feels so good, and I want that and see that for other people. Because of my life experiences, I believe that I have a unique ability to pull that out in a fun way (though it's sometimes not fun).

The topic of how I got into this 5-MeO-DMT community is really auspicious. Out of life and death necessity, I've been seeking my own inner freedom, seeking liberation, seeking resolution, seeking stability, and just seeking help. Since I was about 13 or 14 years old, I've been receiving therapy, boot-camps, hospitalizations, institutions, rehabs; you name it, I did it, or I've tried it. I've had this dialogue of self-help for a long time, which I believe has been my early spiritual awakening of just unraveling at this seemingly snail pace.

And so, I found myself, after turning my life around (having been a victim of sex trafficking and abuse) when I became a mother 11 years ago, in college, emersed in this very intellectually stimulating environment for the first time (because I didn't graduate high school) and I was a train wreck before. But finding myself in these environments, a whole world opened up to me about psychology and consciousness and human rights. Everything was just kind of percolating inside me. I ended up following the track of my Master's degree into consciousness and transformative studies, which was like, Holy Shit! Now I have a language to talk about this transformation that's been happening with me over the span of my life.

I've had very deep and profound revelatory experiences along the way. Even though I really wasn't able to get my shit together, I was I was having these very profound experiences that led me to the next stage of my human development. While I was in my degree program, I learned about plant medicines and non-ordinary states of consciousness which you could achieve through breath or drumming or ceremony. I was already very familiar with ceremony because of my ancestry and being a yoga teacher. I started having dreams where ayahuasca was coming to me in my dreams and haunting me night after night, and I had never had any other experience like that.

So, it was a culmination of these seeds being planted, this idea of expanded states of consciousness and intuitively feeling like, shit, I need something more than talk therapy. I need something more. I need the big guns here. If not, I'm going to die. I made so much progress and won so many awards (from my work combatting human trafficking and sexual abuse) and was able to have some stability, but in those times, that story of self-destruction and hopelessness would turn on and it would grab me. It was dangerous and it was dark. I wondered what it was going to take to finally heal this thing.

Between having the dreams and then these seeds being planted, I was getting really curious. I was going through what I would consider a kind of a shamanic initiation when I had to lay down my life on this hospital table when I was pregnant with my last child. For about 3 months I knew that I had a devastating fatal disease or condition where, during the pregnancy, the uterus starts to grow like a cancer into the wall of your body. You're at risk of bleeding to death at any moment, and there's no way to save you except to give you a blood transfusion. They knew this was coming, and I had to be within 5 minutes of a hospital at all times. They had to schedule an early delivery, and it was going to take about 20 people. The only way to get the baby out would be to remove all of my female organs. They expect 98% of the women to need a full-body blood transfusion and to be in the ICU, because your lungs start to give out a lot of times. So, I was planning to be in the ICU on a breathing machine. Normally the baby comes out just fine, but 10% with this condition die, even with all these precautionary measures and planning.

When I laid myself on that hospital table, it reminded me of a DMT experience I'd had in the past where I was I dropped through all these layers of consciousness and I found myself laying on this metal hospital bed in the DMT experience. I could hear this woman, and it was kind of like the spirit of ayahuasca, now, looking back on it, but I heard this woman, and all these people were panicking, and this woman was in charge. The other people were saying, "She's not ready. Robin's not ready. She's not ready to go deeper. She's not ready for the full she-bang!" And then this woman was like, "Hold on. I got it. Let me help her," and she was kind of troubleshooted something, and then she realized, "OK. Yes. It's not time," and she released me. And then my DMT experience opened up to something fun, a circus, or whatever.

Facilitating 5-MeO-DMT

But when I laid myself down on that hospital bed to birth my child, it was that same feeling, exactly like laying on this table in the DMT experience, putting my life in someone else's hands with all these wires and things. I had this opportunity when they told me to take a breath of the anesthesia to surrender and I thought, "I don't know if I'm going to wake up . . ." I had to write a will for my children. I just felt that feeling of full surrender of like, "OK, universe, Creator, whatever; here I go! Take care of my kids!" I really believe that that moment prepared me for being introduced to 5-MeO-DMT.

About less than a year later, I was asking my friends who served ayahuasca about drinking it. I really wanted to try it, but no doors opened. I don't know why, but when someone mentioned the toad, I felt ready; I was a warrior, and I needed this warrior medicine. Everything lined up, all of a sudden, and I'm in this ceremony that was set up in such a beautiful way with integrity and a lot of preparation. I felt really comfortable, though I was scared as shit, but I knew that things were about to change.

Coincidentally, I had discovered that I had an eye tumor the week before I had to go into the ceremony. It was crazy. I felt I had nothing left to lose, so, "Creator: take me all the way! Just do it! I'll do whatever it takes!" Right before I took my first hit, I was scared and I thought to myself, "I don't want to trust these people. I don't want to trust this situation. But, I can choose to trust and maybe win everything, or I cannot choose to trust and get nothing." So, I just chose to trust. Surprisingly, I found that it was so much easier to surrender than I had thought. Just by the sheer power of my will I was able to surrender again and again and again. What ended up happening was that I had this reflection on my tragically beautiful life, and all these difficult and dark things I had gone through, from a different perspective. I wailed with my whole body. There was no story attached, just this beautiful crying, and I had a tiny experience of what you might call the divine. I say tiny because I've later had bigger experiences with peak periods of the divine, and of my own divinity. It was revealed to me that I was that love and the healing that I had been fighting for since I was a 13-year-old little, suicidal girl. It was shown to me to be true and that my inner guidance was telling me, "Don't kill yourself. Don't die. Keep going, It's there. It's there somewhere."

It became real. It was shown to me as real. I just bowed down to God, to myself, to that inner knowing that love and healing was available to me, and that I was right that talk therapy and everything I was doing just wasn't the end game. There was so much more. I found that it was infinitely more.

Then I went for a second round, and that's when I had the nondual experience. I projectile vomited decades, lifetimes, of trauma. Then I read about that in your book about the those "champagne cork" vomits, and it was just like you described. There was surrendering even in that because it was like infinite throw up. I didn't know up from down, left to right, but I knew I was vomiting and releasing, and it was great! So that obviously had a big impact on me, just as it does for most people, and I just saw it in unspeakable reverence. There was unspeakable reverence for what I was shown, and I was almost frightened that I was allowed to see such a deep mystery. It almost filled in all those feelings of unworthiness to be able to peer into this deep mystery. I've had to spend these years afterward working through that feeling of unworthiness. It's so profound and so precious.

It's so beautiful to hear you share all of this. I really like that you've just mentioned this idea of feeling unworthy because it's interesting how often that does show up for people, especially people who have had a difficult past or a difficult life, and that sense of unworthiness that people hold against themselves. The irony is that of course you're worthy! How could any of us not be worthy of the infinite love that we all are? Yet that's the way that the ego works. It tells us that we're not worthy or that we didn't deserve that. But it's really transformative when you have these deep purges and letting go on 5-MeO-DMT where it feels like the whole universe is turning inside out through you, and it feels like it's never going to stop, but then you're cleaned out and you feel new. And then the ego comes back and says, "You weren't worthy of that!"

Afterwards, I felt this call, as many people do, to give back. Some people who taught me leadership said that when you enjoy something, when you want to know about something, you get involved. I was pretty shy growing up and it was hard for me, but I knew it worked for me, it helped me, so I immediately set the intention to get involved. How can I serve? How can I get involved in this community? I went to WBAC, and that changed my life because I met such wonderful people there, and there I met a teacher whom I've since been mentored by, and just having another woman to speak to on this path on this level is so helpful. It makes me feel so safe and rooted in my life. Then people just started asking me to help, so I ended up creating the "Heart-Centered Integration Group" on Facebook. There was already a very popular toad group on Facebook that had about 7,000 people, which is wonderful. Participating there was a way that I was able to process and connect, but I also saw a lot of meanness and cruelty and criticism going on there. It wasn't directed at me at first, and then it started to be directed at me. I was like, man, am I creating this, or what?

I thought, why don't I create another space that is centered around certain cultural values of respect and speaking from the heart, and matters of the heart, like a heart focus? That felt important and real to me. As the leader of that group, I can determine what's allowed, or what's not, and set the standards. You know, no shit-talking or

FACILITATING 5-MEO-DMT

character assassination. It's curious to me why there's so much of that in there on social media. We're dealing with an experience that is filled with such beauty and love, but the conversations on social media don't reflect that. I am curious about why that is, and so that's why I stopped participating in the already-established group. I just felt a need for a safe place for people to talk about matters of the heart regarding integrating these experiences.

I wonder if we can go back to something that you mentioned with your introduction to the medicine. You said that there was a lot of preparation before going in. That's definitely one of the issues out there in the Toad/5-MeO-DMT community in that there are some people who serve the medicine, and my understanding is that they basically don't give any kind of preparation. It's just kind of, "Here you go . . ." My own approach to it, when I was facilitating 5-MeO-DMT with clients, was to give people an extended preparation before ever taking the medicine. Quite significantly, Johns Hopkins University has just released a study that was done with participants of the Temple of Awakening Divinity, which is where I was first introduced to the medicine, where there is a great deal of preparation beforehand. The recent Johns Hopkins study was basically saying that this emphasis on preparation has a direct impact on people's ability to trust and let go and to have a full mystical experience. So that preparation, and also integration, is very important. I do think it's a little startling that there are people serving out there that don't really offer either preparation or integration and it's just kind of, "Here you go," and then, "OK, next person, here you go." So, I'm curious; what kind of preparation did you get?

The preparation that I got was from the facilitator's assistant, who kind of organizes all the people because she's the first entry point that people have. She's just so loving. She hops on the phone with people, and she shares her story – not in depth – but her gratitude and what she's experienced, and so potential clients can develop a sense that this woman is being vulnerable with me, and I can be too. You can feel that she's sincere. That makes me feel I can trust her, and that I can be vulnerable too, and ask my questions.

You get the first intake call, which is kind of a screening call, and once I had that, then I had a very lengthy intake form that went into my trauma and my life experience. It also had me reflect on what kind of outside support I had in general, like who can I talk to about it? So not only is that good information for the facilitators, but it's good information for me to know, like, who's on my team? Do I have anybody on my team? And to know that I have support afterwards. So that was really helpful, and then there was some preparatory questions that were for my personal reflection, such as: who am

I? How do I identify myself? What is life? – those kind of existential questions. Following that, there was a brief call with the actual facilitator – maybe a 15 or 20-minute call. I was able to ask any questions I wanted. I was able to express any anxiety I was feeling. He was also available by email. I had a lot to share, so he jumped on another call with me. I was probably a special case given my past difficulties. Then we had a group orientation call with everybody, and for people who were local, we were able to come in person and have a group orientation (and the people who weren't local called in) and then came the day of the ceremony. We were able to have hours of time beforehand to kind of settle in and then congregate as a group and do a little bit of process work. I think that's really important. And then he added a small ceremonial piece where we gave reverence to the sacrament, and said a prayer, if prayer was in our practice, did some cleansing, and then we were ready to go.

Reflecting back on that, now that I've experienced many, many ceremonies, and been through boot-camp-style trainings, and things like this, I feel that there there's some wiggle room there. There's room for creativity in expressing what's true to the facilitator, what they believe, and what feels important for them and their style. But it is startling to me to that people can be doing kind of the drive-by method of like, "Oh, I'm in town! Here! Light it up!" But at the same time, I just don't know. I don't know if there's not some divine intelligence kind of orchestrating it all. But what I do know is if it's in my consciousness to honor and to value a certain way, then that's for me, and that's for me to do and follow and promote.

I like what you just added there: the idea that there's there is a divine intelligence behind it all, and that's definitely a statement that I would agree with. At the same time, I personally think that preparing people is important, and offering some kind of support afterwards is important, too. But, the drive by-method might be fine for some people. Also, picking up on something that you said earlier, there's a lot of judgment out there. There's a lot of really negative talk about people and practices that goes on within the 5-MeO-DMT community. And even in the broader psychedelic community, there seems to be just a lot of passing of judgement and a lot of it is very ugly. And a lot of it is driven, in my observation, by people who themselves might not be the most stable individuals. It's interesting that even you yourself mentioned that in putting yourself out there, some of that started to be directed towards you. Perhaps you've experienced: why is everybody jumping on me for being wrong or not being part of their circle or whatever? There are people putting up boundaries and putting up accusations. It's curious. Maybe one of the reasons is that 5-MeO-DMT can dissolve the ego on a temporary basis, but then sometimes it does come roaring back.

Facilitating 5-MeO-DMT

They talked about that in my Master's degree program about when you have an expanded state of consciousness (either spontaneously or via entheogens) that it's like a rubber band. You have a center of gravity and then you can go "boing!" when you get triggered, you go backwards, or you can go "boing!" and go forward. We can go either way, and if it's too extreme, it can ricochet and basically go backwards in your human development because the ego tries to, like you said, reinstate itself so strongly. It feels so threatened. I think that's part of it. I think another part of it is just the pulsation, the dichotomy, the duality. For those of us that feel adamant about it being done with integrity, and safely, and in an honorable way, if we didn't see that dark, crappy stuff, then we might not be as compelled to do it in what we feel is a good way.

I think we should allow that different people will feel comfortable in different contexts and situations, and not everyone is the same. Personally, I like to put out what I feel is the best information, from my perspective, and people can use that anyway they want, but it doesn't necessarily mean that someone who does things a different way is wrong or that they're bad, because we all have our different perspectives on this. Anyone who facilitates, or anyone who coaches, or anyone who offers integration and support, they're going to be coming from their own heart, and allowing for that diversity is perhaps a good thing. But what concerns me, at times, is that there seem to be elements of control that comes in there where people want to control other people and control the way that things are happening. What I've found most valuable with 5-MeO-DMT, and with life in general, is the more you let go, the less you try and control, is that ultimately the more at peace you are going to be, and the richer your life is going to be. Even in the most difficult circumstances, the more you let go, the more you're going to get, and so that's why I personally try and step back from all of the fighting that goes on. I don't want to be involved. That's why I really honor that you put up your own page of heart-centered integration and support. So let's talk a little bit more about what you're offering in terms of heart-centered integration and support. How does that look for you? How does that work?

To be honest, I'm pretty annoyed with the word "integration" because I feel like it's thrown around a lot and everyone has different ideas of what it means. I decided to use it so people had the general gist of what I was trying to create. I feel integration is: OK, now how do you have a good life? OK, now so what? And that's going to look different for everybody. I feel like if you're leading with the heart, meaning you know your inner guidance, what your truth is, what feels true, what feels good to you, what you want, what you desire, then you're going to be able to follow the breadcrumbs of what it is good for you. I don't think there's one cookie-cutter way of doing it. The principle would be curiosity – just staying extremely curious. And as you say, it's about that lesson of surrender: how much can we keep letting go? Let go of that state of consciousness. Let go of that identity, here, and this desire here. And having community to bounce that off of and get feedback. We're all wanting connection. That's what the medicine gives us. That sacrament gives us a connection. It gives us the ultimate connection, right? And then it's like; OK, how can we keep seeking this connection in our daily life? And let's talk about it, because I don't have all the answers! You don't have all the answers! But together we can inspire each other.

And then there's another aspect of actually making sense of things that were shown to you, like; Oh crap! I had the nondual experience, and now what? How can I digest this? It's taken me a couple of years to digest the first experience. I went through phases of being angry about it, almost a panic. I find that it comes back to me piece by piece. For example, I was sitting in a meditation the other day and I was having a lot of anxiety. I'm in this third dimension like I've got to provide, I need to take care of the kids, I'm moving, or you know, blah blah blah! And I was like; I need to breathe! So I sat and I began to breathe and I began to seek my inner wisdom to please guide me. What washed over me was a memory of my first experience when I was shown divine trust, and it was like; there was no such thing as safety! There was no such thing as survival. It was like; it's all good! It's all fine. You can trust. And through that little tidbit of a revelation, I was able to remember how it felt in my body when I was on the on the medicine right here, right now, and so that gave me ease and comfort. To me, that's an integration.

I had that experience, and now I'm bridging it to this day in real life when I am anxious about being a human. I can remember, "Oh yes. I can trust." It might just be a little bit, and then a little bit more. So that's an example of how I see integration. I don't market myself as an integration coach or anything like that. What's coming through to me is that I'm seeing people come into my sphere who want to step into leadership, who either experienced this sacrament, or not, or they're just doing other transformational work and they really want to step into holding space, like ceremonial space. I feel that all the all the things that I would teach someone about integration and the things I've learned through 5-MeO-DMT are things that I would teach people if they wanted to start facilitating transformational work. These are all the principles that have been shown to me and in as non-dogmatic a way as possible.

I really resonate with the idea that it's about people being true to their own path, true to their own wisdom, of what is true and what is helpful for them, what their way is to transmit truth and revelation. And so that's the work that I'm stepping into more and more. I am creating a leadership program where I believe that I can have a powerful impact on the next wave of ceremonial facilitators, and it doesn't necessarily mean

FACILITATING 5-MEO-DMT

people who want to serve medicine. That would be a whole other level of training that would have to take place out of the U.S. (for legal reasons). I teach people how to step into their integrity and their leadership in the well-rounded way that I've been shown and that I'm doing. I'm thinking of starting a mystery school, because that's really what we're talking about: inquiry into the deep inner mysteries that reside in all of us. And they're going to play with their own individual consciousness in a different way so I can tell you: it's in this Mexican lineage way, or it's in this Native American way, or it's in the way that you right now are experiencing it and we provide opportunities for you to awaken, and that's kind of what my experience with the medicine was.

I've had the medicine over 150 times now, in a short period of time. What I've been shown and taught by it is all around having great humility as a human being, and around community, and right relationship, and deep listening to the self, like no matter what's coming at you with the people assassinating your character, or doubting you, or thinking that you need someone to ordain you as a priestess, or tell you that you're enough. I want people to be clear that you just initiate yourself and choose to liberate yourself. Here, fine: I'll give you permission to do that and the container to explore it in, but it has to come from yourself and not someone or something outside you.

I think something that you're speaking of is that it really comes back to personal responsibility, and also comes back to personal choice. Even with something as powerful as 5-MeO-DMT, there's still personal responsibility and choice. Sometimes people approach it with the idea of, "Oh well, this will reveal all the answers to me," and, "This is going to fix all my problems," and, "It's going to change my life." It holds some of those potentials, but the ultimate lesson, I think, is always that it comes back to: who are you? What do you want? Are you choosing authentically, or not? Are you telling yourself stories, or not? And that is a responsibility that arises in every moment of every day and 5-MeO-DMT isn't going to turn that off for you. It's not going to tell you what to do. It's not going to be like: this is what you must do! *It still comes down to:* what's in your heart? What are *you going to do?*

I love that and it makes me so happy and pleased and I feel so lucky that, thank God, I turned out to be a decent human being. It could have gone so many other ways and I'm so thankful because it feels like grace. I chose to keep taking personal responsibility, no matter what. I've been through a lot of weird, extreme situations with sex trafficking, and I continued to choose the higher road. I continued to choose to assign my own meaning to it that got me to the next stage, and I think in stepping outside myself, I think that's glorious. How can I inspire other people to make that choice if that's what they want?

Martin W. Ball, Ph.D., Editor

I think really the best leadership role is finding how to inspire others so that they make their choices for themselves. Something that I see, even in medicine circles, is that there is a lot of, "Well, if I just sit with this person…" or, "If I go and get this ceremony…" or, "If I get this authentication…" There's still a lot of that out there with this idea of the right person in the right place, the right lineages, the right whatever. That's really overlooking the questions of: who are you? What is true for you? Just because someone over here does it this way, that doesn't mean it's right for you. It's about self-empowerment. For me, it's not about the right lineage, or the right organization, the right affiliation, the right belonging. It's what is right within your own heart? Are you activating that? Are you operating from that place? That's really the inspiration is for the empowerment, and then we can see a beautiful amount of diversity. We can see a beautiful array of approaches, and ways, and techniques. If it's coming from the heart, that's really what's most important.

I'm just reflecting on the community and reflecting on my personal path. I want to be vulnerable, to stay open. It's been hard to find and strengthen that part in myself, to not doubt myself, and to also not be grandiose of like, "Oh yeah, I got it! I'm going to do this and I'm just going to bulldoze these people." It's in between. I learned this through my ass getting kicked by life, but it's this rooted humility of, "Yes, I'm powerful. Yes, I'm here to do something cool and fun and righteous, but I'm also just a tiny speck of dust in this grand web of things, and I am still teachable. I still need community. I still need my mommy. I still make mistakes. I'm still healing. I can learn to stand in my wounds and my strength at the same time." This has been a huge part of this path, and it's scary, especially when you're stepping into some big shoes or dealing with powerful transformation. You don't want people to doubt you. You want everyone to pat you on the back and say, "Yeah! You're doing great! Keep going." But it's not always going to be like that.

I generally was so sensitive growing up, so when that started to happen, I felt like it was my own life shaking me and I needed to stand still in my own heart. But it was hard. I felt so sad when some people questioned my sincerity online. It might be only a couple people out of a bunch of nice people, but you still feel that. And even people in the medicine community, I've had a couple of fallings-out with other medicine women who, for some reason, I just irked in some way, and they were not in celebration of me, and it broke my heart. I felt so unsafe and so betrayed, to not be seen in my sincerity. I'd gone around thinking I can just be vulnerable with everybody and tell them all my darkest secrets and everybody is still going to know how sincere or great I am. But I'm finding that it hasn't been that way, and that you have to use

FACILITATING 5-MEO-DMT

discernment on this path. It's stepping into your heart and believing in what you're doing as long as you are willing to be self-responsible. Even if I make a mistake, I'm taking responsibility for that because it was my choice, that was my creation. It's been hard, but beautiful in strengthening myself as a facilitator of transformation. It's the joy of the journey. It's my life to be had, my offering, and my joy to be in service. My hope in my heart is to be a good and inspiring example of what it is to be tragically human and helpful.

No amount of transcendent experiences, no amount of smoking 5-MeO-DMT, or anything else, is ever going to override our humanity. In many ways, it is going to amplify it, and that's really the beauty of the gift. God, the divine, has chosen to manifest itself as human beings, and we can fall into the ocean of that universal oneness and consciousness and experience that as ourselves, but it's never going to override or obviate the conditions of being a human being, and having human emotions, and human failures, and human tragedy, and our thoughts, emotions, and physicality, and interpersonal relationships. It's all still going to be here. There is no magic pill to make everything great all the time. We still have to make choices, and the more we do that with integrity, and at least with some clarity within ourselves, then the more trust we can have within ourselves and with reality as a whole. But we still have to make choices, and we're going to make wrong ones, and we're going to not listen to ourselves, at times, we're not going to not listen to our heart. We're going to overthink things, we're going to be self-critical, or going to be judgmental, we're going to experience these emotions with other people. So really the best we can do is to collectively and personally navigate this together and hopefully do it with an open heart and without just giving into judgment.

I've actively been working on that a lot. When I first came into the 5-MeO-DMT community, I felt frightened of some people. Someone with a big ego freaked me out, or I'd catch someone in a lie. I've been reconciling that in myself of recognizing that I'm carrying that judgment, and that it wouldn't feel good for me. I know I'm safe in my own body, in my own life. I don't need to be afraid of associating with or sitting next to this person or talking to this person. I've softened around all those judgments. It comes piece meal, like the slow integration process of recognizing that here's judgment. I see it. I'm willing to forgive this judgment. And then you keep doing it, and over time, it just softens. I would love to be in a place where I'm just able to sit at the table with the people that I used to judge the most. That would be ideal.

WHO DO YOU SERVE?

by Rak Razam

Editor's Note: This submission was transcribed by Rak from an interview we conducted for The Entheogenic Evolution Podcast specifically for the purpose of creating an entry for this anthology. In crafting his entry, Rak has removed the conversational aspect of the interaction and presented it as a single discourse.

Psychedelic de Jour:

5-MeO-DMT is the current psychedelic de jour, celebrated by medical science hungry for a short-lasting chemical to help relieve the mental turmoil of the ego, and by spiritual enthusiasts eager to reveal the Divine within in ceremonial and psychonautical contexts. The sheer power of reconnection, of dropping the mind to reveal a sacred geography within our very being, is overwhelming. A sense of belonging, gratitude, oneness and meaning beyond the duality of other psychedelic experiences has propelled a large majority of those who have experienced this grand initiation to want to share it with others. Despite the absence of a pronounced lineage for the serving of 5-MeO, a new generation of facilitators has emerged, growing almost exponentially, with the natural growing pains, pangs and joys of service. And yet, this role in facilitating the sacred is itself a sacred act. Like midwives of the Divine, 5-MeO facilitators are helping rebirth God consciousness back into the collective. And in doing so we must ask: Who do you serve?

I was introduced to the medicine of 5-MeO-DMT in 2006, in the jungles of Peru, in a very unorthodox set and setting, whilst wearing an EEG helmet and having my brainwaves read by Dr. Juan Acosta and tended to by the "Gringo Shaman," Ron Wheelock (see www.aya-awakenings.com/film). They were my first facilitators. Ron had sourced a synthetic version of 5-MeO and the experience completely changed my life. It set me on the course of documenting and communicating what both ayahuasca and 5-MeO-DMT were about, to create media containers for the sacred initiations and to share the essence of the wisdom that channeled through me. It became a seven-year plus journey to make my book and film, *Aya: Awakenings*, during which I didn't go near 5-MeO again, as I was still integrating.

And as that cycle completed: boom, 5-MeO entered my life again in 2015 via Dr. Octavio Rettig, the now infamous Mexican practitioner who had himself been healed from his addictions by the medicine of the *Bufo alvarius* toad, native to the Sonoran Desert in the north of Mexico. Toad medicine has its subtle differences from the synthetic version, with over 17 different alkaloids including 5-MeO-DMT contributing to an entourage effect, but the destination was the same: home.

That ceremony was a grand initiation into the medicine of 5-MeO, the Mexican lineage Octavio had kickstarted with the Seri tribe and style of ceremony he brought out into the world (Note: I do not condone Octavio's now controversial practices, some of which have resulted in death and injury, do your own research). Where nine years before I had received 5-MeO with just my two friends holding space, the mélange of a community ceremony, drawing upon ancient traditions, songs, and ways to hold space, captivated my heart. Coming back from the "full release" of 5-MeO in 2006 I felt alone. By 2015 a global tribe was birthing, and everyone had a role to play as seeder, sporer, server. An archaic revival was burgeoning, and a new generation of medicine holders was manifesting to be in service – and I was right there at the coal face of the Divine.

FACILITATING 5-MEO-DMT
God's Back Door Access Code:

I could see that in many ways, 5-MeO-DMT was becoming a modern global sacrament. It's found in plants, seeds, grasses, animals, mammals – and us, humans. 5-MeO is endogenous to consciousness, like "God's back door access," a cheat code to remember Who and What we really are. Mario Garnier, the director of the *World Bufo Alvarius Congress* (www.WBAC.info) likes to say that "the molecule has its own agenda," whether it's synthetic or toad. And it's not the molecule, obviously – it's the spirit in or behind the molecule, or the force that is revealed in the fullness of the 5-MeO-DMT experience, which I believe is the active intelligence of Source consciousness itself, shaping its creation.

Having felt an ultimate intelligence and getting a glimpse of understanding of the way that it is working through us and through this culture, it has directly affected my perception of 5-MeO facilitators and the role they play in the dissemination of this molecule into the world.

If 100 people drink ayahuasca, maybe three will think that they want to serve the medicine, maybe one, or maybe none – because it's challenging, it's purgative, it has all these skills and sensitivities that need to be learned over many years of sacrifice. With 5-MeO-DMT it seems like one in five people want to serve the medicine. And the growing proliferation of servers emerging into our community with little to no experience reflects that. But *this desire to be in service doesn't mean you have to be a facilitator.*

In fact, in some ways you could say we're all facilitating the integration of this medicine back into the culture and into the species. And so essentially, if you take a top-down or a holistic approach and you're not looking at it from the human ego – here I am as a 'facilitator doing a nine-to-five job' – but if you realize the molecule and the intelligence behind the molecule is actually permeating through the collective, it adds weight to the urgency with which people who have experienced 5-MeO want to share it …

What we have learned is that *5-MeO-DMT is a replicable technology of the sacred.* It is endogenous to all mammals, including human beings – we already have the on-switch. We have the ability to have this connection without synthetic medicine or the toad, but we've needed these training wheels to *remember that we are the medicine.*

Martin W. Ball, Ph.D., Editor
Default Mode Networks:

When you have a unity experience like a full release 5-MeO-DMT journey, many things happen. Essentially, the ego mind is lowering: the neuroscience has proven that as well as the traditional psychedelics that affect the Default Mode Network and the 5ht2a receptors, 5-MeO also targets extra areas of the brain. My neuroscience data came from working with Dr. Juan Acosta and others (see: *Cosmos and History: The Journal of Natural and Social Philosophy, vol. 11, no. 2, 2015*), who showed in their data collections that 5-MeO is working on the Default Mode Network and the parietal and frontal lobes of the brain to shift electrical activity to the gamma frequency, as the egoic sense of identity melts into hyper-coherence.

Neuroscience studies have pattern matched EEG and MRI scans on monks meditating (https://braintap.com/study-of-meditation-and-brain-waves-in-buddhist-monks-confounds-wisconsin-researchers) which are identical to scans of people on 5-MeO-DMT. What this means in that external 5-MeO-DMT is simply 'lowering the gate' of the egoic mind, in the same way that years of meditating or breath work or mantras also lower the egoic mind. *The mind is just a filter between you and Source consciousness within.* So, what are you facilitating then, exactly?

As the ego mind lowers, we know that there can be healing effects, there can be a release of trapped energy in the energetic body, in the emotional body and all the fine gradation of layers of being. And this is what the majority of the Western Psychedelic Renaissance and the planned legal therapy with 5-MeO is focusing on: 5-MeO-DMT as a replacement for SSRIs as an antidepressant to heal mental imbalances and traumas, etc. Facilitators in this model could one day work with insurance companies, medical staff and public clinics that serve 5-MeO in the traditional therapist template. But that's still the very thin edge of the wedge – it feels like the mental and energetic healing are peripheral effects as you cleanse and open to the fullness of your Divine being. The medical model may be getting more than it anticipates.

The corporate establishment is also trying to deconstruct the psychedelic component of psychedelics and still have some sort of positive biochemical shift in being. But as a 2019 Johns Hopkins study on the mystical experience clearly showed (https://www.sciencedaily.com/releases/2019/03/190318132628.htm), it is basically the ego reduction-dissolving-letting go of the ego mind, the "full release" that engenders the healing. That full letting go helps reduce our separation of the egoic filter, which allows for that physical-emotional-energetic healing. And that tangible healing is all that they want from these "drugs" in the Psychedelic Renaissance paradigm. And yet, 5-MeO is so much more, which facilitators must know.

Facilitating 5-MeO-DMT

The Western medical establishment compartmentalize these substances and views them as products – and to a degree they are. But they have no real idea of the ramifications of the person taking these products having an intimate sacred experience beyond their paradigm to understand. So, I have faith that again, everything is orchestrated by a greater power and our ego just nibbles at the edges and tries to compartmentalize stuff. Big Pharma may think 5-MeO is going to be a product that can be sellable and work within capitalism, disseminated by therapist-priests, but it's freaking crazy because this thing is beyond all "isms." 5-MeO in the therapeutic model may enable an unforeseen transformation of the medical establishment into more of a mystical-mystery-school.

> *Remembering our Divine nature is fundamental to understanding what we are doing as facilitators of this medicine.*

Reconnecting to Source:

The Latin for *religion* means "to re-weave, or to reconnect," and what are we reconnecting to but the divine Source, our true nature? So, we all have the capacity to remember IT, but it slips off the conscious mind like a dream. And yet in the energetic opening to what is within it feels like IT reformats our whole being. And by letting go of our trapped trauma and opening up to this Divine presence, we're re-initializing our connection with our deepest self. The Indian holy text *The Upanishads* talks about the "seed of God" that we all have within us – you could call it Buddha nature – this flickering or potential activated over many lifetimes to essentially anchor God in the human form, to bridge heaven.

This is what a lot of the Indian mystic Eastern-meditation traditions point towards – that the whole process that they engage with meditation, breath work and their modalities, is to clean out the organism, to clean the *yamas* and the *niyamas*, all the things that we energetically hold onto, all the *samskaras*, all the filtering layers that we create that obfuscate and separate us from our Divine nature within. In the Indian traditions many of their gurus and holy people have achieved this bridging state – they call them *Jivanmuktas*. They embody the idea that you can be God – on earth – while conscious and having a sublimated ego. Again, no one's trying to destroy the ego with the 5-MeO experience; just remind the ego that it is in service to God, that it is an extension of God – a sub-program.

So, all of this is memetic architecture to describe the process that I believe is involved when we are facilitating this medicine. Essentially, when we have a full release on 5-MeO-DMT, or through an endogenous mystical experience, it initiates this process of that seed of God germinating and growing in relationship with us. In this lens, we are acting like pollinators, activating the God nature within, far beyond a simple psychedelic "drug" peak experience. We are acting as vessels for a higher consciousness to work through to activate a psychic maturation of the human condition latent and waiting to be awakened within us all.

Our modern culture has shunned the traditional world religions, good and bad, and so even in the psychedelic community we shy away from religiosity. We don't have the nuance of language to differentiate, but the 5-MeO experience is archetypally a religious experience. People frequently say in the fullness, or returning from it, "oh my God, oh my God," not as a linguistic approximation, but as a descriptor of the real, tangible, felt experience of the oceanic God consciousness within. Maybe people don't have different words for it ("God" is only a label, after all), but they have felt it in a deeper level of their being that is beyond words. They know. And so basically, at that moment of knowing, they become a convert. And then they want to share that experience of Divinity with others.

Sharing This with Everyone!

"Oh my God, my mom has to do this! My dad has to do this! My friends and family have to do it!" But this is the ego-filter talking, the ego that has come back from full God frequency and is making sense of its experience. And the quality of wanting to share it – to be in unity – is strong. But then we come back to duality. And so, we instinctively sort of migrate towards this idea of switching on the others. Tim Leary had this great quote in the 1960s – as well as the "Turn on, Tune In, Drop out" – there was "Find the others." And you know, as a counterpoint, Ramana Maharshi says: "There are no others," right? And in the unity field this is exactly it.

5-MeO-DMT is similar but different from all the other psychedelics in that it is endogenous to the human organism. So too is DMT, but the tryptamines in general seem to overwrite the other psychedelics. That is, once you've had this activation of that seed of God within you, then anytime you perturb or alter your Default Mode Network it can just sort of bleed through and come into the other experiences. 5-MeO seems to be the higher vibration and it wants to come into our vessels. We are in relationship with it, as the potential for "reactivations" shows.

So, this is all to say that the people who want to be facilitators – it's the ego filter thinking small. It's like, all right, there's a religious impulse to share this experience but the thing you've got to remember is this experience is dormant and it's in everyone right now. Everyone is God on earth, but they haven't opened to the awareness yet. Some people that have had the external 5-MeO experience may interpret it as simply a drug experience or they might not have the vocabulary, or the let's say energetic complexity to understand and hold the immensity of IT. But they're still getting switched on.

And again – these catalysts through toad and synthetic 5-MeO are external catalysts to remember our internal capacity. But essentially, when people want to share this medicine, they often don't fully think it through. They may be like, okay, well, you just light a pipe, right? What is there to it? They're not thinking about the mechanics and the role of the facilitator in the world and the interface with the client/facilitator relationship. They're just awash with this awe, with this desire to connect and this desire to share and behind that, what I really believe is happening is a species activation which is coming through in everyone and spreading this activation of 5-MeO-DMT.

And so essentially, that impulse and that connection behind that impulse is what drives people to serve. Now this doesn't mean you have to be the person lighting the pipe and taking the great and grave responsibility of looking after people's health and well-being and being the rock that holds that space. You might not have the skills for that – but there are many ways to serve. A facilitator needs the support of a team before, during, and after a session to be in greater service to their community. Integration is vital. For me, I took my enthusiasm from my first experiences and poured it into service to support others who were facilitating and forming community. Eventually it came to this fruition point where I deeply felt it was time to serve myself – in countries (like Mexico) where this is legal.

The intelligence in the medicine is guiding all of us, I believe, and when we connect, and when it promulgates through our communities, it self-organizes to create a container for itself.

The Good, the Bad, the Holy:

Ultimately, I believe we are vessels, and as a facilitator who has experienced this medicine, it's really about the capacity you have in your being and in your vessel to serve. It's all an entrainment by Source itself. And you know, what we see in the community – there are good facilitators and there are bad facilitators, regardless of their intentions to give service to the community. And yes, Virginia, it takes all types, so don't judge the facilitator book by the cover. Like Smurfs, there's a 5-MeO facilitator that fits every archetype you could relate to or need.

Martin W. Ball, Ph.D., Editor

On a fundamental level there are things which can go wrong in the ceremony and there are checks and balances and things which must be maintained in a safe, sacred and sound container to do the work. Check out www.theConclave.info, which has some of the best guidelines for Best Practices, Ethics and support on the mechanics of serving–in countries where this not illegal (see Appendix B for an edited version of the "Best Practices" document by The Conclave).

We have all seen people serve and there are many ways to do so. Some people serve clients one-on-one in a therapeutic model; some people work in a more shamanic model; some people work outside, some inside; some people serve standing up or sitting down. But all should have an underpinning of safety and sacredness in the ceremony or therapy container: that's the basis for the work.

I recommend to anyone who is feeling like stepping into service to get more experience first. Even though 5-MeO can be very similar for everyone, it's about the lens of their ego and how they react to the revelation. So, you need more experience to see other people and how they react and the best way to do that is to sit with many facilitators and see the different styles of practice and response.

Before people get to work with the medicine, they should be pre-screened to look for medical conditions, psychological issues, et.al – you also want to also establish in that process a rapport with the client. This is something which is such an incredibly large initiation on a psychic and physical level that you don't just rock up to this and then rock out again like a businessman's lunch and go back to work. This is something completely transformative and you need trust in your facilitator. The client needs trust, and you need to establish a rapport, so all of these subtleties really start to modulate the way you hold space and the container you hold space in.

And as you grow, you will change in your ability and understanding of what is a safe container and the style that you will develop to deliver the medicine. You can learn from other facilitators both what to do and what not to do, and through trial and error finding a style of facilitation that is right for you. Trust the process.

One of the concrete differences perhaps between a lot of the Western styles of facilitation and the Mexican indigenous style is the potentially controversial issue of doing a little bit of medicine at the same time as a client. This challenges the use of medicine for just letting go; in this instance a handshake or such activates but should not debilitate from functioning in ceremony. It reminds me of the first times you do ayahuasca – it can be overwhelming and that's the same with 5-MeO. But what I've learned is that I can take about 20 to 25 milligrams of toad and be functional in the space.

Facilitating 5-MeO-DMT

As a facilitator you have a duty of care to hold the space and to keep the space sacred and to be in service to the client. So sometimes taking a small amount of medicine yourself would potentially not be a good thing whilst holding space for other people. But I find it can lower the egoic function and open to the Field. In combination with the witnessing consciousness and an empathic presence with the client, it can enable Source to use my vessel to be in service in ways the flatlined ego cannot. You become a vessel for this bridging of Source consciousness to work through you. It doesn't mean that you can't do this without taking medicine. Find your groove.

Midwives of the Divine:

Now there's a big overstep that can happen if you are projecting onto a client. I believe at a fundamental level we simply hold space. And I say to people, I'm not a shaman, I am a facilitator, but the closest archetype is a midwife or a doula in that this is a natural process that people have within them already that is being revealed, and we are facilitating that process like midwives of the Divine. We're not healing them, but we are in service to their awakening and to their healing and to the process that 5-MeO initiates.

A lot of therapeutic techniques are vitally relevant in a 5-MeO session. For example, I try to be careful about projection both from facilitator to client and vice versa; I try to stay out of their line of sight and yet if they do catch my gaze, I will hold it. Sometimes that person needs to connect, needs eye contact or physical touch, needs to be held and loved. But there can be a lot of interpersonal issues that arise that are relevant to the serving of 5-MeO-DMT that study and practice in a therapeutic set and setting can entrain. I'm sure other writers here will cover some of the more practical steps and advice.

Ultimately, though, what I believe is that this is not a clean therapeutic Western psychoanalytic container or process. This is a sacred mystical initiation with many forces at work. There are so many variables that you really shouldn't and can't talk about most of them in the public arena because they will be out of context and can be misunderstood.

As a midwife, this is a natural process of rebirthing, and if the 'baby' gets stuck, then there will be an intervention, there may be some touch, etc. and getting consent for touch beforehand and explaining the general parameters of what that may mean is essential. But generally, I say this is your process and your sacred space which will be respected. If there are energetic blockages, I may draw attention to those areas – I use rattles and feathers in a more shamanic approach. I usually use recorded music indoors, but the set and setting is all consciously orchestrated to create a flavor in the space that supports the client, not to draw attention to itself.

If people's egos react to the medicine in a big way – if they're really screaming their head off, then the rattle has an energy to it which will peak and carry and seem to energetically complement their peak of energy. What I'm attempting to do is to complement and assist in any shifts of energy that need to happen within them. If they're stuck, it may be more dynamic help, if they're not stuck and they're just processing then I'm holding space without getting in their face or interfering. But there's a delicate art of engagement which can only be learned through a lot of practice and through a larger exposure to different ways and different modalities from multiple practitioners.

Client Screening and Rapport:

When many people who have these experiences then want to be a facilitator of 5-MeO, I believe they think that everyone's going to have their same experience. 5-MeO reveals a holy geography that exists within us, but to get to the core of it you've got to work through all your layers. And everyone has trauma, and everyone has an ego and filters between them and that central holy core. And this is why, I believe, that you fundamentally need to have a relationship with the client before you get into the ceremony. You need to know that their heart's in good condition, their blood pressure is good and they're not on SSRIs. You need to know if they've got any trauma and you need a questionnaire and a medical induction form to elicit as much information from them as you can to know what is arising in their healing release.

You can iron out a lot of problems that may arise in a session beforehand through proper screening and relationship building. If a man or woman client has, for instance, been sexually abused, I will ask if they want a support person, or another woman to be present and try and minimize my own triggering presence in that field. And you need to know these things because it cuts down on the things that can go wrong. But essentially one person's experience is not going to be your experience, even though the destination is the same. And that is really important to understand by seeing a wide spectrum of people's presentations or responses to the medicine.

We know that psychedelics are having a renaissance and that all the major Western media is positively pushing psychedelics. It's creating an increase in the demand of people wanting to experience this medicine. There's also a lot of issues around the business of spirituality and how we can ethically create a container for this work. But essentially what I find is: it becomes a path. And the path is walked one step at a time. And that's all you have to do: say yes to each step of the path. That will lead to fractal pathways for more collaboration, meeting other facilitators and learning from them.

Keeping it Clean:

I've always been conscious of the money and the medicine interplay and try to separate them ethically. I believe this is an integral and spiritual path and that there are larger forces at work in it. Now you deserve to be reciprocated and nurtured on a financial level, but you've got to set your own parameters for that on the cultural level. And then just let that go. It's not about chasing the money, or the fame, or the fortune. Those are all ego games. And with all the psychedelics, we know they can be ego dissolving, but the ego bounces back. And the danger is the ego can be like, *oh my god, I'm a shaman!* And that's not why you should be doing this work. Not for any ego game, but for service to others and to Source, and to your higher self.

I mean, framing this work as spiritual midwifery underlies it's a holy pursuit. And it's a very old archetype in service to the human community. We are birthing ourselves – rebirthing ourselves – and if we keep a spiritual perspective, it keeps us clean. So, what I really see happening is this is hard work, and after a while, when the honeymoon phase wears off, it can become light that pipe and there's another client and put the money in the bank and then go home. It can be desacralized. So, you've got to keep fresh, you've got to keep clean and connected to Source consciousness yourself.

After your first initiation with a peak experience, the spiritual traditions of the world tell us the next step is purification. So, as part of your integration you don't just go back to normal, you're activated, and you need to maintain that activation by keeping your vessel pure, clean and operable for use by Source working through you.

As 5-MeO-DMT crests into the mainstream we're seeing both the good and the bad news; we're seeing all the dirty laundry on facilitation hitting the socials and issues around abuses of power by facilitators. It's important that we work on these issues as a community as well as on a personal level. As with other medicine communities, there can be power dynamics around money and sexuality, all of these things are reflections of our own shadow.

Our shadow as facilitators permeates the ceremony, it permeates the way we approach people and how we hold space. Say you're in a ceremony with a beautiful woman and there's an energy there. Of course, we know there are ethical protocols for how to engage with people, both men and women, and refraining from sex with clients is one of the golden rules. But it goes further than a 'rule' – energetically our energy sets the tone for a ceremony and the choices we make, the number of participants, the energy we can hold space for. We need to be aware of our shadow and our own purification process.

The medicine and the intelligence in the medicine, i.e., Source consciousness, is continually grooming facilitators to be of best service, because we are essentially vessels and bridges to then switch on other people as this species activation and remembrance of the Divine within us is occurring. And so, we have a sacred responsibility and perspective to be the best us, the best vessels to serve Source consciousness.

And after a lifetime of service, maybe one day you will look back at and remember the faces of all those souls you have helped rebirth. So many souls, all part of the One soul awakening. I like to think that as more and more people remember their sacred essence, that essence gets stronger, like a million lights viewed from space, illuminating continents. A "samadhi-mesh network" that feeds into itself, eight-billion vessels and growing, but all the one Source working through its awakened vessels. The molecule is terraforming the species, making room for the Creator in the Creation.

And this is Who we serve.

And this is why we give thanks.

All is One!

Help me
Become the person I have always longed to be.
Give me the strength to serve,
And the knowledge to know where I am needed,
The perception to step forward when the time is right,
And the tact to withdraw when the job is done.
May I be true to my ideals,
Flexible in the ebb and flow of daily life,
Yet unswerving in upholding the truth.
May I find joy in my interactions with others
And practise kindness in the face of our mutual shortcomings.
Help me see the eternal in each human being,
Thus, releasing the goodness that this world so desperately needs.
I offer myself as an instrument

Facilitating 5-MeO-DMT

Of the higher intentions of this school.
For I believe in the future.

— from *Initiative: A Rosicrucian Path of Leadership,* by Torin Finser

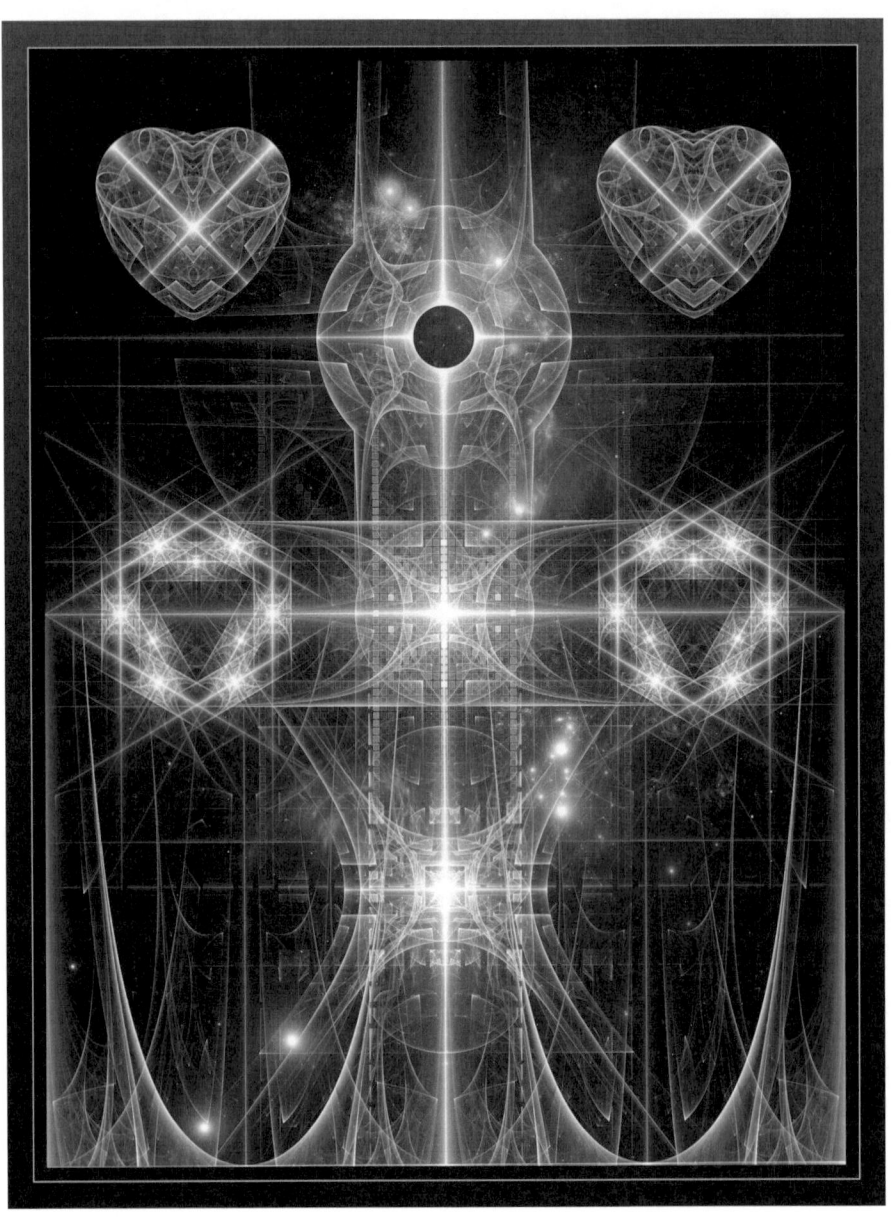

The Ultimate Un-Conditioning

by Issa Mariska Karuna

There is not one true condition in this world of appearances, although the illusive mind proclaims conditions constantly. The central one is: I am a person. 5-MeO-DMT can override this illusionary sense of being an independently existing entity. Swiftly the compound neutralizes the filter that usually keeps our experience limited to being an apparent separate self, and we can feel ourselves as all-there-is. After witnessing the disappearance of the perception of separation numerous times, I sense this formless unconditioned unity outside of the 5-MeO-DMT journey, also. I do not put any conditions on it. I recommend no certain preparations, and do not reject them either. Follow your own inner callings; there is no certain way of being or doing anything. All conditions are concepts arising in the mysterious no-thing containing all possibilities. Life has no agenda; it is just living. This is the ultimate un-conditioning; the freedom of all freedoms offered by 5-MeO-DMT: just being, beyond concept and context.

When I started facilitating private 5-MeO-DMT sessions in the beginning of 2020 there definitely was still a sensation of being a true facilitator; a separate being who has to do things in certain ways in order to ensure the session happens in the most optimal way for another. 5-MeO-DMT demolishes the apparent boundary between self and other, and quickly erased that shred of the sense of a me being in control. As a yoga teacher and bodyworker, I had already experienced strikingly that classes and sessions seemingly unfold smoothest and most satisfying for all when the apparent separate self gets out of the way. When there is no effort to be a good teacher or bodyworker there is just yoga-ing and bodywork-ing happening. When I feel one with all and I am not thinking about what to do, there is just what is happening without conditions. There are no expectations about how it should go and no doubts about what to do. In this state of simply allowing what is unfolding as it is unfolding, transformations occur which can shift the experience of this existence profoundly.

This is It; What is Happening:

After taking 5-MeO-DMT three times in group sessions, I embraced this entheogen as the ultimate eraser of the illusion of separation. Following a variation of spiritual practices in pursuit of awakening, I had been diving into nonduality. A glimpse of freedom that had been simmering for a while had come to a boil: what if this sensation of being someone is just an illusion? What if there is no one that has to become enlightened? What if there is no real outside world that has to be changed by someone separate from it in order to be able to happily live in it? Maybe existence is like a dream, generated by thought and feeling. And maybe I cannot wake up from it because there is no I anyway. This is simply it; what is happening. It is already awake and it knows no limitations. And because this mysterious existence is unlimited there can also be the perception of being limited; of being un-whole and seeking to become whole. When the sensation of being an incomplete I is absent, there is just what is. No condition is being put upon existence by an apparent separate self.

No Entity Running the Show:

The more radical the nondualistic message was, the more authentic it felt. The drive to be free of falsehood is sustaining my willingness to let everything go, including my identity: being a person. Beyond the intellect deeper understanding started to arise that there is no separate entity running the show called life. Whenever a sharer of nonduality would come with suggestions about 'how to integrate nonduality into daily

FACILITATING 5-MEO-DMT

life,' or 'how to become more nondual,' there was a drive to move on to a more progressive messenger. The idea that there is something wrong that needs to be fixed is a concept arising in flawless totality. Only when you sense yourself to be separate from the rest of perceived reality, conditions are placed upon life. Obviously, I am not referring to the circumstances that keep the apparent organism alive: air, water, food, shelter. Searching for wholeness is the inclination of the human individual. This is being looked for in for example the ideal partnership, a successful career, a fulfilling social life, the perfect body.

Just Perfect Being:

To the apparent individual it feels as if the self is never good enough. At the core of the human experience is a fundamental belief that one cannot exist just as one is. There is a sense of being separated from everything else; a feeling of incompletion. The seemingly separate self desires to transform itself into a more worthy self, or to get rid of itself. The goal of enlightenment is to become free of the burdened me which persists in wanting fulfilment. This desired liberation of self emerges from the conditioning of feeling oneself as a flawed separate self. When the sensation of separation is absent, there is just perfect being. The self is experienced as a unique expression of the formless all-there-is, or God, Great Spirit, Zero Point Field; obviously there is no accurate description for the all-encompassing mystery. The shift of perception of separation to awareness of (n)oneness is not truly happening to anyone. No one can make it happen, yet fascinatingly it seems that 5-MeO-DMT can play a pivotal role in this realization.

High Velocity to Non-Existence:

Shortly after my third experience with 5-MeO-DMT I was reading Martin W. Ball's book *Entheogenic Liberation* during the breaks of some group 5-MeO-DMT sessions I was witnessing at my community. Its subtitle, 'unraveling the enigma of non-duality with 5-MeO-DMT energetic therapy,' had attracted my attention. I sensed that 5-MeO-DMT was completely different from other awareness altering compounds like DMT and psilocybin. This so-called crown jewel of psychedelics truly appears to have unique properties. The main one is its potency to actually completely override the sense of being a separate individual. Other compounds are road markers while 5-MeO-DMT is a high velocity vehicle, taking the separate self straight to non-existence. As I was devouring the book swiftly, I came to the chapter about being a non-dual energetic practitioner. All of a sudden, I knew I was going to offer 5-MeO-DMT sessions, and how. As a bodywork practitioner I had witnessed acute transformations within the receivers and myself which seemed to be the perfect prelude to (the facilitation of) a 5-MeO-DMT experience.

The Unified Essence of All-There-Is:

Through giving and receiving touch and attention various discernible shifts happen. The central nervous system relaxes, the breath slows down, thought constructions lose their dominance, receptivity increases. Overall, there is a sense that all is well as it is, in both apparent receiver and giver of the bodywork. As practitioner I experience the unified essence of all-there-is regularly during a massage or treatment. There is the sensation of feeling unconditional love for the one I am giving my attention to. I can feel the wholesome effects in my own apparent body and being. By generating a connection beyond our identities – the mes and their life stories – I can perceive we are truly equal and we are desiring the same in the human experience: to exist, to be seen, to be appreciated, and to be loved – as we are. A tangible vibration of love and trust emerges, which seems to be an impeccable breeding ground for surrender. The ability to surrender contributes to the intensity of the 5-MeO-DMT experience, seemingly. Who is it that surrenders though?

At Odds with Reality:

Since there is no separate individual, there is no true free will. No one is choosing anything; things are simply seemingly happening, including humans. We are the mystery human-ing, trees are the mystery tree-ing. Atoms, the building blocks of matter, consist of subatomic particles which are composed of quarks. New technology will provide an even deeper look into matter. The further we dive into the rabbit hole, the less conditioned and predictable reality is. Quantum physics, the study of matter and energy at the current most fundamental level, discovered bizarre things that are completely at odds with how things seem to work in the world. Quantum particles behave like particles located in a place or like waves distributed all over space in several places at once. How they appear seems to depend on how we measure them. Before we observe them, they seem to have no definite properties at all! So what is the nature of reality? What are we? According to science we are definitely not the autonomous individuals that we take ourselves to be.

FACILITATING 5-MEO-DMT

Complete Mental Mayhem:

When an apparent individual takes 5-MeO-DMT, there is no choice to let go as there is not anyone separate from what is unfolding who can choose. When the sensation of being someone has diminished, the phrase letting go makes no sense. Who needs to let go and of what? The second time I took 5-MeO-DMT I felt a nervousness that bordered on anxiety as I now knew the immense power of the so-called God molecule. As I inhaled, I repeated the affirmation "I am calm and centered." When the illusionary self started to be ripped apart, complete mental mayhem broke out as the concepts of an I and a center were totally pointless. At the peak of a so-called full release 5-MeO-DMT experience it is unquestionably clear what you truly are. What you really are is limitless and therefore is indescribable. People say they experience themselves and all else that exists as God, love, light, the no-thing that is everything, source energy, home, all-there-is … One has to experience it; the mind can only conceptualize and 5-MeO-DMT eats concepts for breakfast!

Insights about Life and Oneself:

On average a 5-MeO-DMT journey goes something like this: the receiver inhales and keeps the vapor in for a while, during this phase the apparent separate self already starts to disintegrate. There can be resistance, wonder, confusion. Then at the peak most people are gone, especially the first time, meaning they are not aware anymore of their body and surroundings. Time and space disappear. Even while the 5-MeO-DMT peak only lasts about ten minutes in the world as we usually know it, when dissolved in all-there-is, it can feel like a lifetime! As the receiver returns to the conditioned world and self as (s)he knew it, the experience of being (n)oneness is integrated in the apparent conscious mind. Of course, these words do not describe truly what is happening; there is never a going away, a returning and a coming together happening for real. All these apparent events are taking place in the unified all-there-is. As the body metabolizes the 5-MeO-DMT rapidly the illusionary sense of being someone returns. There can be ecstasy, grief, relief. In this phase a stream of insights about life and oneself pours in

Un-Conditionality of Reality:

Soon after I started offering private bodywork and 5-MeO-DMT sessions I was confronted by the ruthless un-conditionality of reality. Although there are common effects, every 5-MeO-DMT session unfolds completely uniquely. My intention for offering bodywork as a preparation for the psychedelic experience was to facilitate an easier surrender to the potency of the most powerful entheogen. Yet it turned out to be no guarantee for an effortless letting go. Even after a two hour long physical and energetic bodywork session and several doses of 5-MeO-DMT the illusion of being a someone would not budge for some receivers. Life is a mystery that cannot be conceptualized in words. In this mystery concepts seemingly arise in the mind of an individual which are the scripts for the movie the apparent person calls "my life." For example, if the concept is that living life is a struggle, that it is difficult to get what you want out of life, then that is the basic theme of the movie, psychedelic journeys included.

The much-desired 5-MeO-DMT full release experience does not occur.

It is Always Perfection:

The question is: does that even matter? If there is no real separate incomplete individual anyway that has to find wholeness outside of itself and make sure to merge with it completely, then the experience of dissolution of self is not even needed. It either apparently occurs or does not occur within the mystery; the already complete all-there-is. Initially I started facilitating these sessions to offer others the opportunity to experience themselves as all-there-is. To wake up from the dream of being a separate self and experience life as a playful and graceful blessing instead of a task that has to be done right. After witnessing several mind-blowing sessions, I understood that this was a condition as well; this desire to help others become free of the illusion of being a separate individual by getting to the ultimate destination of a full release 5-MeO-DMT experience. There are not even any others! My intention is no intention. I sense the already present perfection in anyone and anything. 5-MeO-DMT can be a reminder of this perfection or not; it is always perfection.

To be Loved Exactly as One Is:

Many receivers come to do a session with certain intentions. Some for example are fascinated by the possibility to experience themselves as all-there-is, others want to

Facilitating 5-MeO-DMT

break through conditioning that keeps their apparent self stuck in a loop. The unified mystery expresses itself as all these unique appearances with their own drives and dreams. They are all equal; there is no higher and lower, just what is. There is an almost mystical power hidden in graceful allowance; unconditional love that sees and embraces everything as it is. I discovered it when I studied cranial sacral therapy. This light touch treatment is all about just letting things be, being with them as they are. When an obstruction or contraction is encountered, it is simply held until it dissolves on its own. Loving attention from another human – another expression of all-there-is – is enough to set about transformations. It confirms to the receiver that (s)he is worthy to exist and to be loved and cared for, exactly as (s)he is.

No Conditions, Whatsoever:

Oftentimes receivers express to me after their sessions that to be held lovingly while experiencing deep feelings of unworthiness felt very healing. A journey with 5-MeO-DMT is certainly not always a full bliss trip; an apparent shedding of conditioned beliefs can occur before you shoot out of the illusionary bubble of being a me to dissolve in the mysterious no-thing that is everything. This can be expressed in wild repeated movements, purging, or screaming for example, in which the restraining conditionings are visibly released as energy through the physical appearance. The word energy is very tricky here as the mind directly correlates it with the concepts of *kundalini* energy and *chi* life-force energy. There is no true energy as it implies movement, change. All-there-is is constant, unchanging; it has no properties. It cannot go from a certain state into another; it is all states simultaneously and therefore no state at all. It knows no conditions whatsoever. As you are all-there-is, there is no true you releasing something.

Mind-Blowing Experiences:

This unconditionality of reality that the appearances we call saints and mystics talk about can be experienced in the 5-MeO-DMT journey, yet it is always happening. It is what is. A session does not have to unfold a certain way to be so-called successful. The apparent separate self has an agenda of becoming more whole and unified with all-there-is through having certain intense experiences. Conditions are placed on the 5-MeO-DMT trip in the form of expectations, and there is an urge to mentally analyze and understand the experience. After a couple of absolutely mind-blowing sessions the unconditionality of reality could no longer be denied. I had to simply trust that what unfolds is always perfect. One of those sessions involved a receiver who felt a deep longing to go home. Another drive for her desire to experience 5-MeO-DMT was to get an insight on how to handle the abundance of *kundalini* energy she felt in her body. Minutes after inhaling the first dose she did not feel anything, so I offered another larger dose. Again there was no noticeable effect at all and she asked for a third.

A Perfect Effect:

The absence of any effect turned out to have a perfect effect. After her request for a third dose, I told my client what I intuitively felt; that taking more would have no effect whatsoever. There seems to be in general a certain time frame after inhaling when administering another dose has not much effect. In her case I sensed that there was more going on since the first two doses had had no effect at all. She expressed again that she just wanted to go home, and I replied without thought: this is it, this is home, that is what it is showing you. She said she knew this to be true, acknowledged the difficulty to accept it and started to cry. Her partner and friend who were present just sat with us in silence as she felt her emotions. When she became quiet, they played some music. Silently she observed her apparent inner world. Half an hour later she was smiling excitedly and shared with me that she had no idea why she had made such a fuss about *kundalini* energy! She felt relieved, centered, and at home in and as her apparent unique self, being whole and complete.

Paradigm Shifting:

A similar experience had already shaken up my belief in the essentiality of the intake of the 5-MeO-DMT itself. A client who was doing a weekend-long retreat with me had been doing a lot of research about 5-MeO-DMT prior to her session. She watched the videos I recommended, and just like me she was enchanted by the book *Entheogenic Liberation*. We had many eye-opening and paradigm shifting conversations about 5-MeO-DMT and nonduality. During the days she stayed with me I witnessed profound transformations in her. She seemed to become more lighter, less burdened by thought. When the actual moment was there to inhale the 5-MeO-DMT, sitting on a beautiful wild tropical beach, she looked at me and shook her head. At that time, I still experienced myself as a someone who has to make sure she is doing things in the right ways. Immediately the thought arose: should I encourage her to take it, to make sure she gets the full experience of my offering? It was followed by the reassuring feeling that everything was perfect as it is. I just let her be.

FACILITATING 5-MEO-DMT

Complete Trust:

A life-changing experience with 5-MeO-DMT knows no condition, not even taking the compound itself! This was again confirmed when a friend invited me to stay with her and offer sessions in her community. After witnessing the profound changes in her flatmate's health following the bodywork and 5-MeO-DMT session she did with me, my friend booked one for herself. The prior night she dreamed that she died and experienced a ripping apart of self. Everything she believed to be true, all the conditions she apparently placed on herself and life, showed themselves to be illusionary. She canceled her session and stayed at home integrating her experience by writing about it in her journal. I offered her bodywork which she declined. By then, after several paradigm shifting experiences, I felt complete trust that all was perfect and that neither I nor the compound necessarily had to add anything to the apparent process as it is unfolding. These three sessions are definitely not exemplary for an average journey with 5-MeO-DMT, but in my view they are showcases of the molecule's tremendous transformational powers.

Simply Following Intuition:

In these examples the natural thing to do seemed to be nothing at all, except assisting the receiver to process the experience by talking about it. Other times I seem to play a bigger role as facilitator. That what I do is what is happening through what I appear to be. There is no true separate self arranging the right circumstances for another self to have a certain experience with a desired outcome. These are all conditions, arising in the illusive mind. The feeling of being truly unlimited and absolutely free seems to arise most effortlessly and gloriously in the condition free space of allowance – for lack of better words. I admit that this statement is a condition in itself and therefore a contradiction; it is impossible to express the mystery in words. Truth can't be spoken about. Being can't be done. Simply following my intuition in the moment, while massaging someone or facilitating a 5-MeO-DMT session, seems the most so-called beneficial thing to do. This is constantly confirmed by my receivers' experiences.

Feel the Joy to Be as You Are:

When there is just the unfolding of the moment without an illusionary self focusing on what to do or not do next, it is very clear what needs to be done or not done by simply doing it or not doing it. I have experienced many pivotal moments in sessions where touch was of great support according to the receivers: to not feel all alone in the experience; to feel safe to let go; to sense the unconditional love of this existence through receiving loving touch in the midst of the disclosure and release of pain. All of a sudden, my hands will reach for and hold the receiver's lower back, chest, back of head, feet, hand; there is a direct clear knowing what to do. Just as suddenly the receiver will indicate through a moan, movement or other sign that (s)he is getting into what I call the empowerment phase. 5-MeO-DMT is not only about disintegrating the false self but also acknowledging the unique and sovereign expression of all-there-is that we each are. You feel the joy to be exactly as you are, to be alive as this mystery, and as your unique appearance of a self.

The Empowerment Phase:

In this phase the primal ecstasy of existing as one is expresses itself through, for example, laughter, body movements, monologue, sitting or lying completely still in total amazement, and many other variations. I can clearly feel this shift from shedding identities and paradigms – after going through the eye of the needle of non-existence – to enjoying and embodying the unique expression of all-there-is. I immediately release the touch, sensing that to empower their self-empowerment they are now better off being on their own in their experience so-to-speak. They are perfect, whole and complete and they can sense it. There can simultaneously still be a release going on of the irrationality of feeling oneself to be separate and the suffering that comes with it, expressed through sudden screams for example. In my experience it is easy to be tempted in these moments to support them through touch yet oftentimes they will indicate somehow that this soothing energy now is obsolete.

Natural Evolution:

There is no technique someone first has to master in order to facilitate 5-MeO-DMT sessions. Like with all that seems to be unfolding in this mystery, there is a natural evolution occurring as an event is seemingly repeated. Just follow your heart, go with the flow and trust your intuition, is my reply if someone asks what they should

FACILITATING 5-MEO-DMT

do in order to become a 5-MeO-DMT facilitator. The best tip I received myself was to first shed the last shreds of fear concerning the world's most powerful psychedelic by taking a sizeable dose by myself. Even with the strong drive to start offering this mystical molecule in private sessions with bodywork, I definitely still felt fear when I sat down for my first solo journey. The experience confirmed that I could trust my passion and make it my current purpose, yet it took several more sessions before the anxiety totally disappeared. Simultaneously with the fading sense of being separate the fear for the 5-MeO-DMT experience dissolved. If you can feel yourself to be exactly the same as everything else, fear makes no sense.

Back to Factory Setting:

Absence of fear benefits the receiver, I feel, as it assists in generating feelings of trust and relaxation. A 5-MeO-DMT experience, like any moment, is an apparent co-creation of many seemingly separate factors playing their unique role in the unfolding. Yet there are no true separate ones who can consciously choose to do certain things and who need certain outcomes. It's like the chaos of throwing jigsaw pieces in the air, and the following order of all of them falling in exactly the right spot to create a perfect picture. When there is no sense of being separate and no need for certainty, no fear – am I doing it right, is everything going right? – there is clear seeing that the picture is always perfect. No matter in which place each piece falls, the picture can be whatever it is. This order, everything flawlessly falling into its place, I sense clearly in a 5-MeO-DMT experience. I call it going back to factory setting. It includes oftentimes sensations of physical releases and resets followed by a delicious flow that rebalances the energy (for lack of better words) throughout the whole body.

Fascinating Connection:

The ecstatic sensation of experiencing oneself as all-there-is expresses itself also through, for example, the feeling that the body is totally capable of self-healing as it contains all possibilities. This can set about profound transformations in the so-called daily experience of existence. This apparent world is generated mysteriously by the perceived feeling about it. When there is a feeling of being life itself there is no need to control or even trust in it. Oftentimes receivers share at the start of a session repeatedly that they are feeling nervous. I already feel the state of total relaxation they will be in after the two hour long physical and energetic treatment I am about to give. The cranial sacral techniques I apply at the end of the bodywork session can, just like 5-MeO-

DMT, inactivate or decrease the sensation of being a separate self who has to protect itself. I feel there is a fascinating connection between cranial sacral therapy, 5-MeO-DMT, and quantum physics waiting to be explored!

The Primal Benevolence of Life:

Like no other entheogen 5-MeO-DMT seemingly supports the direct experience of total freedom. Within seconds the contracted lens through which existence is experienced – alone and separate from the rest – zooms out to infinity. Suddenly you feel you are the beginning-and-endless all-there-is; the no-thing that is everything we seemingly experience, ourselves included. For many receivers, not all, this feeling goes accompanied with a deep understanding of the primal benevolence of life. It can't be anything else than self-supporting as it contains all within itself. And no matter what is apparently happening, it is not what it seems. What we perceive to be life is a mirage generated by a mystery. In a typical ayahuasca ceremony the apparent journey of dismantling and shedding old identities to being reborn as a clear channel of your unique expression of the mystery, can seemingly take hours and sometimes much purging. Knots of misunderstanding and suffering apparently untangle, allowing the experience of being the gracious mystery that one truly is.

Nothing to Protect Yourself From:

Another freedom feature of 5-MeO-DMT, in its vaporized form, is that it is not linked to any tradition. Shamanistic dogmas related to psychedelics sustain the concept of separate beings on their way to wholeness. Prayers to Great Spirit request protected journeys, ancestors are pleased through rituals, visions are received to improve life. No real separation means that there are no true entities who need to be addressed nor is there anything outside of yourself to protect yourself from or enhance yourself with. Everywhere you look; everything you experience; everybody you encounter: it is all you. This can apparently become utterly clear with the assistance of 5-MeO-DMT, in my experience. Every time I take 5-MeO-DMT – whether it is a small, medium or larger dose – it feels as if I receive an upgrade, like computer software. The ability to sense reality as it is – without the overlaying with concepts based on a true separate life story – seemingly increases. It is as if the filter of separation through which we usually experience all-there-is slowly but surely is evaporating.

Facilitating 5-MeO-DMT

We Are in This Together:

In each session I take a dose of 5-MeO-DMT myself, whatever is left vaporizing after administering it to the receiver. It is not a condition; currently I simply feel like taking part in the molecule itself when facilitating. Just as the bodywork session beforehand my partaking in the 5-MeO-DMT journey in my experience supports feelings of unity, love and trust; we are in it together, both facilitator and receiver in this unfolding freedom. The size of the dose I take does not matter; when the receiver goes deep, I go deep. When the receiver feels obstructions, I feel obstructions. When the receiver senses infinite bliss, I sense infinite bliss. After more than a decade of sharing bodywork and feeling its effects clearly in my own apparent being, I was already very familiar with this sense of being the other and the other being me. When this sense of oneness is present, it is no challenge to be of service. Just like all the cells in the body innately know how to serve the whole, there is a natural inclination to act or not to act as facilitator in the experience.

Smooth Processing:

When I don't act, I am quietly sitting, feeling, observing near the receiver in a spot that feels good. In the beginning of facilitating 5-MeO-DMT journeys I followed the advice from the book *Entheogenic Liberation* to position myself as facilitator straight in front or right behind the receiver. Now at times this happens, other times it doesn't. My exact position or that of others present at the session, is no longer a condition. Having the apparent physical form(s) in symmetry definitely seems to be of support to smooth processing of so-called energy. Yet it is no hard rule or condition as there are none. Sometimes I gently unfold receivers and bring them into a symmetrical position when I sense this to be appropriate, other times I leave them in a fetal position for example, feeling that they are going through a profound process, and it would be interrupted by moving the body. This action without agenda – not doing certain things in order to attain an expected result – contributes to the sensation of unconditional love. Everything can be, and is perfect, as it is.

All Is the Condition-less Mystery:

In the 5-MeO-DMT experience the receiver can sense this utter perfection. Afterwards doubts might arise; the sense of being separate has reappeared and now the apparent individual wants to get something out of it. It is constantly seeking to complete itself; whether it is through finding a soul mate, getting rich, reaching enlightenment, or having a proper 5-MeO-DMT experience. A 5-MeO-DMT journey is not a holiday from the me to which you have to return after the trip is over. The essence of I – the appearance and experience of the totally unique expression of all-there-is that you also are – is never gone. There is no true departure from a real body into an I-less realm. All that seems to be happening is the condition-less mystery, including the sense of being all-there-is and the sense of being a separate me. The apparent individual is seeking to get something out of everything to complete itself. Even its own apparent death in a 5-MeO-DMT experience becomes a desired destination if the me feels it might help accomplish wholeness.

The Promised Land:

An often-heard commentary from receivers is that they feel they could have gone deeper. A sense of self remained, and there is a strong desire to get rid of it. As a facilitator I share openly with my receivers about my own experiences as this seems to be of assistance in the integration, and it supports the authenticity of our connection. One of the apparently most life changing experiences with 5-MeO-DMT I ever had was definitely not a typical full release experience in which the sensation of being a self and having a body completely dissolved. As I took the 5-MeO-DMT I felt the familiar feeling of expansion into infinity, yet there was also the sensation of a body sitting on the earth and the sounds of cars passing by. A feeling of discontentment washed over me… where was this boundless field of light and love I normally went to?! Then a realization dropped in like a bomb. It was as if the whole of existence suddenly screamed back at me: this is it! I opened my eyes, looked around me, and experienced a profound seeing that this apparent world is it; the promised land I had looked for.

Integrating the Mystical Experience:

This very grounding 5-MeO-DMT experience supported the breakthrough in seeing that the psychedelic or mystical experience is not different from so called daily life experiences. There is no other realm or state to get to and there is no one that has to get to it. Everything is like a mirage or hallucination, not truly existing as it appears: separate entities, objects, realms, states. Reality is a timeless, spaceless, condition-less no-thing containing all possibilities. A 5-MeO-DMT journey in which there is the experience of being simultaneously a person and all-there-is – instead of the full release of the sense of separation   can contribute to integrating the mystical experience of

Facilitating 5-MeO-DMT

being the boundless mystery in the usual experience of being a specific human. Metaphorically stated, the two come together: the dual world of time, space and separate things in which we experience ourselves as persons, and the timeless and spaceless nondual no-particular-thing or (n)oneness in which we experience ourselves as no-thing and everything.

Infinity in 23 Minutes:

When I do a session at someone's house or in my session space – the back porch of my house – I like to play a music track especially designed for the 5-MeO-DMT journey, appropriately called "Infinite Forgiveness" by the artist Maok, who also created the soundtrack for the film *Bufo Alvarius The Underground Secret*. In linear time the track lasts 23 minutes. One time during the phase of the journey when the sense of oneself as a person with a life starts to return yet the unconditional loving energy of 5-MeO-DMT is still running its forceful course simultaneously, I experienced infinity within 23 minutes. As I was cradling the head of the receiver and listening to the music, there was no end to the track. I just sat there quietly realizing it was going on forever. I also knew somewhere that this music piece really only lasts a little over 20 minutes. Total wonder washed over me; how was it possible that infinity fitted into 23 minutes?! This wonder is expressed by receivers when they hear how many minutes they were so-called gone. The journey felt timeless, is an often-heard reply.

Event Horizon:

This sense of seeing the dual and nondual as one had already seeded and sprouted during the previously described grounding experience in which I deeply saw and felt that this world of appearances is the formless itself; heaven is earth, energy is matter, no-thing is everything. I am fascinated by exploring the apparent boundary between the two, like the event horizon of a black hole that divides it seemingly from the space around it. All apparent matter is dissolved in its formlessness, timelessness, spacelessness. Before the peak in a 5-MeO-DMT experience there is oftentimes the sensation of passing a threshold or event horizon, like stepping out of the conditioned me into the unconditional all-there-is where there are no certain beings and events. There is a connection as well – which I can sense but can't describe in words – with the wave function collapsing in quantum physics. When there is apparently an observer (a separate self) the unconditionality of all possibilities at once is seemingly conditioned to one possibility. Yet that one possibility contains all possibilities.

Martin W. Ball, Ph.D., Editor

Preference for Private Sessions:

In my experience the initial integration of the 5-MeO-DMT experience happens in the last phase of the journey when the apparent self and its life story have seemingly returned, yet the remembrance of actually being pure love, life, light, God – give it a name – is also present in all its glory and grandeur. To allow for the journey to unfold completely and give the integration chance to take place in all its subtleties, I prefer private sessions over group sessions so there is no one anticipating to go next. Through for example sounds, music, touch, and deep breathing I help so-called energy that is seemingly stuck to move again. This process of release of restrictions can sometimes take a while, and occur as crying, screaming, laughing, burping, shifting from moving to sitting or lying still, and many other variations. The session is only over when the release is finished, yet of course the journey does continue. Days, weeks and months afterwards powerful insights can suddenly occur that put the 5-MeO-DMT experience and possibly the whole of existence in another light.

General Upgrade for Complete Being:

Experiencing unconditional love as the nature of oneself and existence is the core of a 5-MeO-DMT experience. Whenever there is the false sense of an I with a need to be in control, the flow of unconditional love is seemingly subtly interrupted or corrupted. Every 5-MeO-DMT session feels like a general upgrade for my complete being, and a boost in the ability to let a journey unfold as it does without interfering in it as an illusionary outsider. 5-MeO-DMT is seemingly one – maybe the most intense and transforming – of various ways to invoke the remembrance of all to be (n)one and the unconditional essence of existence. The facilitator of the 5-MeO-DMT experience is one of the many expressions of life involved, and, like all appearances, is not a true separate entity with free will. A clear seeing of this apparently can kindle this seeing also in the apparent receiver of a session, like a flame of one candle igniting another. We are God, the infinite field of possibilities, the unfathomable all-there-is. I know this and feel this throughout the journey together and therefore you can know and feel this, as I am you and you are me. There is no separation.

Suggestions for Future Research

Now that we've reached the end of this anthology, it seems a good time to suggest some areas for potential future research. As should be evident from the entries in this collection, there are a lot of differences in approaches, views, and formats in which 5-MeO-DMT experiences are facilitated. For the most part, these various differences have been reported on from anecdotal and personal experiences, sometimes in the forms of online surveys, but more often in discussions in gatherings and online forums. As such, it is still undetermined what scientific research might reveal in numerous areas of interest. It is to that end that I'll make a few suggestions here for where researchers might want to develop research programs and investigations. The ideas presented here are in no particular order. At times, I'm including my own theories and ideas, based not only on my years as a 5-MeO-DMT facilitator (2009-2016), but also as someone who has a great deal of personal experience with this molecule, and my practice of serving as an integration coach and consultant in private practice with clients looking to integrate and understand their experiences with 5-MeO-DMT from a wide cross-section of individuals from around the world who have been served in different contexts and both with toad and the pure molecule.

FACILITATING 5-MEO-DMT

Context and Efficacy:

Everyone who facilitates with 5-MeO-DMT is preferential to his or her or their own style and format. There are a variety of facilitation contexts: ceremonial, religious, therapeutic, spiritual, group experiences, one-on-one, inside, outdoors, retreats, living rooms, medical centers, etc. Furthermore, some people work on their own, others with teams or assistants. Some people have been formerly trained, and others, not. Some devote a great deal of time and effort into screening, prepping, and assisting with integration after the experience. Others take a more casual and hands-off approach. There's a great deal of diversity here.

When it comes to those who are served, there's the question that anyone seeking out an experience with 5-MeO-DMT must ask themselves: is this context *right for me*?

Other than anecdotes, personal reports, and the occasional online survey, we don't have much in the way of objective data concerning efficacy of all these different approaches. The situation is made problematic by the fact that 5-MeO-DMT is illegal in many places, making any kind of research and reporting highly difficult, if not impossible, other than anonymously. None of this has really been studied objectively and virtually all reports are from people who are involved with the scene, in one way or another, so while we've gotten a lot of expressions of preferences and opinions, in most cases, we don't have any real hard or objective data to back up the claims and preferences.

So: how does the context in which one is served 5-MeO-DMT affect possible outcomes? Are there any measurable differences in results between being served outside or inside? Does having many people in the same space as the client (like in a group or context in which many people are allowed to observe and wander about) affect the client's experience? Are people in a ceremonial or religious context more likely to integrate their experiences into their lives given the social nature of the facilitation? Do people in one-on-one contexts have deeper or more personal experiences? Is a group experience more likely to create bonds between people, or does the energy of the experience tend to get messy and chaotic with permeable self-identified boundaries? Do clients who are served by both men and women feel better served and safer? Is trust and confidence in the facilitator paramount, or only a bonus? There's a great deal that could be investigated here and a number of studies could be undertaken to make some determinations.

Martin W. Ball, Ph.D., Editor
Bufo and the Entourage Effect:

While it's clear that secretions of the Sonoran Desert toad, or bufo, contain a great deal more than just 5-MeO-DMT, it remains thoroughly unclear what effect these other potentially psychoactive compounds have on the overall experience. It has been discussed that, among bufo users, there tends to be strong preference for the "natural" form of bufo versus the perceived-to-be-inferior synthetic form, but it's entirely unclear what's opinion and what's reality. While it should not be under debate whether synthetic 5-MeO-DMT is effective, as it clearly is, the question of what the combined effect of all the other molecules in bufo has is unclear and remains undetermined.

Bufo aficionados tend to claim that the "entourage" effect is at play with bufo/toad and is lacking with the pure molecule, whether it be synthetic or a natural extract. The *belief* is that the entourage of molecules in bufo makes it *better and more effective* as a medicine, as a spiritual experience, and as a producer of powerfully transformative effects. However, biases can be so strong here that it is very likely that there's a "nocebo" effect taking place among the bufo-inclined when they encounter pure 5-MeO-DMT. While no one would really claim that bufo and the pure molecule are *identical* in overall terms of the experience, it is a valid question of whether the differences are significant enough to make any kind of claims over which may or may not be "better." Here, we have two very different opinions. There are those who claim that pure 5-MeO-DMT is a smoother and cleaner experience than bufo, while those on the bufo side say that bufo is so clearly superior that they'd never stoop so low as to use synthetic 5-MeO-DMT.

The problem here is that no one's done any real scientific research into whether there is validity to either side of this debate. Opinions and beliefs abound, but data? Sorry. We don't really have any.

At a personal level, I offer consultations with clients who are looking for assistance in making sense of their experiences, integrating, and possibly dealing with after-effects, such as reactivations. I can state that from my experience in working with a wide variety of clients in this manner, I've yet to see anything *definitively* unique about their reports, questions, and issues, with either synthetic or bufo. In other words, both groups of people come to me with the same issues and concerns, which leads me to believe that the differences are overwhelmed by the similarities. But, this isn't the result of scientific investigation.

Let's assume that there is an entourage effect with bufo. It's undeniable that there are other compounds present in bufo smoke or vapor. But what effect does this have on the overall experience, and not just the experience, but the results? Just because there is an entourage effect, doesn't necessarily make it *better*. Maybe it does make it "more powerful," but what if that increased power leads to greater difficulty remembering and integrating? Maybe it's potentially more traumatic. Maybe it has greater healing properties. Maybe it makes it more visual. Maybe it makes it more tumultuous. Maybe it's more "spiritual." Maybe it isn't. Just because there's an entourage effect doesn't necessarily mean that it's objectively better. It might just make it different, and even then, the difference might not be as great as proponents make it out to be. And if both synthetic and bufo give access to full nondual experiences, then how much does the effect of the entourage really matter?

While it's generally true that adding any psychedelic molecule to any other psychedelic molecule tends to produce a hybrid experience, there is also the matter of threshold. Thus, are the other compounds that are present in bufo of a significant enough amount to really influence the experience in one way or another? Given the high number of different molecules present in bufo secretions, it may be the case that none are really present in enough quantity to have a strong impact. But . . . what happens when they're all present in small amounts at the same time?

The thing is, we just don't know. This is an area that's worthy of actual research, and not just relying on self-reporting or the possibly biased views of facilitators and clients. There is soft data in terms of online surveys, but no hard data from direct scientific studies.

One difficulty is that it seems that it would be impossible to produce a double-blind study, which is needed for unbiased results. Bufo secretions can only be consumed via smoking or vaporizing, and its distinctive scent and taste (somewhat like old fish) gives it away immediately. In contrast, pure 5-MeO-DMT has a slight floral or moth ball-like scent and flavor, and when vaporized, is hardly noticeable. Anyone consuming either would immediately know which is which. It would stand to reason that anyone participating in such research would have to have no prior experience with either in order to have a neutral assessment of the results.

Something that does seem clear, at this point, though more research could be warranted here, is that bufo, because of its multitude of ingredients, is more dangerous than pure 5-MeO-DMT when it comes to the possibility of interacting with other medications that an individual might be taking. There are reports from the field of people consuming bufo with a MAOI and having disastrous results, whereas there are also reports of people combining pure 5-MeO-DMT with a MAOI and having great results. Here, the entourage effect seems to work *against* bufo. More research is needed, especially as 5-MeO-DMT is potentially moving into mainstream therapy for treatment of PTSD, addictions, trauma, depression, and anxiety with patients who may already be on psychiatric medication.

Questions of Energetic Entrainment and Transfer:

Some, though not all, facilitators of 5-MeO-DMT consume some of the molecule in concert with their clients. In the modern Western therapeutic landscape, this is considered a big no-no. However, facilitators consuming the "medicine" along with their clients is more the standard practice in traditional cultures that make use of entheogens for ceremony, healing, and personal growth and transformation. It would be highly unusual to go to an ayahuasca ceremony and for the *ayahuasquero* not to consume ayahuasca along with everyone else. The general rationale is that by partaking, the person leading the ceremony or medicine experience is better able to feel into the situations of the various participants and allows the facilitator to more actively direct the experience, as and when needed, in a way that bypasses discursive thought.

For those in the field of 5-MeO-DMT facilitation, those who take it along with their clients often claim that doing so allows them to more directly and intuitively feel into how energy is working, moving, and processing in the client's experience, and therefore allows them to make intuitive adjustments on the fly, as it is occurring, and not according to any pre-established program or routine. According to facilitators, not only does this allow for intuitive guidance and directing to take place, but also allows for a transfer of stuck energy from the client to the facilitator, which the (more experienced) facilitator is then able to process through on behalf of the client (such takes place in ayahuasca and peyote ceremonies, as well).

Furthermore, clients themselves often express that working with facilitators who engage in this style of practice is more powerful and productive than merely being served the medicine from a provider. Though this is not at all a scientific statement, in my own practice of facilitating 5-MeO-DMT with clients, where I always took it with them, I had two different clients who didn't know each other make the identical statement that the difference between having been served 5-MeO-DMT for them to experience in a non-interactive setting versus taking it with me in an interactive setting where we both were experiencing 5-MeO-DMT simultaneously and energetically working together was, "The difference between kindergarten and graduate school."

My stipulation is that by both the facilitator and client taking 5-MeO-DMT together, it allows for a kind of energetic entrainment between the two that just isn't really possible when only the client is served, and the facilitator takes the role of

FACILITATING 5-MEO-DMT

"holding space" for the experience rather than "working with" the client via energetic exchanges and interactions. A rough analogy is that one form is more like a personal meditation, and the other is more like getting a massage. Both are energetic events, but they result in different outcomes and results. It would be interesting to have this studied from a scientific perspective. If it were possible, it would be ideal to conduct this research with both the facilitator and client hooked up to EEG machines to see what's happening at the brainwave level as these kinds of interactions and exchanges take place. Of course, for EEG readings to be accurate, there should ideally be stillness, so it remains how this could actually be accomplished. But, it's a question worthy of further investigation.

Symmetry vs. Asymmetry:

In my experience and observations, when people who are experiencing 5-MeO-DMT completely transcend the ego, their bodies respond by opening into symmetrical postures, and when spontaneous movements take place in this state, they are always symmetrical with the left and right sides of the body mirroring each other. In contrast, when the ego is still present, there tends to be some kind of physical asymmetry present in the body, which might be as subtle as the eyes looking to one side rather than fixed along the center point of one's experience, or as outstanding as flopping around wildly from side-to-side as the body contorts and writhes about. While spontaneous movements can arise while the ego is still present, even if unconsciously, then these movements display asymmetry and side-to-side gestures and articulations.

I see two possible forms of studies on this phenomenon. One is for self-reporting. Do people who display spontaneous physical symmetry report deeper, more powerful, and more clearly nondual experiences than people who display asymmetries in body posture and movements during their sessions? My guess is that people who go into symmetry will tend to describe their experiences after the fact as having been nondual, ecstatic, infinite, and positive. In contrast, I suspect that people who display asymmetries will be more likely to describe their experience as having been challenging, difficult, traumatic, and more filled with the working and projections of the ego.

Of course, many people who experience 5-MeO-DMT exhibit both kinds of body postures and movements at different times during their experience. In my perspective, these alterations can be clear markers and identifiers of when the ego is being involved in contrast to moments of surrender and letting go. In my experience, this difference is so clear that it is extremely easy to "read" videos of peoples' experiences where, simply by marking these differences, one can accurately determine when someone was grappling with or acting through some aspect of their ego and when they weren't.

To do such a study, because people experiencing 5-MeO-DMT often have little-to-no body awareness, it would require video recording sessions and then attempting to correlate instances of body posture and movement with subjective reporting by the client in review of what they recall from their experience in conjunction with reviewing the video. It's important to note that sometimes people subjectively report that they were "perfectly still" and not moving, when video recordings show them flopping around, fighting, or trying to run away, and conversely, some individuals report that they felt like they were moving when they were actually not moving at all.

Furthermore, it is my contention that by intentionally working with bilateral symmetry in the body in sessions with 5-MeO-DMT, the ego can be more easily transcended and thereby making entry into nondual states more likely, even on small doses. This is something that could be studied as well: do people who intentionally seek to maintain bilateral symmetry in their 5-MeO-DMT experiences report greater access to nondual and ecstatic states, or not? Based on anecdotal reports I've received from individuals around the world who have intentionally employed my advice to "stay symmetrical," it would appear to make a significant difference in the subsequent experience. It bears further investigation and is a worthwhile subject of scientific research and study. What such research will reveal, I expect, is that the ego tends to be embodied asymmetrically whereas fully-open energetic nondual experiences tend to universal bilateral symmetry. And, that people can "hack" their way to nonduality by consciously engaging in physical symmetry. Just as in other areas of life, posture and body language are significant factors in 5-MeO-DMT experiences.

Relative Significance of the "Backside" of the Experience:

It has been my advice, as is also mentioned by several contributors to this anthology, that the "backside" of the 5-MeO-DMT experience is highly significant for the overall experience, including how well it is integrated into ordinary life, and this aspect is worthy of further study.

By "backside," what I mean is roughly the second half of the experience where people describe themselves as "coming back" into their body or individuated consciousness post-peak and possible nondual absorption. In general, this is the point

Facilitating 5-MeO-DMT

at which the ego consciously comes back online and the individual regains a sense of individuated being and identity.

Because the ego is reforming at this point, and because the ego is a habitual doer and thinker, it is at this transition that many people immediately start operating from their egos, such as describing what they just went through, start looking around, making contact with others, and otherwise engaging in social interaction with others who may be present, or alternatively, just attending to themselves with various movements, expression, and gestures. As I and others have advised, this is actually an important period for the client to continue to "do nothing," and rest in the remainder of the experience, and just observe and feel, rather than act or try and articulate or figure things out. By just paying attention and staying relaxed and open (ideally in a symmetrical position) at this point, individuals have the possibility of more consciously observing the habitual patterns of the ego as they are attempting to engage, and may even find that with a slight surrender, they can voluntarily "go back in" to the fullness of the experience.

In contrast, those who immediately act out and fully engage from the egoic perspective that is still reforming, miss this opportunity for more conscious observation of the habits of the ego, process the experience with less of a sense of completeness, and might tend to be more ungrounded after the 5-MeO-DMT has completely worn off. It could be worthwhile to study this difference more fully. If it does work as I and others suspect, then this would lend itself to more private facilitation settings where there are less possible distractions of others present that might inspire someone to start engaging from their ego. It would also mean that fully allowing each client to have as much time as they need to navigate this "backside" before moving on to the next client is vital for their full processing. And, it would instruct facilitators to allow space and time, and also encourage them to coach their clients, to really maximize not just the way up and into the 5-MeO-DMT experience, but also to pay equal attention to their exit out and down. The idea is that it is by becoming aware of the unconscious and habitual patterns of the ego, we can release and transform them.

It is also significant that for some, it is during this re-forming of the ego period that many experience the most personal discomfort and distress, and by relaxing and letting go once more, any repressed energies from traumas or behavioral or even thought patterns can be released. Such is often experienced as vomiting and purging during this phase. Most likely this takes place because peoples' egos are "out of alignment" with the genuine energy of being and unconditional love, and by allowing these releasing processes to take place during this more self-aware time period, the individual has more opportunity to transform and ground into a "cleaner" and more "aligned" mode of being.

So, for a study, it would require not only information about what clients did during the backside, but also ongoing reporting on how well they feel they are grounding and integrating their experience and maintaining behavioral or thought pattern changes post-session. Basically, the question is this: do those who remain relaxed, centered, focused, and attendant to "doing nothing" post-peak get more tangible results from their experience, or not? Is it the "big bang" of 5-MeO-DMT, or how it is attended to all the way through, from first hit to return to baseline, that is the more significant factor in post-session integration?

Reactivations:

Who gets reactivations, and when? Learning more about reactivations, and what methods or techniques might lessen them (when they're not desired), could help make 5-MeO-DMT more palatable in a therapeutic context for treating such things as PTSD, trauma, depression, and anxiety. Reactivations that occur at night and disrupt sleep seem to be the most disturbing for people, whereas reactivations that happen during meditation are generally welcome, so just because someone is having reactivations doesn't mean that they are disturbed or unsettled by the phenomenon, but having more data on this could help people understand the risks and potentials more clearly.

My personal theory is that people who leave their session of 5-MeO-DMT with a sense of being energetically complete and grounded are less likely to experience disturbing reactivations than those who don't. This is one of the reasons that I've recommended that sessions with 5-MeO-DMT take place with several rounds of taking the molecule rather than a one-off approach where the client is considered "done" after having a singular big experience. The theory is that taking multiple rounds of the molecule allows for more processing, releasing, resetting, and grounding to take place for the individual, allowing them to go all the way through whatever energetic (emotional, mental, physical, spiritual) process is taking place for them during their session. This orients the session around the idea that it is about the process that plays out, and not just singular experiences. To my mind, it's a question worthy of further investigation and study.

On the question of bufo versus synthetic, it would be interesting to see which group reports a greater number of reactivations, and of what kind and duration. Does one or the other lead to more, or less, appearance of reactivations? Furthermore, do

FACILITATING 5-MEO-DMT

different delivery methods (and here we're specifically referring to synthetic or pure molecule, which is available for a greater variety of delivery methods than bufo, which can only be smoked or vaporized) have any effect on reactivations?

Are there prior factors that impact how an individual is able to manage their reactivations? Do people with more experience with meditation fare better? How about people who are experienced with energetic modalities of physical practice (such as breathwork, yoga, tai chi, etc.)?

On average, how long do reactivations last? Based on self-reporting, it seems that two weeks is fairly standard, with reactivations lessening in intensity over time and eventually washing out. Is this accurate? How about severe cases that last for longer? How often does this occur, and to whom? Can profiles be created based on potential clients, methods, contexts, and approaches?

Regarding nighttime reactivations, sometimes referred to as "night school," there are some who claim that taking melatonin (a closely-related tryptamine molecule) increases the likelihood of having a nighttime reactivation. Others claim that regardless of taking melatonin as a sleep supplement, endogenously-produced melatonin is responsible for the experience (though this doesn't, in any way, answer why it happens to some people, and not others). Personally, I question the validity of these claims. It is my understanding that the body produces melatonin prior to bedtime, not when we're sleeping, so it doesn't make sense that most people who go through "night school" either have a reactivation just as they're falling asleep, or commonly, wake up at 2 or 3 am to find that they're suddenly "having a 5-MeO-DMT experience." How would melatonin be involved in this? Furthermore, this would provide no insight at all into why some people have reactivations at other times in the day, or while engaged in other activities, such as meditation, sex, dancing, yoga, etc. I myself had daily reactivations that I could enter and exit essentially at will during meditation, while my wife experienced 2 and 3 am reactivations that she felt were completely out of her control. Whereas I welcomed and enjoyed mine (though they did leave me wondering what was happening to me), my wife wanted them to stop and found them greatly disturbing. The melatonin hypothesis doesn't really account for these differences in any way. And what about reactivations that last for longer periods of time? For example, when I "cracked open" in the spring of 2009 after experiencing a profound process of energetic recalibration via 5 McO-DMT, ayahuasca, *Salvia divinorum*, and mushrooms, I felt like I was tripping 5-MeO-DMT, to varying degrees, for about 3 months straight (see my memoir, *Being Infinite*, if you want more details). I can't imagine that this was the result of melatonin!

Additionally, what are the best approaches to dealing with reactivations? I have my own set of ideas here, but can we study this more thoroughly? As stated above, it's my theory that people who leave their sessions with 5-MeO-DMT energetically incomplete are more likely to experience unwanted nighttime reactivations. Additionally, I generally advise people who are having such experiences not only to simply surrender to the experience and treat it as a session with 5-MeO-DMT (keep the body symmetrical and open, allow yourself to express and process energy, stay focused, choose to let go and surrender), but also, if they persist and do not lessen in intensity within a few weeks, then go for another session with 5-MeO-DMT to bring the process to a point of relative completion. Based on self-reporting from people who've taken my advice, going back to 5-MeO-DMT has dramatically reduced the experience of unwanted reactivations. It can be counter-intuitive, but it seems to work. This ought to be studied more directly.

Lastly, why are some reactivations "flashbacks," whereas others aren't? By flashback, what I mean is that, for some, the reactivation feels like they are right back into whatever was taking place in their session with 5-MeO-DMT and whatever reactions or content they might have been processing at that time. However, this is not the case for others where it's more of an energetic opening that is related to the here and now and not what specifically happened in their session. It's my guess that nighttime reactivations are more likely to be of the flashback kind (due to being the result of an incomplete energetic process), whereas reactivations through meditation aren't. And there's also the experience where a subsequent psychedelic experience, even if it's not 5-MeO-DMT, seems to pick up right where the 5-MeO-DMT left off.

Effects on other Substances, Post-Session:

Related to the above question of reactivations is the issue of how other substances might be experienced or impacted by a 5-MeO-DMT experience, post-session. For example, some people find that even one hit of cannabis can send them all the way into a 5-MeO-DMT reactivation, whereas for others, cannabis might now seem so tame and mild by comparison, that it seems to have no effect. Also, some people claim that taking melatonin to sleep helps them after their 5-MeO-DMT experience, and others feel that it potentiates unwanted reactivations.

Can we get some more clear data on this?

It's also the case that many people claim that after an experience with 5-MeO-DMT, all other psychedelic medicines "turn into" a 5-MeO-DMT experience, though this effect might only be felt for a limited period of time and eventually wanes. My

Facilitating 5-MeO-DMT

theory is that 5-MeO-DMT, being the most powerful energetic flood a human body can experience, opens individuals up to a higher carrying capacity for the energy of being, and therefore, post 5-MeO-DMT, they can go deeper with whatever other modality they may be engaging with. This seems to be especially the case if someone reaches a full nondual experience and sense of energetic infinity. Once one goes "all the way," this experience becomes much more readily available and accessible. But does it wear off over time? Are there ways to sustain it (if desired), or lessen it (if desired)?

Is there any correlation with this effect, as with reactivations, with endogenous production of 5-MeO-DMT in the body? Normally, there are only trace amounts of 5-MeO-DMT present in the human system, but does this potentially increase after being introduced to 5-MeO-DMT from an outside source? And why this phenomenon with 5-MeO-DMT and not DMT? Both are produced in the human body, but DMT users don't seem to experience reactivations of this kind or report similar impacts correlated with the use of other substances. Is it just that 5-MeO-DMT is that much more profound and energetically powerful? Is it related the duality-enhancing effect of DMT versus the nonduality-accessibility of 5-MeO-DMT?

And, as has been seen in this anthology, some facilitators like to work with 5-MeO-DMT in conjunction with other psychedelic medicines simultaneously or in succession. For some, this could be establishing someone on a "bed" of MDMA before giving them 5-MeO-DMT. Some people serve 5-MeO-DMT on top of a bowl of cannabis. Others serve 5-MeO-DMT after earlier work with ayahuasca, mushrooms, or iboga. How do these combinations work? What effects do they have? Of note is that 5-MeO-DMT in the form of bufo should only be taken at least a full day after anything that contains a MAOI, such as ayahuasca, due to the danger of poor interaction and risk of serotonin syndrome.

Kinds of Clients and Results:

As 5-MeO-DMT moves more into the mainstream and finds its place in the spiritual, therapeutic, and self-exploration landscape, can it be determined what kinds of contexts might best serve different kinds of clients? While some people are very happy to be in highly structured rituals, others aren't. Some people are more comfortable in a less structured one-on-one approach. Do different contexts serve different kinds of people better? What works best for people looking for help in dealing with a drug addiction, or trauma, or spiritual growth? Is it purely an individual matter, or are there significant factors that could help someone decide what might be best for them from a more objective standpoint? Going to a ceremony isn't for everyone, but who is it for? Is it better for a drug addict to be served outside in nature, or in a doctor's office? Who benefits most from going on a retreat? Do people who spend a week or more in a supervised context (such as a retreat or treatment program) gain more benefits? If so, what are they?

Related is the question of who really benefits from having a 5-MeO-DMT experience. Is it effective for drug addicts and does the experience help them? How about people with trauma, PTSD, depression, or anxiety? Online surveys have sought answers to these questions, but more research could be done to really fine-tune the process. As access to and interest in 5-MeO-DMT and other psychedelic medicines spread, these are all worthwhile areas of investigation to best help potential clients decide what might be best for them, and also help facilitators direct clients to the best possible resources and even help them screen potential clients for compatibility with what they do or don't offer in their particular context.

As has been stated by some of the entries in this anthology, some facilitators claim that they've seen people with physical ailments, such as cancer, disappear after experiencing 5-MeO-DMT. It's undeniable that 5-MeO-DMT has a tremendous impact on people mentally, emotionally, and "spiritually," but what about physical issues? Can this be investigated and measured? Is it just a "miracle," or can we develop a more sophisticated understanding of what might be going on? Can "mystical" experiences have a direct impact on physical disease? It's certainly a popular idea in the modern "wellness" culture of New Age healers and "New Paradigm" practitioners, but is it hype, or something more measurable?

Slower Methods, Different Results?

While bufo is only really available to be consumed via smoking or vaporizing, the pure molecule of 5-MeO-DMT is not similarly limited. While the vast majority of those facilitating 5-MeO-DMT experiences rely on smoking or vaporizing, there are other delivery methods available. With the pure molecule, it can also be snorted, injected, or taken anally. There are supposed advantages to different delivery methods as it changes the onset, duration, and intensity of the experience. However, longer, slower, and less overwhelming might not necessarily be better. One of the remarkable things about smoked or vaporized 5-MeO-DMT is how incredibly fast it takes effect. One theory is that it is this overwhelming rush that actually facilitates entry into a nondual state as the ego feels so completely overwhelmed in a "near-death" experience that it can effectively "give up" and "let go," allowing the individual to pass into a unitary state of being. However, with longer and slower methods, the ego might not ever be confronted with a full "ego-death" experience, and therefore might be less likely to have a nondual experience. On the other hand, longer and slower methods might be potentially less traumatic, and more amenable to therapeutic approaches. They also might be less likely to produce reactivations. Or not . . . We don't really know. This hasn't really been studied and it's worthy of further investigation.

Experienced Meditators and 5-MeO-DMT:

Some of the facilitators included in this anthology have stated that they prefer clients with prior experience with meditation, as they feel that such individuals are better-prepared to surrender to the energetic onslaught and expansion that is 5-MeO-DMT. Can we test this?

What we do know, from brain scans, is that both advanced meditators and those experiencing 5-MeO-DMT show coherent gamma wave production in the brain. Gamma waves are associated with intense focus, sense of "flow," highly coherent thought processes and insights, and greater physical, mental, and emotional performance. In theory, skilled meditators ought to be more familiar with the states of consciousness and experience made accessible via 5-MeO-DMT due to this correlation with gamma waves.

However, how does this play out? Personally, I've seen people who have claimed to be experienced meditators have pretty significant freak-outs during their 5-MeO-DMT experiences, and also people with no meditation experience have blissful sessions with 5-MeO-DMT. Why is this?

From what I've seen, at times, people with lots of experience with meditation, particularly when they practice meditation in seated lotus posture, appear to actually use their meditation experience to "hold on" during 5-MeO-DMT experiences and do not open all the way, which almost universally correlates with open, "spread-eagle" body postures. Sitting cross-legged with hands overlapping can indicate maintaining poise, but not necessarily fully opening and surrendering. In such cases, prior meditation practice might effectively get in the way of the fullness of what 5-MeO-DMT has to offer.

It would be worthwhile to do a study that compared the 5-MeO-DMT experiences of those with meditation experience with those without. What are the results and post-session self-reports?

Of great interest would be to see how experienced meditators report the depth and profundity of their pre-5-MeO-DMT meditation experience, how it compares to their experience of 5-MeO-DMT (my guess is that most would say it's more profound, deeper, more energetic, and more infinite), and how their meditation practice is affected post-5-MeO-DMT (from anecdotal reports, it gets bigger and deeper). If all this is correct, as could be studied, then it means that a 5-MeO-DMT experience could be a profound accelerant to one's meditation practice. Yet here, some meditation traditions promote the "slow and steady" approach, so it might not be a welcomed result. But, that doesn't mean we can't study it.

Post-Session Changes in Religious and Spiritual Beliefs:

What impact does a 5-MeO-DMT experience have on individuals' religious and spiritual beliefs, and identities?

For example, 5-MeO-DMT, as "The God Molecule," is notorious for radically challenging the worldviews of atheists and agnostics. Furthermore, people who previously adhered to a specific religious tradition often report that their experience of *being* God doesn't really jive with their religion of *believing* in God, or accompanying theology and doctrine (see Appendix D for more on this). People who formerly "worshiped" God might find acts of worship, prayer, and devotion meaningless upon encountering themselves as identical with the Universal Being and Consciousness: who are you worshiping and praying to, at that point? For others, it might inspire them to become religious or spiritual whereas they previously had no such inclinations.

It is widely agreed that a full 5-MeO-DMT experience can produce an ontological shock in those who have experienced it, inspiring many to completely reconfigure their worldviews and beliefs. People change their affiliations, identities, and beliefs, as a result. Can we investigate this more fully, and is there anything here we can quantify?

I'll use myself as an example. Prior to experiencing 5-MeO-DMT, I was Buddhist-leaning philosophically, and while not necessarily a "believer," accepted that concepts of reincarnation and karma, and the path to enlightenment, were potentially true and valid. However, after 5-MeO-DMT, the entire idea of individual reincarnation struck me as radically wrong and a product of egoic thought and identification. If I'd just experienced myself as God, then it certainly meant that I wasn't some kind of soul or stream of individuated consciousness (this is a tricky question for Buddhism, which rejects the notion of individual souls, yet still retains the Indian presumptions of reincarnation and the effects of karma) that was inhabiting different bodies in a succession of linear lifetimes, as I was already God, and that meant that I was simultaneously myself, along with everyone and everything else, right here, right now. There was no "I" remaining to be reincarnated across multiple lifetimes because every

FACILITATING 5-MEO-DMT

living thing, and every object, is just God "pretending" to be that one or that thing. So, the whole Buddhist program of getting rid of karma to prevent reincarnation, and to categorize "enlightenment" as an "extinguishing" of karma (*nirvana*) just came off as radically misguided and pure projection, not related to anything that actually takes place in "reality" as I'd just experienced it. Furthermore, it was at that point that I became comfortable using the word "God," which I'd formerly associated with the Western theological traditions of Judaism, Christianity, and Islam, all of which, in their dominant forms, posit that God is "other" and "transcendent" of "created reality," whereas what I'd just experienced was the fact that God *was reality* and was in no way separate from it, beyond it, or above it.

So, how does this play out for other people? Many people who seek out the 5-MeO-DMT experience are already disaffected from their prior religious identity or upbringing, so a good number of people looking for 5-MeO-DMT are self-identified "spiritual seekers," which is what I would have identified as, as well. However, what happens after you find "it," and all the old systems no longer make much sense? Now that you've found "it," what seeking is there left to do? And, what happens to those who are still religiously-identified, but then experience 5-MeO-DMT? Do they continue participating in their religion, or not, and even if they do, has their understanding and appreciation of it changed? For example, someone might now reject the doctrine, but still appreciate the social connections that religious identity provides.

And of course, there's also the possibility that for some, the 5-MeO-DMT experience is taken as *merely* a drug experience, albeit probably a very interesting and unique one. Not everyone experiences it as a profound shift in identity or worldview. Some prefer to remain atheist or agnostic. For some, the nondual experience is just a possibility within consciousness, but isn't taken to mean anything about the nature of reality itself. These are interesting results. I'd be curious to see it all quantified with rigorous studies.

On the other hand, do some people *become* religious about 5-MeO-DMT, such as desiring to join a 5-MeO-DMT church, or even join a 5-MeO-DMT cult (based on reports I've received from clients for my integration sessions, there are various cults out there with all the trappings such as charismatic leaders, doctrines, special clothing, separation from society and family, etc.)? And some effectively create religions around the toads, as well. From a sociological and psychological standpoint, this is all quite fascinating. There's plenty of room for graduate students to create research programs around to earn their degrees!

Martin W. Ball, Ph.D., Editor

Conclusion:

These are just some of the thoughts, questions, and queries that come to my mind as I contemplate the diversity of ways in which 5-MeO-DMT is facilitated, its growing global popularity and interest, and the diverse panoply of people who are seeking access to the experience. Back in 2008 when I first experienced 5-MeO-DMT, no one was doing any kind of research on it. It's a very different world today. Online surveys have been conducted, and universities and research institutes, as well as healthcare product developers, are creating new studies about 5-MeO-DMT, so we're at the precipice of having a lot more information about this amazing molecule. There are still many questions that can be investigated, and I've shared my most pressing ones here. But what have I missed? What questions do you, as a facilitator, as a client, or as a 5-MeO-DMT-curious person have? Where else should the sights of research be set? What do we need to know? What do we not know? How can we collectively create the best information about The God Molecule, its use, applications, and results?

The answers, like the molecule, should be fascinating ...

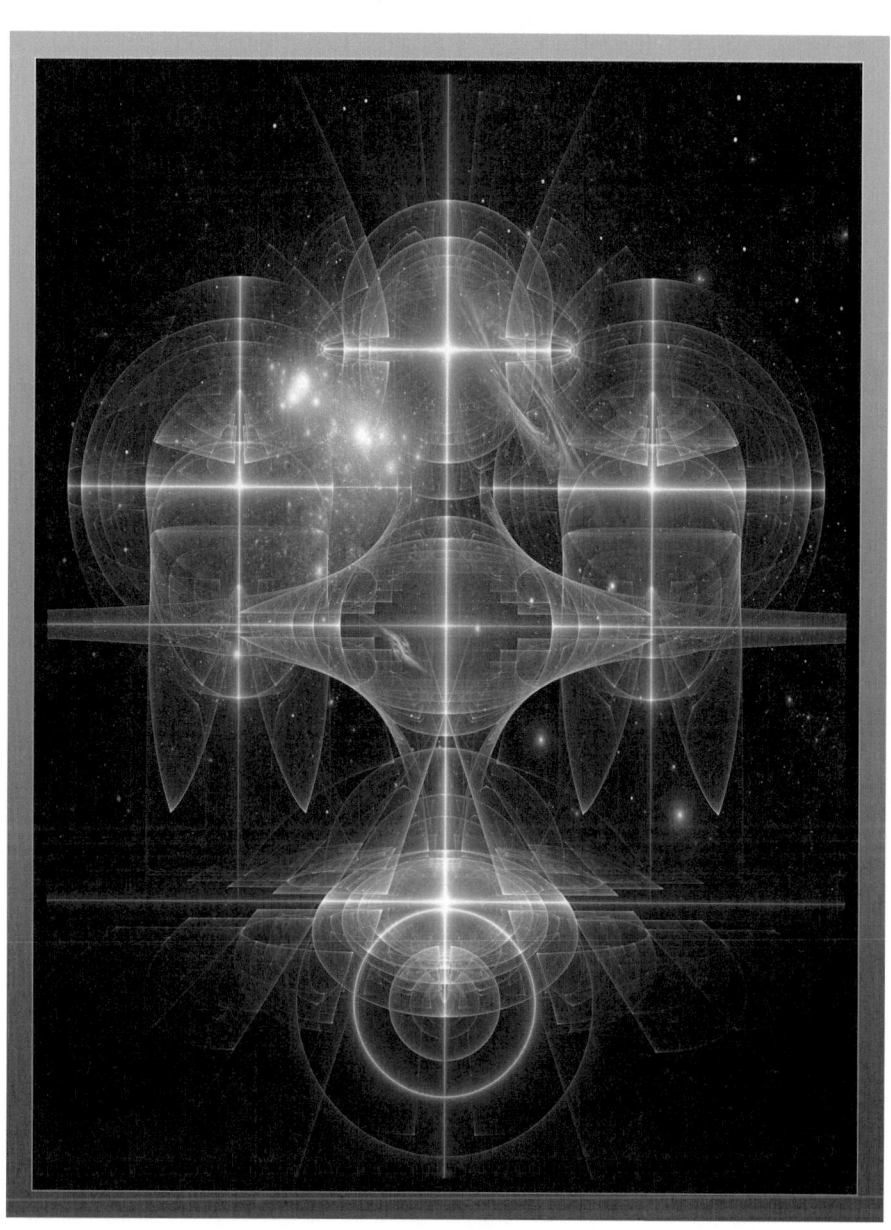

Appendix A: Integrating 5-MeO-DMT

Embodying Your Relationship to Yourself as the Divine

by Martin W. Ball, Ph.D.

I've written and spoken elsewhere at great length on the topic of integrating 5-MeO-DMT (see, in particular, my books *Entheogenic Liberation* and *The Entheological Paradigm: 2021 Edition*), but feel that it is worthwhile to share a few words of wisdom here as an appendix to this anthology. Back when I was undergoing my own personal transformation and opening with 5-MeO-DMT, "integration" wasn't a thing that people talked about or emphasized in the psychedelic world the way that it is now where people like myself work as integration coaches and programs are being developed to certify individuals as integration specialists and psychedelic therapists. When people ask me what I did for "integration" while undergoing my own process, I tend to answer that I simply focused on the process, and most importantly, saw it through to its natural conclusion and ultimate transformation (see my *Being Infinite* for the full account of personal details of my process). The point is that "integration" wasn't a thing at that time, and my process was so profound, so unique, and so decidedly *different*, that I had no one and nothing in particular to turn to for this laudable ideal of "integration" as I really only had myself and my own experience.

FACILITATING 5-MEO-DMT

And here's what I learned: the *entire process was about learning how to embody my individual relationship to myself as the divine*. Nothing more, and nothing less.

There will always be room for philosophical and theological debate in terms of questions of *what actually is*, and whether 5-MeO-DMT literally grants individuals access to the direct nondual experience of being God, Source, Pure Consciousness, The Divine, Absolute Reality, etc., but what should be clear by this point after having read through all these accounts by facilitators of the 5-MeO-DMT experience is that *this is precisely how we can describe the experience and the process of personal awakening and transformation* that 5-MeO-DMT potentially triggers in individuals. In that sense, it doesn't really matter *if it's actually real and true* (I'm of the firm view that it is), because that's what people experience, and having such an understanding of the magnitude of this perception and direct experience is crucial for helping people integrate, make sense of, and ground their experience into everyday life, behavior, thought, and action.

It is therefore important that anyone looking to either experience or facilitate 5-MeO-DMT, especially as it becomes ever-more-mainstream and potentially available through licensed and regulated therapists, understand that the phenomenon of 5-MeO-DMT is an experience of the nondual nature of the divine and the unitary nature of the self. In other words, anyone working in this realm has got to be comfortable with the topic of God, Absolute Being, or whatever we may want to call it, and the reality that people are going to experience themselves *as that*, to varying degrees and with varying levels of personal insight and perspective. Whether this is actually *true* or not is irrelevant, because that's the overwhelming impression that is consistent and fairly universal and is what people need to grapple with and accept as part of their process of integration and potential personal transformation.

While it's possible to treat all this agnostically, I'm not sure if that'd be helpful to anyone. In my opinion, I think it's far easier and more productive to just take it at face value when we're dealing with full nondual experiences and realizations. Someone discovered that they're God (just like everyone else)? Great! Now, the question is not "Was that real?" but rather, "How do I learn to embody this truth within my being, here, as a human being embodied in this particular life with this particular perspective?"

This is not a religious question or an issue of belief, faith, or doctrine or dogma. It's just how the situation presents itself to the individual. And, importantly, it initiates changes and processes of energetic transformation within individuals. The question then is: how does one navigate and integrate the process itself (and not just the event of experiencing 5-MeO-DMT)?

When it comes to the question of "integration," I've seen lots of things promoted that I think are actually rather superficial, potentially misleading, and while perhaps, at times, relevant, not really getting to the heart of the matter. First off, let's make it clear that anyone looking to help individuals integrate or otherwise "make sense of" or "understand" what their 5-MeO-DMT experience was all about, and what it might indicate of where they are in their process, needs to have not only a great deal of personal experience with 5-MeO-DMT themselves, but must also have a great deal of experience in either facilitating this molecule or, at the very least, ample experience carefully observing numerous and diverse cases of individuals under the influence of 5-MeO-DMT, and also awareness of the issues they describe as arriving in the aftermath of a 5-MeO-DMT experience. In other words, I cannot possibly imagine that anyone who goes to a "psychedelic integration" school or certificate program who does not also have these necessary requirements in regards to 5-MeO-DMT could ever legitimately be qualified to work as a 5-MeO-DMT integration coach or therapist. I see ample and diverse personal experience as *fundamentally necessary*, and anything less is superficial, generic, and possibly terribly misguided.

At the generic level, people put out some of the following suggestions for "integration": meditation, yoga, diet and eating good foods, journaling, spending time in nature, "grounding" (the thoroughly scientifically dubious practice of "grounding" energy by being barefoot in the dirt), reading spiritual literature, adopting a spiritual practice, joining discussion groups, getting acupuncture, receiving massages, etc. While these are all potentially legitimate aspects of generic "self-care" as is widely promoted in contemporary wellness circles, they honestly don't have much to do with 5-MeO-DMT in particular, and are so generic and non-specific that they don't really address the full magnitude of what 5-MeO-DMT presents.

For example, if someone is having disturbing reactivations post-5-MeO-DMT session, telling them to meditate (which might activate a reactivation), getting a massage (which also might lead to a reactivation), or practicing yoga (same goes here), is not necessarily helpful. Or, telling them to take walks in nature as they're succumbing to a full-scale panic attack is also of dubious value. Same goes with suggesting they take their shoes off and stand outside for 15 minutes every day, or changing their diet. It's unlikely that any of this would help in a meaningful sense. And, it can reinforce the egoic perspective that *there's something wrong*, and the mistaken notion that there's something concrete that can be done about it with a "problem/solution" mentality. Sometimes, such works as a placebo effect, but just as often, it doesn't, and the person feels more and more distressed as none of the "integration tools" are really making a difference. Trust me – I'm speaking from direct experience here as a professional 5-MeO-DMT integration coach and consultant and deal with individuals from around the world on a daily basis who need assistance reflecting on what they're going

Facilitating 5-MeO-DMT

through, and these generic suggestions don't cut it. Simply put, clients need more, and primarily what that more is is that they need to have personal insights into what's going on with them, and how best to engage with it in a meaningful and personal way that works for them and their current reality.

Something that I find helpful is starting from the position that we are beings of energy – everything we experience is a form of energy: thoughts, emotions, sensations, sights, sounds, tastes, everything. And the ego itself is a collection of energetic patterns of habitual thought and action and embodiment with which we've identified. When we work with 5-MeO-DMT, we're potentially bringing our energetic experience to a state of being infinite or without boundaries between self and other. Thus, it challenges, resets, releases, changes, and transforms our more personal expression and experience of energy, and this process takes place across all energetic aspects of our being. Put in this context, we can see that what's taking place is a process of energetic reformatting that its simultaneously universal and intimately personal and individual. Starting from here, we can understand that each person's process is going to be unique, and understanding how someone has inhabited, embodied, and expressed themselves energetically, and how they're changing, and becoming more present and authentic with themselves, is the best way to help them integrate and process what is happening to them.

So, here's a different approach: what you're experiencing is the after-effects of going through a radical process of energetic reconditioning and recalibration that has been set into high-gear from your consumption of 5-MeO-DMT. The discomfort you're feeling is all the places in the energetic constructs that is your ego that is out of alignment with your true and authentic energy as a direct embodiment of universal consciousness and unconditional love. While this phase of the process is uncomfortable and mentally and emotionally disturbing, if you can look at it as an opportunity to fully feel yourself, surrender, and open to the energy that you're experiencing, you'll start to feel better and more grounded. Rather than trying to make any of this stop, what's important is to *allow* the process to unfold without interference or trying to make it anything other than what it is. In extreme cases, it might indicate that the energetic process got opened up by your session with 5-MeO-DMT, but you left your session without having had the opportunity to fully ground out that phase of the process in your session, so the energy that arose then is continuing to seek to sort itself out and have an opportunity to ground into your embodied being now. In such cases, you might benefit from going in for another session and consciously choosing to fully surrender to the energy and the process. It might be scary, and it might get messy. You might throw up all over yourself and scream and cry or strip off all your clothes, but if you embody that energy in the session fully and without any filter or control, you'll find that your energy naturally re-balances on its own, and you'll feel better. Most importantly, you'll feel more available to authentically be yourself, to embody your genuine thoughts, feelings, and emotions, and express them in a way that is genuine, authentic, and direct, and less clouded by egoic narratives and constructs. If you're having reactivations, rather than fighting with them or trying to make them stop or go away by applying some technique or receiving some form of therapy, treat them as sessions with the medicine. Open up your body symmetrically, feel into the energy, and let yourself embody and express it as it is happening with movement and sound. Don't think about how it looks or sounds: just surrender fully to it and allow the energy to be however it is. Once you've fully embodied and expressed it, it will pass, and you'll find yourself in a new embodied state of being and more energetically grounded. You deal with it not by trying to deal with it, but by embracing it and accepting that you signed up for a profound process of energetic reformatting, and this is what it looks like for you, right now, but it won't always be this way.

As you move through all this, accept that *understanding* is not as significant as feeling. There is no need for you to *know what is happening, or why*. You can trust that energy will naturally sort itself out, if given the opportunity. Here, you have the potential to really *feel* all the places where you're out of alignment and where your ego, through its habitual and unconscious patterns, are attaching you to false beliefs, constructed narratives, and artificial standards and expectations. Understand that much of your ego was shaped by choices you made as a child, so as an adult, you're likely not even aware of when and where you made the choices to conceive and construct yourself into the individual that you've become. Each person has a unique life history and energetic trajectory through which their life has been lived. This is why the effects you're getting are different from others you've observed or witnessed. Your process is *your process* and is thoroughly unique to *you*, while also universal in the sense that we must all individually navigate our personal relationship to ourselves as individual embodiments of the one universal consciousness. Because it is so individual, *your process* will never be identical to anyone else's, and what you will need to support you and help you navigate through won't necessarily be the same as anyone else.

Take this as an opportunity to really feel into where you think you are withholding love and authenticity from yourself. Does your energetic expression and embodiment align with what you truly think and feel, or are you putting on a show for yourself and others? Do you lie to yourself? Do you lie to others? Do you try and hide your true thoughts and feelings? Do you act out of self-love, or out of fear of being rejected, or judged? Do you internalize judgements of others and use them to govern yourself? Do

Facilitating 5-MeO-DMT

you allow yourself to be free? Do you extend that freedom to others in your life? What's in your heart? Do you give yourself permission to feel the contents of your heart, and express them, or do you stuff them down and repress them?

You are a unique, individual, embodied expression of the unconditional energy of pure love that is the universal consciousness. Are you trying to be something in particular, or have you accepted that your only real job is just to be yourself, and be that self fully embodied and present in reality, here, now, in precisely this moment?

A common refrain I hear from my integration clients is that they are grateful to have someone they can talk to about their experience who understands it from the inside out, and can help them reflect on how their experiences relate to their sense of self, their energetic expression and processing, and their relationship to the nondual state of being without introducing spirituality, religion, or metaphysics. Sometimes simply having someone with deep knowledge tell them, "What you're going through is normal and here's how to appreciate it as an energetic process," provides a deep sense of relief and opens the possibility to trust what they are going through. To really get at where they're at, we often have to investigate the context in which they were served 5-MeO-DMT, what happened during the event, how their body responded, what they expressed or held back, and how others who were there responded to them at the time. Furthermore, we often have to investigate childhood ego developments, how they were raised, whether they developed the ability to express themselves in their thoughts and emotions, and what kind of religious or even political upbringing they had. We also look at how they treat themselves, and those close to them, such as romantic partners, parents, children, etc. We dive into how they respond to the question of "Do you love yourself?" We also spend a great deal of attention on how they embody themselves and what their body language tells us, and how it relates to what they expressed and embodied in their 5-MeO-DMT session (having video recordings of sessions to review is profoundly helpful in this regard, and also being available for video calls to make immediate observations and provide feedback about body language and expressive patterns as exhibited in the call). We also might examine what kinds of physical activities they engage in, and how conducive such practices are to their energetic expression and embodiment. We look at whether they have creative and expressive outlets, or not (writing, making music, doing art, public speaking, video blogging, etc.). Furthermore, we might need to get into a chronological history of their psychedelic experiences so that we can start to form a picture of what kind of process they may be going through and how different themes have developed over time and across different experiences that are emblematic of their relationship to themselves across multiple levels of being. Sometimes, we need to dig into spiritual practices and experiences. And of course, if there are traumas in their past, we'll need to get into that too, and also if they've gone through major changes in worldviews (such as leaving or joining religious, spiritual, or political communities). All of this becomes relevant as it gives us a picture of where someone is at in their process of simply becoming themselves, free, embodied, authentic, and genuine.

In my experience and opinion, there are some kinds of people I'd never recommend going to for help integrating a 5-MeO-DMT experience. For one, certainly not anyone who has no experience with 5-MeO-DMT. This applies to people who may have extensive psychedelic experience, but if they're lacking significant experience with 5-MeO-DMT, it's highly unlikely that they'll be able to understand much of what one is going through, so just a generic "psychedelic integration specialist" isn't good enough. In some cases, speaking with a therapist can be helpful, especially with emotional content, mental struggles, or behavioral issues, but again, unless the therapist has personal experience with 5-MeO-DMT, they will not be able to understand or relate to the profound energetics of the experience and will have little to offer when it comes to 5-MeO-DMT-specific issues. Trying to talk to a priest, minister, rabbi, imam, guru, or other forms of spiritual and religious teachers will most likely be worthless, as they'll not be able to relate and will have their views colored by doctrine, dogma, and beliefs. Even nondual spiritual teachers or therapists might not be of much help because the energetics of 5-MeO-DMT are so unique. Many "spiritual teachers" are highly biased against psychedelics (though this is changing), and often see them as polluting, cheating, or "fake" spirituality. Shamans can be of little help, given that much of shamanism is highly committed to various forms of metaphysical and ontological duality, and are often not equipped to deal with nonduality. And certainly, speaking with an astrologer, channeler, psychic, or medium, is far more likely to get you fancy stories with made-up meanings and make-believe stuff than anything truly relevant and worthwhile.

It can also be problematic to speak with other people who have had a 5-MeO-DMT experience because their level of experience might not be extensive enough to really give worthwhile feedback, and also opens people up to comparisons. There's a sense of belonging in 5-MeO-DMT communities that can be rewarding, but sometimes even there people don't feel understood or heard. For example, there might be a group that attended a retreat, and everyone but you seemed to have had an easy time, but for you, the experience was terribly challenging and maybe even terrifying. In such cases, people feel like they're the odd one out, or that they must have done something "wrong," or are somehow a failure. Revealing such to even well-meaning

FACILITATING 5-MEO-DMT

others can open one up to having to endure all kinds of interpretations, speculations, and opinions, none of which might be helpful and productive.

For example, I've seen some people post on social media forums that they felt a dark energy during their 5-MeO-DMT experience, and then I've seen commentors chime in that they must have a dark entity attached to them, and need to perform some kind of cleansing or exorcism ritual. Or someone else might chime in with that's their karma from a past life that they were processing, or maybe their ancestors. Or another interpretation might be that it came from someone else who was present at the time, so it wasn't really their energy to begin with. These responses might be well-meaning, but honestly, they're more destructive and harmful than anything else, in my opinion. They are using beliefs, metaphysics, and spirituality to provide interpretations and actions that can be very confusing for someone in a difficult passage. Often, you have to buy into the whole belief structure of the commentor to accept the interpretation. It's not helpful, and might profoundly get in the way of someone owning their experience and taking responsibility for themselves.

If we can start with the understanding that each one of us is the unique individual that we are, and also the universal and unitary being that is all of reality, then we are better poised to understand what is taking place in 5-MeO-DMT experiences. And, if we ground that in an understanding of the energetics of being, even better. We can view the human ego as a collection of energetic patterns of expression and embodiment with which we have identified, which may or may not be in alignment with our authentic expression, and then we can see that by flooding the system with intense nondual energy that transcends our limited self-concept and identity that we are initiating an energetic process of recalibrating and reconditioning our entire energetic system, which is always housed, expressed, and experienced in the body.

To that end, it's worthwhile to pay attention to all the energetic asymmetries of the ego, especially in contrast to how bodies open up and freely articulate with perfect bilateral symmetry in the peak of the nondual energetic expansion of the 5-MeO-DMT experience. We can then start to learn how the "character" of the egoic self with which we've identified is in fact a construct, and generally a restrictive and constricting one, at that. In contrast, the freedom, spontaneity and open balance of the energy of nonduality, the energy of the ego is conditional, imbalanced, and limiting. By embracing our true nature as nondual beings of the open energy of unconditional love, we can start to restructure the character we live through to be more open, more balanced, more genuine, and more authentic, and less constricted by beliefs, desires, attachments, and projections, thereby rendering us more able to simply be with what is, as it is, in reality, and not in the constructs of our minds. And this is a process. It doesn't happen with just one experience, and sometimes not even with many. It takes focus, concentration, and deep levels of trust and willingness to go through the process, knowing that it will often be challenging, confusing, and sometimes even downright freaky.

But it's worth it.

That's why people go to 5-MeO-DMT. It's what they're looking for, at the deepest level: genuine knowledge of the self and the ability to be who and what they are without imposing unnecessary limits on the self as both an expression of universal being and individuated humanity.

If you're not embodying it, you're not really doing it. And what you're embodying is your relationship to yourself as a unique human individual who is also simultaneously a direct expression of the universal being that is all of reality. At the heart of it is your heart, which is also the universal heart, and in that heart, the flow of unconditional love is always seeking expression. It's up to you to embody and allow it as the unique expression that you are.

Appendix B: A Recommended Model for Best Practices

by The Conclave

Editor's note: The following text has been provided by "The Conclave," which is an anonymous group of 5-MeO-DMT facilitators, educators, and enthusiasts. While I was personally present for the foundational gathering of The Conclave in Ashland, Oregon in 2017, I have not been an active member and participant in the group. Though they will remain unnamed, some of the contributors to this anthology are active in The Conclave. Additional materials are available at www.theconclave.info. The aim of The Conclave is to establish and share community-sourced guidance on best practices, ethical principles, and effective facilitation and integration of 5-MeO-DMT. As such, their work dovetails nicely with the focus of this collection, with the understanding that this is their presentation of "best practices," which has not necessarily been the aim of this collection of personal accounts. As stated in the introduction, the book itself is meant as a window onto the world of 5-MeO-DMT facilitation and should not be taken as suggestions or endorsements of any particular facilitator or methodology. However, adding this submission from The Conclave seems suitable and valuable as an appendix to the collection so that readers can see what issues have been considered significant to a number of people in the 5-MeO-DMT community in an effort to ensure safe and secure access to the experience by skilled facilitators who strive to uphold community standards. The document, as presented here, has been slightly edited to correct minor typographical errors, remove clearly redundant sections and statements, and has also been formatted to fit with the overall formatting of this volume and therefore will appear differently than it is available at The Conclave website.

5-MeO-DMT has been used in organic plant form in brews and snuffs in the Amazon by indigenous tribes, but there are no proven and established indigenous traditions or lineages associated with its use in a smoked or vaporized form. Most facilitators or practitioners have themselves been initiated by other practitioners in their own various styles, which have essentially evolved by trial and error, and many facilitators believe their way is the way.

There are, however, many different approaches to work with this sacred medicine for varied intentions and outcomes within a more generalized holistic model; from small doses to a "full release" experience, from a psychotherapeutic setting to a more shamanic practice, from non-interference to active guiding. Our understanding is that every approach affects the journey and best practices essentially serve as guidelines or ways to approach the 5-MeO-DMT experience to secure an optimal outcome: ensuring the safety and best result for each participant.

A positive "session" can result in many feelings, such as: opening, letting go, purging, catharsis, releasing, healing, remembering, reunification, trust, love and bliss, amongst others. It may take more than one session to establish trust and rapport with a facilitator, to develop greater facility and ease in the internal process and to learn to fully let go, or to shed a lifetime of suppressed energy. A skilled practitioner listens and learns from each participant and their connection with the medicine and adjusts accordingly. One person's perfect dose may, metaphorically, be another's poison.

If the participant has not been able to open, or if the energies opened up have not been fully expressed, supported and integrated within the session, ego-fear, blockages, trauma, confusion and related energies can remain and even re-emerge in "reactivations" after the initial session. There is no goal, no striving, no right or wrong. Everyone's journey to the same central Truth is unique, while the essential Truth remains the same. The best practice is to trust yourself and the process, to open to love, and to let nature take its course as it reveals Who and What You Really Are.

There are three effective stages to the process of providing an optimal experience with 5-MeO-DMT (or any other entheogenic/psychedelic substance for that matter). We have defined these under the broad categories of: Preparation, Initiation & Integration. Responsible practitioners will strive to develop and fully incorporate these three stages into their sacred work.

Those seeking to work with this sacrament would be wise to review these "best practices" when considering selecting an appropriate practitioner to work with and

FACILITATING 5-MEO-DMT

should feel free to ask questions of any potential practitioners before choosing to work directly with them. These recommended practices are offered in the spirit of love, communion & community, so that those approaching this important and most sacred work may be fully informed and that practitioners undertaking this sacred duty may do so responsibly and confidently with all the necessary tools and information that we can afford them.

May this Great Work be done well and held sacred by us All.

BEGINNINGS:

Questions People May Ask When Selecting a Practitioner or Guide:

- Who is this person you are going to be working with?
- Who is recommending them to you?
- What is their specific background in working with a particular sacrament?
- Do they have a particular expertise, or are they working in an apprenticed tradition or lineage of some kind, as in traditional Ayahuasca, Peyote or Iboga ceremonies?
- Are they authentic, relatable and trustable?
- Are they knowledgeable and intimately familiar with their particular ceremony and sacrament?
- Do they have any other background or skill set that aids them in their Work, such as a psychology or psychotherapy background or other healing modality that they utilize?

These are just a few of the basic things that should be established in advance of choosing whether a particular facilitator, practitioner, ceremony or sacrament is right for you. And any practitioner or facilitator should always be more than willing to answer any of these basic questions for interested persons before they choose to participate in ceremony.

Martin W. Ball, Ph.D., Editor

Health Considerations & Addressing Health Issues:

First, unless you actually are a medical professional, you are not qualified to give health or medical related advice directly to a potential participant and should clearly state that you are not a doctor and therefore cannot offer medical advice or counsel.

Participants must be in good physical and mental health before participating with the sacrament. This includes screening for pre-existing cardio-vascular disease, significant high blood-pressure, respiratory disorders, stroke or other neurological conditions. They should also be screened for significant food allergies or other conditions that could affect or be exacerbated by participation with the sacrament.

Participants should also be pre-screened for any history of psychological conditions including schizophrenia, psychosis, manic-depression or bi-polar disorder, PTSD, OCD, ... etc. Although some conditions such as PTSD and depression may be benefitted by participation, these considerations must be made very carefully and on a case-by-case basis.

Should any concerns arise, they should be clearly and openly addressed and communicated with the prospective participant during the health screening process. All information provided by potential participants is considered completely private and confidential and shall be treated as such.

On occasion practitioners may choose to informally consult with medical professionals in making their determinations for a given participant and should be encouraged to cultivate these professional relationships. Participants are also strongly encouraged to consult with their own personal medical provider before participating with this sacrament if there are any health-related questions or concerns.

PREPARATION:

Screening your Practitioner – What do I ask and look for?

Be sure to ask the practitioner's history and experience with the medicine. Some have made the distinction between terms such as a "provider" (one who provides medicine and holds space) and a "facilitator" (one who holds space and can assist in shifting the energy with a participant). While some may find these distinctions useful, we find that it is more important to ask what specific capabilities your practitioner has and how they interface with the participants they serve.

How long have they been doing their practice? How many individuals have they served or worked with? What style or approach do they offer (psychotherapeutic,

FACILITATING 5-MEO-DMT

psycho-spiritual, shamanic, mystical, etc.)? Is it a group circle or one-on-one session, inside or outside, etc., whether they take small doses of medicine with you or not, what kind of dosage will they serve you and how long will it last, whether they do multiple rounds to build to a full experience or go directly into a "full release," etc., and what preparation and/or integration support do they offer? They should be able to answer these questions directly and/or provide materials that address these questions prior to your participation. Make sure this all feels like a good fit for you, and that you are physically and mentally ready for the experience.

Establishing rapport between participants & practitioners:

Rapport with participants begins with the first outreach, in person meetings, phone & email correspondence, etc., and should continue through the session or ceremony and into the integration period and beyond. Both participant and practitioner should feel into each other's personality, their ability and readiness for the session, and be open to questions and feedback. Are they authentic, relatable and trustable? Are they knowledgeable and intimately familiar with the sacrament? Do they have any other background or skill-set that aids them in their Work, such as a psychology background or other healing modality that they utilize? Be sure you are both a good fit for each other's needs. Both men, women and transgendered individuals need to feel safe with the practitioner, their style of serving and the space within which the session is conducted. These are just a few of the basic things that should be established in advance of choosing whether a particular facilitator or practitioner is right for you.

Providing Clear Written & Spoken Communications & Essential Introductory Information:

5-MeO-DMT provides, possibly, the most powerful entheogenic experience one can have, opening and revealing deep states of Source consciousness within the Self. A participant should always be as informed as possible on what to expect and have access to further links and information in order to make an informed choice if this is the right step for them at this time. The practitioner should provide such information in advance of participation. This can be accomplished through written communication, e-mail, telephone, or they may provide a full orientation gathering in order to address these questions adequately. It is also highly advisable to complete some form of health screening prior to participation to better know and serve the needs and suitability of each participant. Does the facilitator or those working to make their arrangements communicate clearly? Are they providing you with all the adequate information about what they do and what you can expect?

Answering Any and All Questions in Advance as Necessary:

Answering any questions forthrightly, truthfully, and in a timely manner helps to create trust between participant and practitioner and transparency in the relationship moving forward. Are they providing detailed reference and written material in advance of the ceremony that is clear and understandable and provides all the details you'll need to know before your participation, including conducting any necessary health screenings or providing information about dietary, pharmaceutical or other restrictions? Are they open and willing to clearly address any questions, special needs or concerns in advance of your participation?

Other Necessary Information for Your Participation (Diet?, dress?, sexuality?, menstruation?, etc.)

Various practitioners approach these kinds of preparation differently, so it is generally best to check in with them in advance. There can be varying degrees of dietary preparation for a 5-MeO-DMT experience, because it is usually smoked, vaporized, or insufflated, thus bypassing the gut. In general, the cleaner your body and energy are, the more aligned and able it will be to fully experience the energy that is opened by the medicine. Some suggest that, at a minimum, to fast for several hours before participation. Others suggest longer time periods, or abstaining from meat, alcohol, sex and drugs for 24 hours or longer beforehand.

As with other plant medicines and diet, it is more about purifying your energetic field than any physical contraindications. Other practitioners may have less stringent or more rigorous requirements. It is good to know and understand these and follow their lead. Feel free to ask questions as to why they feel this is important.

Similarly, there are generally no restrictions regarding menstruation or sex before or after a session with 5-MeO-DMT, but energetically, if you are feeling low energy or sick, for example, it may not be the best time to undergo such an intense experience and you may wish to consider rescheduling. This is especially true if you may be contagious. Loose-fitting, comfortable clothing that allows you to move and feel free are recommended, as well as removing any restrictive garments, jewelry or adornments that may become cumbersome or entangled. Participants may also wish

FACILITATING 5-MEO-DMT

to consider refraining from using excessive make-up, heavy perfumes, or essential oils in ceremony.

Editor's note: use of perfumes, colognes, and essential oils in any kind of group experience is generally understood to be highly inconsiderate of others. Scents and smells can be perceived as highly intrusive on others' experiences, so while you may think you smell great, others in your presence may strongly resent your choice to impose your smells on their space and experience. Facilitators who choose to use oils, smudges, scented water, etc., should also keep this in mind. Highly Sensitive Persons (HSPs) do not ever appreciate the imposition of scents of any kind into their personal sensorium.

Providing a Clear Overview of What to Expect from the Experience through Integration:

There is a common geography that is revealed in the fullness of the 5-MeO-DMT experience, often referred to as an oceanic space within. Still, each individual brings their own unique energetic signature, sensitivity, armoring and understanding to accepting that central space, and each practitioner should endeavor to communicate this spectrum of experience to the best of their ability. How an individual responds outwardly has been termed their "archetypal presentment," and how someone is presenting outwardly may have little to do with what is actually going on internally for them.

Participants will be best served by refraining from attachment to outcome or comparison with others' experiences, including their own previous experiences. Practitioners can explain that the energy that is opened with the external/exogenous 5-MeO-DMT catalyst is the deeper nature – or "ultimate reality" of the participant's being – and that energy, once awakened, is a relationship to be nurtured ongoingly throughout the participant's life. Participants should be empowered to know that this energy may "reactivate" or BE activated, and that with a practice this dynamic state can be sustained to a degree within a healthy body. Participants should be given ample integration advice and counsel in order to maintain, manage, maximize, or minimize this energetic relationship as best they see fit.

Privacy & Confidentiality:

The privacy and confidentiality of all participants, practitioners, locations and details of sessions and ceremonies are essential for the protection of this work and the

Martin W. Ball, Ph.D., Editor

respect of all involved. This is especially true in areas where the legal status of the use of this sacrament remains in question. Each individual's experience should be considered wholly their own and that experience should never be shared with anyone by another, unless express permission is given by that individual to do so. Different practitioners or groups may have different protocols in regards to their privacy and confidentiality policies and these should be adhered to by all participants for the safety, security, and continuance of the work for all involved.

Individuals may be encouraged to share their own personal experiences with others close to them; however, tact and discretion in this regard is both recommended and requested. In any event, details of the experience should not be shared in an open, cavalier, or casual manner. The privacy of all those participating should be considered sacrosanct. The identities of those present, their experiences and the location of specific activities should never be shared with others. Some practitioners and groups consider the nature of the experience as initiatory, so specific details of the ceremony itself are requested to not be shared with others.

Some may choose to share their experience in more open online forums such as Erowid, 5-Hive, DMT Nexus, or even on various related Facebook groups. It is highly suggested that individuals involved in this vital work carefully consider how their sharing may be viewed by those who may not understand the importance of this work. We strongly encourage discretion in terms of what and how you share about your experiences – and those you may have worked with in these online forums as this can dramatically affect and impact how this movement is viewed by the wider general public, and can have adverse implications if not handled tactfully and respectfully.

Developing Personal/Group Intentionality in Advance of Initiation/Ceremony/Session:

5-MeO-DMT can reduce or temporarily eliminate the sense of ego and identity separating us from the "nondual" or unitive Truth within. With higher doses, all sense of ego and intention may dissolve completely, and yet intentionality can also help prepare for the opening to this Truth. Setting a personal and/or group intention can provide focus on lower doses, can entrain the unconscious and assist to program the conscious mind going into, or returning from, the peak experience on higher doses. Intentions should be carefully considered and crafted before a ceremony or session. Intentions should be clear within your mind, and some may even wish to write it down in a succinct manner. Hold this intention lightly and be prepared to surrender that

FACILITATING 5-MEO-DMT

intention if and as necessary in order to be present and open to what actually shows up for you.

Dealing with Nervousness, Anxiety and/or Fear:

C.G. Jung aptly stated, "What you resist, persists." And when it comes to facing our fear (or inner shadow content) no statement could be closer to the truth. Fear can be a mind-killer; a little death. Fear can close us off from experiencing the fullness of Love. Yet, fear and anxiety are natural artifacts of egoic consciousness. And the ego may be trying to protect itself, to avoid facing something that needs to be addressed, or to distract the participant from facing or experiencing the ultimate Truth: that you are not your ego.

A skilled practitioner can assist, coach and guide individuals through or around this anxiety simply through their way of being, with their words, with the establishment of trust, sometimes with touch, with song, or with any number of ancient or modern techniques that allow the participant to feel safe. Some practitioners utilize a first round, smaller "handshake" dose of medicine to establish a connection with its energetic signature, to relieve anxiety and empower the participant to consent to a deeper medicine round.

Likely the best way to address fear is to accept and surrender into it. To embrace it, to make fear your lover. It is also said that, "Courage does not exist in the absence of fear." So, developing a courageous sense of being is to face our fears, by relaxing and breathing deeply into them. "Ego death" can be a reality within the 5-MeO-DMT experience and learning to let go of the egoic structure can take practice in order to fully experience ego transcendence. Practitioners should be able to offer effective advice, counsel, coaching and support regarding this effectively before, during and even well after initiation.

Fear can also be a profound teacher and a natural part of the experience as it plays an integral role in letting go and dissolving the ego and moving into Source energy. In a certain sense fear can serve as a gateway or portal. Should fear come up in a session or reactivation, do not resist it, but, instead, work to stay present and observe it with curiosity as you allow it to move through. Remember that moving through the fear has a purpose and a message, and it's important not to get stuck in the information that it is trying to impart. Don't deny the fear, but realize it is a choice. The fear that something is somehow "wrong" or seems "different" or "not normal" are all fear-based beliefs. Refuting the rationality of these beliefs helps one surrender to the process.

Martin W. Ball, Ph.D., Editor
How is the Facilitator Influencing the Set in Advance of Initiation?

Almost everything the practitioner does from the very first contact will influence the mindset of the participant in advance of the initiation. Some practitioners may take a more therapeutic, hands-off approach, while others may draw on various shamanic lineages and use song, instruments and/or prayer to layer the ceremony. Others may use ceremonial techniques to frame or contextualize the 5-MeO-DMT experience.

From the moment of outreach, the practitioner's tone, words, or lack thereof, and style, can influence the participant's mindset and expectation. The practitioner should also be in good health, dedicated to the service and space-holding of each participant, and be responsible and completely able to handle whatever energies or circumstances that may arise both physically and energetically within the participant or within the general space of the session or ceremony. In any event, practitioners must do everything in their power to hold space for and positively influence the mindset of each participant in advance of, during, and after the 5-MeO-DMT session or ceremony.

Individual Sessions or Group Circles:

Different practitioners may offer the 5-MeO-DMT sacrament in various ways. Some work directly, one-on-one, with individual participants. Others may work ceremonially with small groups, bringing each person through the experience one at a time, while other participants are instructed in how to effectively "hold space" for those going through their release. Still other practitioners may offer more advanced group work, where experienced participants may enter into state together. However an individual practitioner may be offering the medicine, they should be well-versed and experienced with the context of their offering and clearly communicate their particular approach and explain their specific methods and techniques clearly and cogently.

Some people compare 5-MeO-DMT to an ego death and rebirth, with that same dynamic energy of a baby being born – and this can be a great way to approach this deep initiation. Whatever their specific approach, a practitioner should be fully focused on each participant, or the group as a whole, and their specific needs within this death and rebirthing process. This should take place without rushing, without expectation, and in full service to what is arising and needs to come through, for the full duration of the experience.

Some participants may require multiple rounds of medicine in order to shed energetic layers and open to the fullness of this experience, and in doing so, they are extremely sensitive to the set and setting of the space. The medicine can dramatically

FACILITATING 5-MeO-DMT

increase the level of psychic perception and sensitivity of those partaking in it. If others are present at this "rebirth," every word and movement within the setting can affect the participant's consciousness and experience while in state. Therefore, everyone present must be instructed in the proper methods of holding space and must do so with focus of attention, while maintaining a state of "loving presence" for those undergoing the initiation.

If multiple people are experiencing medicine at the same time – which should really be considered an advanced practice for those that are ready and prepared – their release and flowering will undoubtedly affect the others within the collective field of opening. Simultaneous group work can be deeply bonding and entangle individuals in the awareness of All is One, as Source does not differentiate between the petals of a flower. Group work such as this should really only be undertaken by those experienced with the powerfully energetic opening that this particular sacrament alone affords. And individual participants should never feel pressured into participating within a particular setting within which they may be feeling uncomfortable or unready for.

Appropriate Compensation & Energy Exchange:

Financial matters and compensation should always be handled transparently and in a forthright manner. Some practitioners host retreats and charge a fee for this. Others may ask for a requested contribution for services received. However a specific practitioner may handle monetary compensation for their work, it should be clearly communicated to a participant well in advance. Some may ask for non-refundable deposits in order to hold a participant's space. Some work on a sliding scale basis and may wait to handle money exchange until after the ceremony to have the participant base their contribution on the value they receive from their experience. In any event, practitioners should request a fair amount for their services and consider alternative solutions for energy exchange as may be necessary, such as partial or full scholarship funds or payment over time for those who may need this.

INITIATION:

Creating a Safe, Solid, Sacred & Secure Container for the Work (Setting):

5-MeO-DMT can be experienced inside or outside, as long as the container for the work is safe, solid, sacred and secure. Outside spaces afford a unique connection with the unified field of nature itself, as all five senses receive the broadcast signal, deeply connecting one to the natural world. Inside work can feel more held, secure and contained, and can minimize external noise, energies or potential interference ensuring the safety of those participating. We define these aspects as follows:

"Safe" refers to an environment that is suitable to the physical, psychological and spiritual safety of the participant. Safe space means no dangers, inside or out, and the more comfortable and open one feels, the more a participant can relax. This involves wisely choosing a space that maximizes the comfort and well-being for both participants and practitioners, where no one is likely to get physically harmed or injured due to the nature of the environment.

"Solid" refers to the conditions within the environment, including things like weather, if outside, that will not dramatically shift or change for the duration of the ceremony or session work, and interior spaces that are suitable that will adequately hold the level of intensity released within the session or ceremony.

"Sacred" refers to the setting up of the inherent psychic and/or "spiritual" conditions of the specific location or space by utilizing shamanic, mystical, or liturgical ceremonial practices to create a "container" that will effectively hold up and support the participant both physically and psychically for the duration of the initiatory work. Practitioners and participants do not have to hold any specific belief in the "sacred" to hold a sacred space; what is meant is that the space is not profane, that it be dedicated to the work and removed from the mundane and pedestrian flow of life. One should not just do 5-MeO-DMT at a bus stop or randomly at a festival event. However, many different spaces can be made sacred by the intention of those creating and holding space. A certain sense of "spiritual" esthetic can also be helpful.

And finally, "Secure" is defined as a space within which all present are protected and held and where the ceremony or session will be uninterrupted and undisturbed by any inside or outside influences. A designated Temple space is highly recommended whenever possible. This could be a dedicated room, specifically set up for this kind of sacred work. Or, if need be, a living room or similar space could be utilized after removing any non-essential furnishings or covering TV monitors, which is a good idea if they are present. Also, an individual may be assigned to serve as a "guardian." Outside spaces should be chosen carefully in terms of privacy and should be set up taking the comfort of the participant in mind. In certain instances, practitioners may need to be agile and adaptive in determining what works best in particular circumstances. In any event, all these factors should be carefully considered by practitioners and participants alike before a ceremony or session begins.

FACILITATING 5-MEO-DMT

Ceremony or Contextualization:

It has been said that, "In true religion, there is no sect." Some practitioners may draw upon indigenous shamanic lineages and affectations utilizing various ceremonial methods of approach including ritual items, altars and iconography. Some make up their own, or have a minimalist–zen approach. Some practitioners use invocations, prayers, music, and/or songs and various other practices within their ceremony or session work, which can create a sacred setting and energetic to frame or contain the central peak experience.

The depth of the "full release" on 5-MeO-DMT means there is no ego present to hear or witness any of this technique, but the artistry is such that a shamanic or magical ritual can help to manifest and hold the space before and during the peak, and reinforce and help reintegrate the ego upon its return. The neuroplasticity and suggestiveness of the rebirth state is extremely sensitive to words, songs, ideas, energy, etc., and the positive use of such can have as valid a place as the practitioner who holds space through non-action and non-communication. Individual participants would be wise in choosing a practitioner that offers a setting or contextualization that best suits their particular needs. And one practitioner may be better suited than another for any given participant. For there are many paths or approaches to the One.

Holding Space and Witnessing:

Holding space is the active art of being present and holding or anchoring energy. It is effectively a collective agreement between the practitioner, participant and all others present within the field of the container, that they will actively witness, while consciously holding a positively rock-solid state of "loving presence" for each individual and for the group itself throughout the entire process. Providing with absolute certainty the knowledge, understanding and deep trust that each participant will be held, honored, respected, protected and cared for no matter what may be coming up for them in their process of unfolding into the fullness of the energetic awakening; in order that each participant knows and trusts that they can fully surrender into the process. And it is this ability for the participant to trust and completely surrender the egoic function that is absolutely essential to this process.

It can also mean non-action, simply quietly witnessing and allowing the participant to fully express without touch, restraint or interference, as long as there is no harm to the participant or those in attendance. Some practitioners choose to hold space with action, and with the prior consent from participants, may hold space with touch, bodywork, song, words, rattle, etc. as deemed necessary. Every participant has an arc of their own experience, and different stages of that experience may require different needs.

Physical Protection & Safety of the Participant and All Present:

The safety of each participant is paramount within this process and every effort shall be made to ensure the safety (physical, psychological, emotional, social, etc.) of those participating in this sacrament. The energy released from the 5-MeO-DMT experience can lead to a very dynamic physical presentment within certain individuals. If a participant is moving dynamically or in danger of self-harm, it is always a practitioner's and/or the group's responsibility to protect them and the safety of any others present. This means paying close attention and adequately containing any extreme or potentially hazardous movements, while not physically restraining a participant. The general rule of thumb is, "Contain, don't restrain."

Restraining someone in their awakening process can create negative imprints and potentially induce trauma. Participants should be enabled to move freely, to get up, dance, express, etc., while the practitioner and those present create room and safe space within which they can do so. Agreements should be in place for participants not to leave the agreed and protected ceremony space, nor to cause self-harm or do harm to the practitioner or others present. In the rare event of aggressive or potentially violent behavior on the part of a participant, practitioners and those present will do their utmost to deescalate the situation and calm the participant, ensuring that everything is safe within the container before proceeding. In no event should aggression be met with further aggression or violence. All practitioners should be aware that aggressive behavior may arise within a given session or ceremony and take adequate precautions to be able to contain and diffuse it safely, responsibly and non-violently. This may mean having assistants, guardians or others present and available to manage these instances when and if they occur.

Appropriate Boundaries and Physical Touch:

Practitioners should discuss appropriate boundaries and physical touch with participants before a session or ceremony begins. The space that can open up when working with 5-MeO-DMT is the most sensitive sacred space one can experience, so tread lightly and with discretion. Also, previous traumas and imprints may arise creating triggers around touch and boundary issues between participants and the

Facilitating 5-MeO-DMT

practitioner. Better to discuss the need for touch in some cases as a possibility than to surprise and overstep agreements with a participant and break trust.

If the participant has "stuck energy" or is trying to purge or release, some hands-on bodywork by the practitioner can be useful and effective in encouraging this energy to shift or clear. Some practitioners may touch, massage, or tap different areas of the body – but only with prior consent. Some may use feathers or fans to facilitate this energetic movement. Some practitioners may attempt to gently uncurl a body going into a retraction or fetal position, or may adjust the participants body to assist in purging or releasing or to avoid choking, aspiration or similar issues. Pouring water into the mouth, nose or throat to instigate the breathing reflex is an extreme tool that should be avoided by more careful consideration of dosage and sensitivity of the participant. It can result in water in the lungs causing aspiration and other complications. If necessary and requested, small amounts of water can be easily given to participants in state with a squeeze bottle, allowing the practitioner to administer small amounts of water directly and safely if water is required.

A participant's journey is as slow and long as needed to open and express their ego death and rebirth or whatever may be arising for them – and this process should be savored and allowed to unfold in fullness. It cannot and should not ever be rushed or hurried. Each wave comes to shore in its own time, and if forced, may cause distraction or even potential harm to the participant. No one should ever be forced to their feet, or forced to do more medicine without their full consent or appropriate time between rounds. No one – NO ONE – should ever be galvanized to move by any external device that removes their consent. Such activity by a practitioner should be considered a violation of their sacred trust of service and duty to participants. Each soul flowers when the bud feels safe to open, and not before.

The 5-MeO-DMT experience is one of incredible intimacy, great depth and beauty. It can also be powerful and challenging for some. Practitioners should work diligently to create an environment of safety, comfort and well-being where all communicants can feel held and supported within this place of great sensitivity and vulnerability. As the nature of this unfolding is one of deep and abiding Love, creating a safe and conducive environment for the free and unrestricted expression of that Love is a high priority and of major importance.

We have found that powerful sensual, sexual or "kundalini" energy can be released through the experience of the medicine; the participant should feel free to personally express such without shame or guilt, and to be held in a safe, conscientious, compassionate and professional manner by the practitioner and those present without indulging or reciprocating such energy. Appropriate conduct and decorum within such an environment demands a high level of emotional literacy and social maturity on behalf of all those participating in order to respect the personal boundaries of participants as well as to guard the sensitive psyches opened within the process.

Some practitioners believe it is best to remove themselves as much as possible from the line of sight of participants to remove ego identification; at other times it may assist a participant to remember that someone is there looking after and tending to them and that they are not alone. Other practitioners may put themselves front and center of the participant, serving as an anchor point. As long as the participant does not confuse "the finger that points at the sun with the sun itself," the bond between guide and those guided can be visible and supportive.

Practitioners should remind participants that they are merely facilitating the medicine experience, but they are not the medicine. Everything that occurs within the 5-MeO-DMT experience is part of the participant's own revelation of Who and What they Really Are; of Source Consciousness within them. A skilled practitioner can assist in engendering an openness to the experience, but it is always the participant who is opening, and remembering, the practitioner is NOT doing this to them or for them. And this is vital to both understand and represent. Egoic attachment, transference, projection or entrainment onto a practitioner serves no one and practitioners should be at pains to avoid engendering such attachments. Sexual energy may arise in a participant in ceremony and a facilitator's role is to hold space, not engage with that. It is not being encouraged, simply acknowledged, that ethical protocols should be generated and adhered to by practitioners in regards to establishing appropriate boundaries in terms of any potential romantic and/or intimate relating with participants beyond the ceremony. This should provide for an appropriate amount of integration time to occur (allowing for any projections or "guru" imprinting to dissipate) before engaging in such activity.

Finally, it is important for us to include a general definition of what we mean by "consent." We are choosing to adopt four principles for evaluating consent as valid given by ethicist Morten Ebbe Juul Nielson ("Safe, Sane and Consensual – Consent and the Ethics of BDSM" – The International Journal of Applied Philosophy 24:2 (2010): 265-288)*. Nielson asserts that consent draws its moral force from the idea that individual freedom and autonomy is a basic human right and cannot be given to acts that destroy autonomy. For consent to be valid it must: Be Informed, with both (or all) parties fully understanding the activities they are agreeing to perform and their risks; Must be whole-hearted and intentional ("enthusiastic"), not being used as a bargaining chip; Consent must be voluntary, not compromised by the threat of force or harm; Consenting individuals must be competent (not intoxicated, under extreme

FACILITATING 5-MEO-DMT

emotional duress, underage, etc). * Thanks to Rev. Teri Ciacchi of Living Love Revolution and Interdependence & Autonomy LLC for this contribution.

Body Position & Posture, Lying Down or Standing, etc.:

There are many ways to receive 5-MeO-DMT, and each may have a varying effect on the experience. Many practitioners recommend sitting or lying down so as to be most comfortable when receiving the medicine, to not be distracted by the body or any aches or pains, in order to be able to fully let go. If seated in a crossed-legged position, it is encouraged to release the legs outward and gently lay down before going into the peak of the medicine, opening the arms, heart exposed and entering "savasana" or corpse pose in yogic terms, a full surrender. Some practitioners may insist on the participant maintaining a very specific body position throughout their experience. However, we have found that simply comfortably laying on the back, face up, arms wide open and legs slightly apart is one of the best positions to allow the energetic flow that the medicine releases to move freely through the body. In any event, the participant should be allowed to move freely as the energy of the release may move them. Some practitioners serve the medicine outside in nature, standing, uniting heaven and earth, drawing energy from both in an augmented warrior pose. This can be transformational, but also leave some egoic focus on standing and being present or holding on. Participants may also need immediate practitioner help in safely lowering them to the ground when the ego goes offline. Standing is a powerful choice and has its place, but may not be for everyone all of the time.

As well as the psychic opening, 5-MeO-DMT engenders an enormous energetic opening that flows naturally through the body's circuits. Some participants may curl up or go into fetal position, exhibit signs of muscle contractions or begin shaking or vibrating intensely as the energy is released. They may try to hold on or otherwise attempt to escape or redirect the experience. Some practitioners recommend keeping limbs uncrossed to allow free energetic flow, which sometimes results in what has been referred to as "mirrored bilateral symmetry" of their limbs resulting in mudras, asanas, yogic poses etc. Some participants may move or dance and experience free flowing movement in their bodies. Some may feel an overwhelming orgasmic burst, and some may overflow into cathartic sound and release, including primal screaming, or may exhibit glossolalia (speaking in tongues), etc. These are all natural responses to be honored and supported as the practitioner best sees fit.

Martin W. Ball, Ph.D., Editor
Use of Music, Chant & Sound, Aroma:

The session may have music that is live or recorded, structured or free-form, or savored in silence. Some practitioners use specific recorded tracks of gentle, non-rhythmic, ambient music that creates a contextualization or framework that assists in deepening or harmonizing the brainwave state of the participant's experience, such as sound healing frequencies, solfeggio tones, and binaural beats. Each stage of the journey has different needs. Lower doses or initial rounds, and the "re-entry" or initial integration phase is when the participant is most aware of their surroundings and the interactions of the practitioner. Sound or song, chants, etc., at these moments can be hugely supportive and guide the participant in or out more fully. However, such techniques must be carefully employed as not to create a distraction for the participant at any time. Should a participant find that any actions, including sound or music, that a practitioner is employing to be distracting, they should immediately indicate this and the sound, technique, etc. should be immediately ceased by the practitioner.

Certain instruments such as the rattle can shake and push the consciousness that is holding on, and be appropriately employed when entering a peak state. Bells or sharp sounds can create vibration to parallel the vibrating consciousness learning to let go and help release, but at other junctures they can also draw egoic attention to the sound, and bring people out of their experience, as can some music in general. Gentle sounds and instruments like singing bowls, Koshi bells, etc. can be highly effective in layering a smooth and supportive sonic environment for re-entry. Some practitioners may artfully use recorded music to assist in the reintegration of the participant by subtly introducing rhythm and melody which can serve to effectively bring the egoic consciousness of the participant gently back until full body awareness and "grounding" is achieved.

Smell is also highly influential and must be approached very carefully by practitioners. Some practitioners may use burning smudge such as sage, or palo santo, which can similarly support the senses and cleanse the energetic field. Others may use traditional incense blends such as frankincense, myrrh, copal, acacia, etc. to consecrate the place of working within a ceremonial environment. Others may incorporate the subtle use of hydrosol sprays, distilled water infused with floral essences, to clear or move energy or for subtle imprinting of the psyche. In any event all of these techniques should in no way distract from the central unitive experience of the participant, but instead serve to support that experience and should always be used with appropriate craft and discretion.

FACILITATING 5-MEO-DMT

Dialog vs. Silence:

It is said that, "Silence is golden" and that it is ." . . . the equilibrium of perfection." In full ego release no external sound is really necessary, although comforting sounds, songs or music can be complementary to creating a sense of safety and presence for the participant's "launch" and "re-entry." It can also be utilized to cover external noises. However, in general, the practitioner, and those present, should maintain silence throughout the participant's experience.

However, judicious and strategic use of dialogue can be extremely effective at the right moments: "trust, open, feeling, love" and similar words are felt, not heard, and can assist in opening to the fullness of the medicine. Simply whispering "Yes" in affirmation of the participant's opening can be extremely useful. However, one must be very careful in using terms such as, "It's okay," when someone may be re-experiencing a trauma that is anything but "okay." If a participant is experiencing fear or anxiety, simple statements such as "You're safe," can be very effective in calming a participant as necessary.

Intuitive verbal free-forming, sometimes based on the health/induction form around possible traumas etc., can also help reframe imprints and blockages, but such techniques should always be approached with respect, prudence, and caution, and only after developing a robust practice. A stray word during the integration phase, after a peak 5-MeO-DMT experience, can reverberate to unforeseen degrees on the participant's consciousness: be prepared and use discernment in what you choose to communicate in these instances.

Porous or Solidly Held Containers:

A 5-MeO-DMT session is best administered within a safe and focused container for the work. Some practitioners hold a more rigorously held container, controlling light, sound, temperature, outside interference, etc. Others may hold a more porous container that allows natural energies in. Some may seem to offer no container at all, which is not suggested or encouraged. Some believe all participants present at the start of a ceremony or session should remain for the full duration and hold space for others in the group; others may allow group members to come and go as long as it doesn't disturb the overall energetic of the field. The golden rule to remember is everything affects everything else. And it is important to recognize the value of how containers are generated and held by various practitioners and how they can serve to hold, support and transmute the energies released within them in this powerful process of awakening.

Conscious Use of Breath (*Pranayama*):

We have found that it can be immensely helpful to practice some form of breathing exercises before (and after) a 5-MeO-DMT session. Deep, unforced, rhythmic breathing can greatly enhance and assist in the process of surrendering the ego. Entraining participants to be consciously aware of their breath, the precious gift of life which each breath affords us, and the release of all which no longer serves with each exhalation. Various breathing exercises & techniques that can be utilized beforehand such as: square breathing, breath of fire, deep belly breathing, and yogic *pranayama* breathwork, etc., can all help open the lungs and empower the participant to be more conscious of their breath in general. This can assist to alleviate any ego fears about their body stopping breathing in the session, in addition to calming the nerves and energy of participants both before, during and after the experience.

During the activation itself it is recommended to simply breathe deeply, through the nose in an unforced manner. Practitioners should pay close attention to each participant's breathing throughout their experience. Simple techniques, such as blowing gently on the participant's face, rubbing the breastbone lightly with a closed fist, or just placing a palm gently over the navel can offer subtle cues to the participant to take a breath should their breathing become compromised within the session in any way.

Total Permission to Fully Express What is Necessary & Essential:

Whatever happens in a 5-MeO-DMT session stays in the 5-MeO-DMT session. Confidentiality is imperative. And each participant must be given complete permission to fully express what is necessary and essential in their experience – as opposed to what the ego may attempt to act out. The practitioner extends that permission, and encourages the participant to give themselves that same permission.

The participant can rage, scream, cry, laugh, orgasm, move, purge, release – whatever is required that needs to be released without shame, fear, or guilt, because everything that comes up is for their healing. Everything. And the practitioner needs to accept that without qualm or reaction or attachment, without reinforcing or denying, to radically accept with non-judgment and absolutely no shaming. This sense of no-shame can be negated if the session is filmed or digitally recorded – as the camera

FACILITATING 5-MEO-DMT

generally just captures the flesh body; the external "presentment" and not the inner spiritual experience.

Some practitioners may allow for audio recording of an individual's experience for later review. However, any recording of a participant's experience must have total consent beforehand and should never be shared with anyone in an open casual manner.

Editor's Note: while video recording is a sensitive topic and not always welcome by facilitators or other participants, it is important to note that some find having a visual review of what their body was doing while they were under the influence can be very instructive and help to recall specific aspects of the experience (and is generally far more effective in this regard than an audio recording), and can be effectively used for later review with a skilled integration coach who can assist in analyzing the energetic presentations within the body, movements, gestures, and vibrations. If such is desired, it should be discussed with the facilitator prior to the session and here the facilitator's concerns take precedence and should be respected. Of course, no one should ever be filmed without their express consent, and videos should not be shared carelessly on social media. With such video recordings, always keep in mind that those with no experience with 5-MeO-DMT will have a hard time understanding what is depicted and are likely to project their own naïve interpretations and values.

Specific Dosing Protocols (Bufo/Extracts/Synthetic):

Synthetic and organic 5-MeO-DMT sources have different potencies and strengths. There is lab-made synthetic 5 which can be up to 99%-100% pure, organic varieties such as *Bufo alvarius* toad bufotoxin (bufo), and other plant based 5-MeO-DMT extracts, including *yopo* seeds and other variants, which can have significant variation in purity and potency. Practitioners and participants alike should be aware of dosage strengths and other potential alkaloids that may be present in organic materials from source to source, and understand clearly that potencies can vary according to the season, individual creature, age, and batch from these organic sources.

Also, every participant is different, and each possesses their own specific capacity for processing tryptamines. It's a unique blend of potency of material, the participant's personal energetic sensitivity and egoic strength, or ability to let go, and an ineffable heavenly permission and protocol that all combine in every single 5-MeO-DMT journey. Practitioners must be intimately aware of all these factors and not just mechanically bludgeon an ego into submission with large doses of medicine. Regardless of dosage, some participants may experience a "white-out" and not have any recollection of the experience. It is important to note that sometimes there will not be a "linear" memory of the experience, as such, in that this is not a linear experience. It is a "trans-rational" unfolding into the infinite, beyond the parameters of the rational, reasoning memory within what has been termed the "Default Mode Network" of egoic consciousness.

Some people can achieve a "full release" experience on small doses of medicine – and invariably these sensitives are overwhelmed by the average or large dose, and larger doses may be unnecessary or less than optimal. However, some participants can be given enormous doses of medicine and their egos shrug it off or refuse to let go. You cannot force trust and openness. Sometimes starting with smaller doses and building up to a medium, then full, dose allows the ego to trust and give consent to itself to let go. Sometimes less is more. Sometimes the participant just isn't ready in one session – and that's okay, too. Proceed delicately and prudently in this process without forcing.

Participants who experience multiple sessions may also find their relationship with the medicine changes. Like peeling back layers of an onion, the more you release, the less you have between you and fully releasing the next time. The more you can trust and remember the process of opening and letting go, then the more you can do so on each subsequent occasion. And the more you understand that the external 5-MeO-DMT is just a key to unlock your own medicine within, the stronger that ability becomes. It is also important to remember that our bodies create 5-MeO-DMT endogenously and it is a naturally occurring substance within all humans. Some have found that for many individuals, the more one partakes of the medicine, the less is needed in subsequent dosing.

It must be clearly understood that 5-MeO-DMT is a pathway and relationship with the nondual, unitive potential within us all. It is the practitioner's ultimate responsibility to effectively communicate that to the participant and to ongoingly support and assist in this process of awakening.

Up-to-Date Valid CPR and First Aid Training & Kit:

All responsible practitioners should seriously consider taking basic First Aid & CPR certification training on a regular basis and keep their training updated and current. These classes can be easily found through any local area branch of the Red Cross or other such organizations. Having this foundational training can be vital in the case of emergencies encountered within a 5-MeO-DMT experience. Feel free to enquire if the practitioner you are considering has had such training. Also, having a solid professional first aid kit on hand, including a pulse-oximeter and oxygen canister

FACILITATING 5-MEO-DMT

and other related supplies can come in very handy in case of a health emergency while in session or ceremony. Be sure your kit is kept up-to-date and filled with relevant and necessary supplies.

INTEGRATION:

Integration & Suggested Techniques for Grounding:

Integration and effectively grounding the energies encountered within a 5-MeO-DMT experience is absolutely essential in this process. Often individuals may need additional support, both during their experience, and especially after undergoing a powerful entheogenic awakening. Circumstances and issues surrounding reactivations may arise that need to be addressed. Experiencing deep catharsis or re-experiencing a past trauma or unresolved fear may arise. Or perhaps some new revelation has dawned within the consciousness of the newly initiated that needs further processing.

Practitioners should be prepared to offer both written material on the 5-MeO-DMT integration process and create spaciousness to be available to follow-up with individual participants and offer necessary support as they gain their bearings and come to terms with any emotional issues that may arise. Furthermore, they may need to be available to assist new participants in getting used to this higher vibrational frequency that often manifests in their lives after their experience. Practitioners may consider training assistants or trusted members of their communities, well-versed in this process, to aid them in these efforts.

Subsequently, participants should be sure to give themselves plenty of time after a 5-MeO-DMT session or ceremony to give themselves spaciousness before just jumping back in to their standard "default reality." Some may wish to develop a "buddy system" in order to have individuals who agree beforehand to hold space for each other in their integration process. Some practitioners and groups use a sponsorship model, where new participants must be officially referred by an existing member of the group who agrees to assist in their integrative process if and as necessary.

Effective Documentation to Offer for Integration and Aftercare:

Individual practitioners or groups should be able to provide participants with effective documentation regarding integration and aftercare, or at least offer solid verbal communications, explanations, and support regarding their particular integrative process.

Accessible and Ongoing Relationship, Interface and Communication with Practitioner or Network/Community:

Ultimately, responsible practitioners should work diligently to create ongoing relationships with individuals they work with, as well as forming alliances with other responsible practitioners. Establishing methods of ongoing interface and communications with an eye toward creating integrated and sustainable practices and communities of empowered, balanced, sovereign and enlightened individuals. Generating these kinds of networks allow for this important work to expand and grow, giving more individuals the opportunity to participate in this vital, sacred work of planetary awakening, healing and transformation. Individuals should consider how they represent themselves, especially within the wider context of social media. We support those who create effective media platforms, interface and channels of communication that allow for the effective dissemination of necessary and essential information and counsel those who interface within broader social networks to seriously consider what impact they may have through their voices and actions in supporting and forwarding the cause of this movement.

Integration Circles, Directly Hosted or Referred:

Some individual practitioners and/or groups work to create, host and moderate regular facilitated "integration circles" where newly initiated participants can share their experiences – their breakthroughs as well as their and challenges – with one another in a safe, confidential, and supportive environment. Many independent "psychedelic support" groups are being established in major population centers to offer just such support. And a solid, reliable practitioner or group should be able and available to offer and provide any additional integrative support or referrals necessary for individual participants.

Sustainability of the Medicine:

Lastly, a note on pacing. Entheogenic medicines around the world were originally utilized and cared for by indigenous tribes with a direct connection and relationship to their environment. This instilled a deep understanding around the sustainability of

FACILITATING 5-MEO-DMT

entheogens and their correct usage, and it also shaped the availability of some medicines with the seasons. In modern times, we often bring an unconscious, capitalist, globalized paradigm to the consumption of earth medicines. More is not necessarily better, and in the global shamanic community this is even more so. This may also be seen in the rapid degree that some people enthusiastically dive into the practice and facilitation of this medicine with little or no training.

The trend in the West towards combining entheogenic medicines, especially something as powerful as 5-MeO-DMT, is relatively unknown territory. Combinations of other shamanic medicines like the kambo frog poison, ayahuasca, psilocybin, San Pedro cactus, and even sources of DMT before or after 5-MeO-DMT can be dangerous and put extra stress on an already activated nervous and serotonin systems. Any MAO-inhibitor should be expressly avoided in direct combination with 5-MeO-DMT and could be fatal. Let these experiences breathe. Let their wisdom reverberate through you to the fullest extent and integrate that, before moving on to another peak experience on a shamanic smorgasbord.

The sustainability of 5-MeO-DMT, whether from natural or synthetic sources, is also a cause of concern in our growing community. The *Bufo alvarius* toad, one of the main guardians of this medicine in nature, is particularly sensitive to the supply and demand of the global entheogenic market, and we caution seekers and practitioners to utilize this and other organic forms of the medicine wisely and effectively, being conscious of sustainability and our human impact on the beings that host this Sacred Gift, and sourcing from ethical toad medicine collectors that continue to nurture these creatures.

5-MeO-DMT is especially powerful and can continue to reverberate in your life and your being. You can become sensitive to any other psychoactives, which, when taken, may reactivate the 5-MeO vibration that is within you, or with a regular meditation practice, you may dip into that Source consciousness in an ongoing, dynamic relationship.

The long-term activation potential of 5-MeO-DMT within an individual or group is presently unknown, but we are walking that path of awakening together.

Call In, Not Call Out:

We aim to keep the community safe by handling any discordant issues internally to avoid external conflict and potential legal recourse whenever possible.

With respect to our colleagues, we act in good faith, with respect, and do not speak poorly about other practitioners. We strive to "call in, not call out" in matters of dispute.

We take action by being transparent with the information and begin constructive conversations with the individuals involved, offering guidance when we recognize or hear of a practitioner or facilitator that may have fallen out of integrity in the community through either sexual misconduct, abuse of power, financial exploitation, etc. In our own matters of dispute, we request an unbiased mediator, and approach the dispute with the intention of upholding the integrity of the work as a whole for the greatest good of all those concerned.

Redress:

While we continually strive to act in accordance with these ethical commitments, we acknowledge our own humanness. When we have lapses in judgement or create inadvertent harm, we seek to make things right through humble listening, owning our contribution to wrongs, asking for council, and being receptive to correction and redress of grievances.

Appendix C: A Conversation with Hal from T.O.A.D.

Reflections on Being of Service

Editor's Note: Though "Hal" and the Temple of Awakening Divinity has already been prominently featured in this anthology, feeling that he had more to add, Hal came over for a conversation, which I recorded and have transcribed here. While there is some overlap with the chapter, "Welcome to the Temple of Awakening Divinity," I felt that the conversation worked well as a stand-alone piece and have thus decided to include it here as an appendix, rather than as an addition to the aforementioned chapter. My side of the conversation is presented in italics.

Hi "Hal" – let's just jump right in. How were you introduced to 5-MeO-DMT and what was your experience? How did that happen for you?

On February 2nd, 2005, I was lecturing on my favorite topic of discussion, which was the mystical unitive experience in, of all places, Las Vegas, NV. It was a gathering of around 150-200 neopagans, alchemists, Wiccans, and spiritual folk, and I was lecturing on the mystical unitive experience from the perspective of the disciplines of raja yoga, ceremonial magic, hermetic qabalah, transpersonal alchemy, and various forms of *tantra*. Technically, I was considered a theoretical expert, yet I had never experienced a nondual or a unitive state of consciousness at that time. A very dear, close friend of mine was standing out in back of the venue after delivering half of what was a 3-hour presentation with well over 100 PowerPoint slides, and he asked me if I trusted him. I thought that was a really weird question, and I asked him why. He said, "Well, because I want to show you the Holy Grail." At that point, every doubt hackle on my body stood on end because having come through a Templaratic tradition, I knew something metaphorically, mystically, mythologically around the "Holy Grail," and I looked at him and I said, "You're offering me a drug, aren't you?" And he said, "Well, you did say a trusted me…" At that point in my life, I was about eight years clean and sober, so I had a bit of a chip on my shoulder because I had done a lot of white powders in my 20s and 30s, and had had some problems with them. But I said, "Yeah, I did say I trusted you," and so he opened the door to his Burning Man bus, and I went on inside.

It was set up like a beautiful temple and there were two sisters there – priestesses who I knew well and trusted – and another gentleman who basically was a chiropractor by trade who had done a lot of work with the Santo Daime tradition basically functioning as the server. They laid me down on this sumptuous bed, and they put this glass pipe that had a little bit of cannabis in it (which was one of my problem substances) with this very tiny, match head-sized pile of this white powder, and I looked down at it and I looked back up at them and said, "Whatever that is, I don't think it's enough." They laughed and chuckled, saying, "No, we think it's enough. So, we're going to light this, and we want you to inhale it, take it in, then lie back, relax, and let go." I looked at them completely confused and I said, "Let go of what?" I had no idea what they were talking about. But I listened to them, and they lit the pipe, and I inhaled its contents.

It came with mixed reservations about blowing my sobriety, but as soon as my head hit the pillow below me, everything disappeared into essentially what I called "velocity and a little bit of terror," and I was jettisoning backwards down a wormhole faster than the speed of light, thinking to myself, "Oh shit! You've done it now!" My son, who I adore, was born one month and one day prior to that, and as I'm jettisoning back down this wormhole of light, I realized their words were "just let go," but I didn't realize I was going to have to let go of everything, including my life as I knew it, because I was convinced that I was in this process of dying. And so, in that moment, I accepted the experience, and I surrendered into it. In that moment of choice, everything exploded and imploded into what I like to refer to as "everything-all-at-once-forever-right-now," and my consciousness expanded into the totality of all existence.

There was no "Hal" there. There was no sense of myself. There was only the complete perfection of all existence that was culminating in a fully transcendent experience of love. There is no way that I can even try to explain it, but it was massive. After what appeared to be some immeasurable period of time, some small little shred

FACILITATING 5-MEO-DMT

of my ego appeared in the vast recesses of the cosmos, and somehow, I knew that I was going to have to land the plane of my ego back onto the runway of my conscious awareness, my psyche, and my body. It took what was then 15 years of my *raja yoga* training to actually land that plane, and I sat bolt upright with a huge gasp, laughing and crying simultaneously, saying," I knew it was real! I knew it! I knew it! I knew it!" What I meant was I knew that this experience of union with God, union with Source Consciousness, what the yogins call *nirvakalpa samadhi,* was possible while in a human physical vehicle. And the irony that this indescribable experience was brought on by the inhalation of a very small bit of white powder was not lost on my continuing-my-recovering-drug-addicted mind.

After a short period of time, they kind of shuffled me off the bus and back into this drumming and dance environment of this party that was going on, and I went home after that and went to sleep. I woke up the next day, looking at all my friends, and I asked, "Did that actually happen?" because I doubted the reality of it. It was so huge. They said, "Yeah, that actually happened." That sent me on about a two-and-a-half-year process of deep-diving into the academic and intellectual understanding of what I'd experienced. I hadn't really been into psychedelics that much before, but I then found the works of people like Jeremy Narby, I had Terence McKenna books on my shelf, I went back and read Hoffman's work. I really did a deep-dive back again into Aleister Crowley's work on the processes of using these kinds of sacraments which had been around for a while. I found Huxley's work. I spent the next two and a half years trying to ground myself into an intellectual understanding of what actually happened during that time on the bus with the little white powder.

I found James Oroc's first edition of *Tryptamine Palace*, which was very useful, because I hadn't read anything else about 5-MeO-DMT. There was nothing published, at the time. I also found Rick Strassman's *DMT- The Spirit Molecule*, which was helpful, but it really didn't get to my experience as it really wasn't talking about the substance that I had just done.

Then two and a half years later, I had another friend, and one of the same two women that had been present at my first experience in Las Vegas, show up at my home in southern Oregon. He reached into a bag he was carrying, and he pulled out this glass and brass device, and I immediately recognized it as an administrative tool for this medicine. He said, "Do you know what this is?" I said, "I think I do. I believe that's the 'lamp of invisible light' of the alchemists, the lamp that burns with neither oil nor wick," which had been talked about very extensively in the alchemical and magical literature. He was a bit of an alchemist himself, and he looked down at the device. He said, "You know, actually, I think you're right! It is exactly that! Would you like to help me calibrate it?" And of course, my hand immediately shot up and we arranged to do a little bit of ceremony in our own temple space at our home. It was then that I did the medicine for the second time.

On that particular occasion, my consciousness expanded into the vastness of the totality and singularity of all things, but as I was integrating in from the experience, I had a distinctly kinesthetic experience, what I would call an archetypal download, where I experienced the Goddess of Infinite Space and the Infinite Stars. In my tradition her name is Nuit. I had been a devoted priest of hers for almost a decade, and she asked me if I was willing to take an oath to myself, and her, through the catalyst of this medicine, to somehow go out and find the medicine and serve it to others. I had no idea how that was going to happen to create sacred ceremony and begin offering this to others. But not only did I agree to that, but I took an oath to that effect while I was under the influence of the sacrament. As I came out, I had some vague recall, and I looked at my former partner (my wife, at the time) and our friends, and I said, "Did I just take an oath?" And they looked at me and said, "Yeah – a pretty serious one!" My response was, "Oh shit! That's not what I was expecting!" Nor was it what I wanted to do. But I realized that I had taken this oath to the goddess that I had devoted myself to, and so, over the course of the next few weeks and months, I really deliberated whether or not this was something that I was capable of doing.

It was clear that I was to do that within the tradition that I had already been raised in, which is the religious spiritual philosophy known as Thelema, and so I started composing the ritual that I would use to facilitate the sacrament. I acquired one of these lamp devices, which you tell the story about in *The Entheogenic Evolution* because he didn't send me "the lamp" – he sent me this other contraption, which I think you described as, "Having too many parts to possibly be useful." And then I did eventually get a "lamp" device.

I ended up acquiring some *Bufo alvarius* toads online, believe it or not, from a company called Bouncing Bear Botanicals – something I would never do again, because I don't believe that these animals should be taken out of their environment and that we really should protect them. And then on December 7th of 2007, I held my first official ceremony as the Temple of Awakening Divinity, or T.O.A.D. Then I met you fairly shortly thereafter, like maybe just a couple of weeks later, and invited you to the temple. Since that time, I have served almost 6,000 individuals and held well over 1,500 ceremonies, and I continue to offer the sacrament in a safe and responsible way to people from all over the world.

Facilitating 5-MeO-DMT

With the development of this ceremonial structure that you use, most of the structure was already there by the time that you and I first met, which, as you say, was just a couple of weeks into even just starting this. So how did you go about developing that structure? I know you say that it comes out of your preexisting tradition, so it sounds like it was more of an adaptation and adopting that rather than necessarily creating it out of whole cloth.

Yes, exactly. In fact, I would really say that I cobbled it together. So, I use a formula of ceremonial magic, and I use a very specific technique that involves processes of induction, banishing, purification, consecration, check-in, and invocation, and then initiation with the sacrament, and then a process of grounding in, and then integration that follows from there. So, what I did is I took ceremonial aspects of liturgical, theurgical, and thaumaturgical techniques – theurgy meaning what I call working with God energy, thaumaturgy generally defined as miracle working – I call it the application of theurgy towards apparently miraculous means. And so, through this ceremonial magical technique, which is where Leary got his ideas of "set and setting" that he and Metzner and Ram Dass put into place, I just decided to take that a step further and go back to the original roots of that by creating a sacred ceremonial context that would give people a safe, solid, and sacred container within which they would be able to surrender fully into the expansiveness of the medicine. There are antecedent rites or rituals that existed that I then drew sections from to utilize in the ceremony, as well as crafting some of that on my own. I honed that down to the minimum of what it can be, utilizing that contextual ceremonial framework.

Something that a lot of people comment on in their submissions to the book is this idea that many of us who have the experience, the immediate response is, "Oh shit! I've got to share this with this with as many people as possible!" – the evangelical urge – there's a lot of commentary on how that's not necessarily the best thing to follow through on immediately, and there's also the general advice, which I think that you would probably be more than happy to agree with, that, for people who are facilitating, it's really important to see a lot of different presentations of how people respond, so that you, as a facilitator, get an idea of: OK, one person might freak out, someone else might try and run away, someone else is going to strip off all their clothes, someone else might throw up all over themselves, right? So, if we only have a small sample, we don't really know the range of reactions. Like with me, from that very first experience, my thought was, "This is what 5-MeO-DMT does," because I had the full bliss, ecstatic, nondual experience, and I thought: it must just do this. But then, as I kept coming back to T.O.A.D., I started to realize: no, this is the highest potential of 5-MeO-DMT, but this is not the automatic result. I think that you definitely provide a very safe and secure format and setting, but just how do you respond now to that idea that first you've got to see a whole bunch of people, and you've got to study with a bunch of different facilitators, before you even think of giving this experience to others. And yours is also kind of a unique case in that you took this oath while in state. So, your next question here is: how did you become a facilitator, and why?

I would definitely say I did not go seeking this out. There was an aspect of it where the medicine came looking for me. It came looking for somebody who would be its champion, to a particular degree, and I did not set out with the intention being a 5-MeO-DMT facilitator. In fact, after the first occasion, the experience was so huge that I had to compartmentalize a good portion of it, because I wasn't ready, or able, to unpack it right there. I would say I'm still unpacking some of the compartmentalized pieces of my first experience.

I do believe it's in the best interest of anybody thinking of facilitating with this medicine to witness as many experiences as possible. In *The Entheogenic Evolution* book you called them types of journeys, and you listed about 10-15 of what I call archetypal presentments. They're how different people present, and each person reacts completely uniquely to the medicine experience depending on their readiness, their willingness, and their ability to let go of the egoic function. A lot of it also depends on how the facilitation is being brought about. My particular approach is to contextualize something with clear ceremonial structure, and then, once the sacrament – really, the Eucharist – is delivered, to step back and be almost hands-off to allow the person to fully express what is coming up and emerging for them.

The only time to really involve myself in that is if the individual needs what I call navigational assistance in that process, and then, if so, I might use techniques of feathering, which I know you know about, to help move and clear energy. There may be some verbal coaching involved, as minimally as possible. There might be a little touch coaching, if I've already gotten consent from somebody that they're open to receiving touch beforehand. And so, I will then gently – I won't even use the term guide – will provide a gentle sense of loving presence for the individual to be able to provide them with whatever they need within that context, but at the most minimal level possible, because I really feel it's up to them to fully surrender the ego function, and that surrendering has to be a choice. It has to be done consciously, and it has to be done willingly. It cannot be forced upon another.

There are a lot of practitioners who will just kind of bludgeon people with huge amounts of the medicine, which isn't really helpful, and can actually be harmful in a lot of situations, because it can bring on effective overdoses, which might then result in extended reactivations – even though those can happen to almost anyone. Having

Facilitating 5-MeO-DMT

worked with the medicine for over 15 years now, having witnessed as many people as I have, it starts giving you a broader overview of the full spectrum of experiences that you might be able to witness and assisting people in whatever way they may need for them to willingly let go of the egoic function. This seems to really be at the core of what this work is about.

Back then, at the time, as you say, there essentially were no books written about it. While there was Oroc's book that was the self-published edition that he had passed out at Burning Man, and that was the only literature that existed, but it wasn't generally available to the public, and the full published version didn't come out until 2009. So you and I struck up an interesting dichotomy in the sense that you were kind of the background guy with the pseudonym of "Hal Lucious Nation," and I was the very open public voice (via my podcast and books). But now people on the inside of the 5-MeO community know who you are – they know what your actual name is. But on the outside, while you've been more public, it's still been a bit more private and background. We're also at a place now where we don't necessarily need a lot of more public champions because 5-MeO is spreading around the world and there's a lot of voices out there. So how do you see yourself now in becoming more public through the years, but still "background," and still conducting ceremonies, and you've expanded into training programs and integration circles and research with organizations like Johns Hopkins, and more recently Columbia University. So how do you see your role within the movement now, and how has it changed over these past 15 or so years?

Wow, that's a great question. It's so interesting to see the emotions coming up. I've always considered myself a steward in this process in that I recognized the importance of this crystalline key for opening up expanded states of consciousness. I'm being a little influenced right now because I just watched "The Sunshine Makers" last night, which is the story of Nick Sands and Tim Scully and their making of "orange sunshine," and you know in that, just like myself, just like yourself, they were deeply inspired by that particular medicine (LSD), and effectively wanted to turn on the world and really took a lot of steps to go do that in a big way. So I recognize the potentiality of 5-MeO-DMT in its ability to open the consciousness of humanity to hopefully lead us to a worldwide transformation of the transcendent experience, to allow for humanity to wake up to the fact that we really are Source Consciousness embodied in flesh, and we can actually love one another, and we can actually have an environment that fosters peace and progress instead of constant war and strife and all of these things that we're dealing with.

Perhaps I'm naïve. I'm naïve in this process, just as I look at Scully and Sands and seeing how they were naïve, but it didn't stop them from trying. And so, I recognized that this medicine – and I didn't even know that there was anything called a "psychedelic community" even happening at this time – but I saw that this was important, and that it could be contextualized and offered to individuals to kind of maximize their experience. The entire temple work was founded on a simple Taoist idea of, "From small things, great." The idea was that by working very closely with a few other people, we could progressively expand this out to produce what I hopefully saw as the "100th monkey effect" that would have some kind of impact on the greater consciousness of society and of humanity. Looking at it now, in hindsight, I can see that it actually is having an impact. It's just a little slower than I'd like it to be, perhaps, but that's my ego talking. So I've never sought out notoriety. I always kept my practice very focused and very centered on duty of care towards the individual who was in front of me, and that was what was really important. It's what remains most important, and to effectively optimize each person's experience as much as possible.

Which then led me to realizing, fairly early on, that there needed to be an integrative component before anybody was offering integration in any way, shape, or form, before "integration" was even being talked about. And I recognized that the formula of preparation, initiation, and integration was the essential model. I've expanded that now to be preparation including education and orientation, because you have to know where you are if you're going into this place that has no directions and is literally omnipresent. You want to be oriented before you step into that, so that when you come out, you can find your direction and can navigate successively back in the ego consciousness world. And that's when I started to learn that there were other practitioners out there who weren't offering any kind of integrative model at all and were leaving people pretty disintegrated and imbalanced. I started offering those aspects of integration circles fairly early in my practice – probably by 2009.

Now we've got really a lot of younger people who are stepping into this field and stepping into the role of wanting to facilitate, or wanting to at least participate in some manner, let alone have the experience. I've had younger people refer to me as an "elder" in the community and, you know, that's not necessarily how I feel personally, but you have been in this for a long time, versus some of the other people in the book who say they've been doing this for a couple months, or a few years, whereas you've got many years in this space. So, what do you feel is your potential role or responsibility, or it doesn't even have to be responsibility, but what do you have to offer these kids who are getting into it out of really sincere enthusiasm, but as an "elder statesman" in the 5-

FACILITATING 5-MEO-DMT

MeO community, what do you see as your role or relationship, or what message would you want to share?

There are so very clearly two words: pace yourself.

To quote Jim Morrison, "I want the world, and I want it now!" and we all do. There is definitively a long arc that we are moving through in this process of global awakening, and 5-MeO-DMT represents a wild card. It is it is extremely potent, and just as it can serve as an incredible catalyst for transformation, if not handled in a safe and responsible way, it could destabilize. I wanted everybody to know about this, and I was much more exuberant about it in my early years. I've learned to curb my enthusiasm a little bit, not because I'm any less enthusiastic. It's because I realize that it's just more prudent in terms of approach. And so, I would say, do what you can to educate people about what this medicine is, because some people aren't really ready for it. It's not right for everyone, and yet, anyone who desires to partake in it, it should really be considered their birthright.

But there are also aspects of responsibility, of doing appropriate health screening, for example – both physical and mental health – before providing this medicine. This becomes a very integral part of the preparation process that not a lot of people are doing. So if people are thinking of serving this medicine, they really need to do their homework so that they're doing so in a responsible manner. And that means providing effective duty-of-care by doing appropriate health screenings before bringing people in, and having integrative components. Find somebody who's serving this medicine and either see if you can develop some form of apprenticeship, or if people are offering training modalities for this medicine, and there are a lot of very capable practitioners who are out there and doing these kinds of things, so make use of it.

I have been approached by many people over the years who wanted to come in in an apprentice capacity, and so I started allowing people to do that. I found even though I feel that shadowing and working within the context of serving people is probably the best way to learn how to work with this medicine, there's even more to it than that. In 2019 I started our temple acolyte training program and brought a cohort of 10 people through that training process. It was supposed to take a little over a year, but it ended up taking over two years when COVID got involved. But we completed our first cohort in September of 2021, and we are now involved with our second cohort of trainees and should be complete with them by the end of 2022. But that is a full year and a day program that requires intellectual and academic understanding of things, as well as practical approaches to the medicine, as well as people creating their own specific offering.

Martin W. Ball, Ph.D., Editor

The Temple of Awakening Divinity is not an orthodoxy. In fact, more unorthodoxy than anything, because we don't believe in dogmatic and orthodox approaches. Once one has experienced the totality of God, you don't need a book to tell you about it, although books can be helpful. And when approaching offering this particular sacrament, there's a lot to learn. After 14-plus years of serving this medicine, I still learn every day with every single person that I've offered this medicine. One cannot become complacent in that one needs to really always be recognizing that they are learning more about the depth of what this medicine can really offer, especially in applying it. There are safer and more responsible ways of doing that.

Looking over the questions that I've provided for people, I think that a lot of these questions are directly addressed in your protocols and methods document that we're featuring in the book. But I do want to ask you about something that is just a little bit ironic, and I just want your own take on it. You've got this great acronym: the Temple of Awakening Divinity, or T.O.A.D., and as you have already articulated, you did start out with a couple of toads, and you were milking the toads, but then you eventually moved on from working with the toad. You have facilitated and worked with toad secretions, you have also worked with organic extracts from natural biological sources, such as plants and grasses, and you have also facilitated with synthetic, lab-made, pure molecule. This is an area where there is a lot of controversy and a lot of debate. I would just like your take on this: should it be toad, or it should be organic, or what's your take on the idea that synthetic is somehow less-than?

It's a big question, and one that seems to come up over and over again. Having worked with both, what I call the organic medicine, which is the bufo toxin from the Sonoran Desert toad, and the pure molecule from a lab, I'd say it takes the expertise of almost a sommelier to really kind of tell the differentiation, experientially. Our mutual friend, doctor Joseph Barsuglia, talks about the "entourage effect" which is brought about by the many different alkaloids within the bufo secretion, including its primary ingredient, bufotenine, 5-HO-DMT, which is found in all toad secretions (not just *Bufo alvarius*). It's been shown to have healing properties as used in Chinese medicine for literally centuries, but it's only the Sonoran Desert toad that produces the 5-MeO-DMT. There's some process that's happening in the toad that converts the 5-HO-DMT into 5-MeO-DMT. I think there is one reason why it's doing that and it's because there's one thing that the Sonoran Desert toad does but none of these other toads do, which is burrow down into the alluvial soils of the Sonoran Desert and go into a state of suspended animation for nine months at a time in total darkness. I believe it's this darkness component that is causing the toad to, somehow, in its

FACILITATING 5-MEO-DMT

physiology, transmute the 5-HO-DMT into 5-MeO-DMT. In recent scientific studies, they found that it can be up to 35% 5-MeO-DMT in the secretions, whereas before, we thought it was only up to about 15%. So certain toads, depending on their diet, or how healthy they are, produce more 5-MeO than others. When the toads are milked, most of the people who are extracting it mix different animals' secretions together to get a more homogenized mix of the medicine.

I've also worked with a number of different plant extracts; primarily one from *Virola theodora,* which is a woody, resinous tree found in Central and South America. It is a member of the nutmeg family. Theo is God, and Dora is gift, so whoever named that plant really knew what they were talking about. I've also worked with some *Phalaris* grass extracts, but those are not optimal for a number of reasons. And, I've worked with high-grade, lab-made synthetic versions of what I, and others, refer to as the "pure molecule." Having worked with all of these variants, I have found that I have preference for the pure molecule. All three of these variants do precisely the same thing. Because what we're talking about is the 5-MeO-DMT molecule itself and what it does. It allows for the ego to completely dissolve and for us to experience that which exists beyond the egoic structure. The other reason is I prefer working with pure molecule is because it requires far less material. It's about a 7-1 ratio, so 10 milligrams of pure molecule is the equivalent of about 70 milligrams of the bufo toxin, but that's going to have seven times more cardiovascular constrictors in it – all those other molecules in bufo toxin. So just from a health and safety point of view, I find that the pure molecule that's cleanly made is usually the best approach.

I'll take those medicines and I'll bring them into our ceremonial environment so that as we're working in ceremony, there is actually a spiritual charge, if you will, that's then brought into the medicine itself, because a lot of people who may be producing these medicines may be doing so for any variety of reasons. And so, we want to ceremonially bring the substances into being the actual sacrament, and we want to tune them to the work that we're actually doing.

Something that's not on the list of questions, but I think it's really relevant for you, because you fit into a special category, is that you are running a "temple," and we are now in the era where we've got a number of lawyers who are actively working on creating protections for entheogenic sacraments by applying the Religious Freedom Restoration Act for exemptions to federal drug laws. I know that you have gone to great lengths to fulfill all of those requirements as would be expected by law, yet also, you are not looking to take the Temple of Awakening Divinity into a public forum as some people have done in creating entheogenic churches. The question is why not? Why keep it underground, in private? And what then are your thoughts about the more public churches which have not yet been tested in the court of law?

Currently, we only have three successful exceptions – The NAC, Santo Daime, and UDV – and to a certain extent we can look at Soul Quest Ayahuasca Church of Mother Earth in Florida, which failed, at least in being recognized by the DEA, so the fact that we have governmental organizations like the IRS and the DEA determining who is a legitimate religion, and who's not, I find to be problematic to begin with. I was already an ordained priest at the time that I started working with this medicine, and I became an ordained bishop shortly thereafter, and I'm working within the context of my general spiritual tradition. My entheogenic experience was a confirmational experience where, through the medicine experience, it just confirmed what I was already doing and focusing on. It just became obvious to me that this was a religious, spiritual experience, just as it became obvious to you as a professor of comparative religions. I just didn't see anything else other than to do it that way and offer it as a form of ceremony and sacred initiation.

It was only later in 2015 that we incorporated, and we started putting together all of the essentials of the 14 points that the IRS is looking for and bringing that forward. There's a part of me that is still resistant in applying for 501c3 status, because even having a corporation, a fictitious body that serves as this interface between the secular and governmental authority, feels really inauthentic to me. I'm doing it because it provides a certain amount of potential safety, which could be an illusion. It was an illusion for the local Santo Daime church leader, Jonathan Goldman, when he came home to find a S.W.A.T. team surrounding his house and interrogating his children. I cherish my personal liberty. I cherish the fact that I can live in a society that says its primary foundations are on freedom, liberty, and justice. But sometimes it doesn't feel that way. I don't know that I want to be the poster boy for testing that.

Now, there are others who are choosing to be, in recent years, far more face-out than I. If they would like to undergo that ordeal, they are welcome to do so. If I have to undergo that ordeal, I will, but I'm not personally choosing it because my work is best done with me free and bringing this to as many people as possible who would choose to partake in it. I can't do my work inside of a prison cell. So I'm choosing not to, and I do I believe that the laws around this are unjust. Slowly but surely, especially here in Oregon, where we are starting to see that change very slowly, and there seems to be a momentum in this thing called the "Psychedelic Renaissance," or the "Entheogenic Reformation," that is allowing for these ideas to be brought out.

Facilitating 5-MeO-DMT

If there were a test case that went forward with a 5-MeO-DMT church that was successful – let's say they go to court just like here in Ashland, Oregon with the Santo Daime church – and it gets recognized, and it perhaps opens up the implication that this is not just limited to one particular state or one particular area (as was the result of the Santo Daime case), but the federal government says, "We can make an exception for 5-MeO-DMT because it does fit the category of a religious sacrament," would that inspire you to go above board and be public, or would you prefer to remain more in the background, even if it looked like things would go positively for you?

I would love to be able to be more forthcoming and transparent with what I'm doing. But just like the early Christian churches under the dictates of Roman authority, that could cost you your life, or at least your freedom. Roman Catholicism is a very different form of Christianity than the original Gnostic sects that started it, and I'm wary of institutionalizing something that has no place within the context of secular governmental authority. Now, do I believe that it's a good idea to have some forms of regulation to make things safe? Absolutely. But is that best instituted by the Drug Enforcement Agency? I don't think so.

The thing is, the government seems to be worried about the unraveling of the fabric of society because people are using these substances. Well, I've got news for you: the fucking fabric of society is tattered and crumbling before our eyes, and it has nothing to do with people using entheogenic and psychedelic substances. It has everything to do with the fact that we are trying to control humanity, that corporate culture is absolutely out of control, and that we are not looking out for the common people, and we are basically selling ourselves to corporations and not really stewarding our planet in a way that's going to allow for our children, and their children, to potentially be able to survive. We are clearly on a spiraling course to potentially the next mass-extinction event, and if we don't wake up to that really quickly, it's not going to be fun over the next 100 years.

The core of this issue – and for both you and I, this is very personal --- but by the standards of authority, we would both be classified as outlaws for doing entheogenic work and service. But both of us are members of our local community, we are parents, we are raising kids, we are not outlaws, we're not anarchists, we're not out there causing trouble. We just want the world to be a better place. With that in mind, what would your final message be as someone who facilitates, as someone who is an ordained priest, as someone who is a father, as someone who is my dear friend, what would be your final thoughts on all of this that you'd like to share, in closing?

Martin W. Ball, Ph.D., Editor

Be kind to one another. Celebrate your life, because it's the only one you get – one precious life – that's all you get. And if you recognize that we're here because Source chooses consciously to not only embody within us, but to embody *as us*, that Source has created you as a unique expression of itself, and there will be no one like you again, ever – that is a precious gift. And to use our lives to celebrate that gift with others by making life itself better for those around us, that's what I believe the message of this sacrament is. The message of Source is a message of love, ultimately. It is only love that we can rely on to bring us through, recognizing that we live on a paradisaical planet – literally on a paradise in physical reality. "Heaven" exists right here. It's not someplace else, because when we shuffle off this mortal coil, when that physical body dies and perishes into dust, when the thing that we've always known ourselves to be disintegrates and we merge into that infinite and eternal totality that knows it's the only thing that exists forever, consciously, and that it embodies itself as an act of love, so it can experience itself as other – when you recognize that it's not going into that state that's a miracle – it's recognizing that we're embodied in physical incarnations and that we have this opportunity to love each other here – now that is the miracle.

APPENDIX D: 5-MeO-DMT and the Obsolescence of Traditional Theology

By Martin W. Ball, Ph.D.

Human beings have had access to psychedelic and entheogenic plants, fungi, cacti, and elixirs for thousands of years. Via modern scholarship, though we don't always know the specific ingredients and recipes in many instances, we can state with a fair amount of certainty that psychedelics have played both major and minor roles throughout most of the main cultural areas of world throughout human history and have had an ongoing impact on religions, spiritual traditions, and cultures. However, with only a few exceptions among indigenous cultures in Central and South America, there's no direct evidence that the vast majority of humanity has ever been exposed to 5-MeO-DMT... until now.

As a final thought and concluding reflection on this reality, I thought it would be fitting to finish off this anthology with some speculations on how 5-MeO-DMT renders traditional theology largely obsolete, and how its widespread acceptance and presence across human cultures might affect religion in general. As facilitation of the 5-MeO-DMT experience grows and expands, which is now happening at an exponential rate across the globe, we have an opportunity to consider how this direct route to full God Consciousness might create something entirely new in the human experience: immediate and reliable access to the absolute nature of being without any need for religion or even spirituality.

Martin W. Ball, Ph.D., Editor

As someone who has earned his Ph.D. in Religious Studies, something that always struck me was how theology (the logic of the study of God, here loosely termed) hasn't ever seemed to have anything to do with reality or direct experience so much as it has always been about identity and belief. As such, theology is more about personal and group identity than anything to do with God or reality, and often rests on interpretation rather than anything we in the modern world would consider to be valid evidence. To illustrate this problem, I'll give some examples before diving into how 5-MeO-DMT radically disrupts all this navel gazing and identity contesting.

The Council at Nicaea, 325 C.E.:

Early Christianity had *major* identity issues. Not only were there multiple and completely contradictory versions of Jesus, his life, teachings, meaning, and message, but his basic identity itself was in serious question. Some early Christians didn't think he was an actual historical person. Some thought he was "adopted" by God and was a prophet. Others thought he was partially God and therefore participated with divinity, but wasn't identical with it. And some others thought he was "fully God and fully man." Some thought he was crucified and resurrected, and still others did not believe this aspect of the Jesus story to be actual fact. And not only were there all these differences, but different Christian identity groups were often in conflict with each other, sometimes violently so, and accusations of heresy were thrown about in all directions simultaneously, with each Christian identity thinking that *it was the correct one.*

Questions of identity were further fueled by the fact that the majority of Jews did not accept the new religion of Christianity as being part of *their* tradition, though for the first several hundred years, there was a distinct sect of Jewish Christians. However, the majority of new Christians were from Hellenic, Greek-speaking culture around the Mediterranean. Here, beliefs that had no official root in Judaism were commonly held as true. Among them were beliefs in immortal souls, and the existence of an afterlife – neither of which are considered orthodoxy in Judaism. For Hellens, these weren't controversial beliefs in Hellenic paganism and mystery cults. The majority of early Christians held no group identity with Jews and did not see themselves as limited by Jewish theology or doctrine. Furthermore, in Hellenic culture, the idea that someone could be descended from the gods was commonplace and widely accepted, whereas this belief would be considered heretical within Judaism.

Emperor Constantine, who moved the center of power of the Roman empire east to the conveniently-renamed Constantinople, in looking to consolidate power and impose uniformity on the now-"Christian" empire, called the Council at Nicaea in 325

Facilitating 5-MeO-DMT

C.E. to get this Jesus mess sorted out. It was the first of several such councils, as differences in doctrine and theology remained, but it did start the process of cementing what would become orthodoxy in the Imperial Christian Church, which would later split (over theological differences), into the western Catholic "Universal" Church and the eastern Orthodox "Correct Belief" Church. To greatly simplify all this, it was at this time that various versions of the Jesus myth and doctrine were deemed to be heretical and wide swaths of then-practicing-and-believing Christians were labelled as unorthodox and needing of conversion, with many of them being labeled "Gnostics," and as having false beliefs.

This is all theology in action: identity-based beliefs centering around issues of interpretation, and also disagreement over what, if anything, was "factual" about the Jesus story and mythological character. Basically, we had a bunch of men sitting around arguing over just who and what this Jesus guy was, what it tells us about the nature of God, the nature of reality, and just what-the-fuck we're all supposed to do about it. They had no historical sources to base their conclusions on, as there were none. No one here, almost 300 years after the supposed time of Jesus, knew anything personal about Jesus or what *he* might have thought about all these different views and takes on him and who and what he was. Rather, we had different representatives from different Christian identity groups arguing over who was right and who should be in control of the imperial Church and who would be left out, converted, or killed.

And of course, *no one asked God directly* to help sort this mess out, because God isn't available in that way.

So, belief and identity (and proximity to temporal power) were the only sources for resolving the fundamental theological issue of Christianity at the time. *That's the reality.*

Augustine, the "Father" of Christian Theology:

Born about 30 years after the Council at Nicaea, Augustine of Hippo, who converted to Christianity from a very different religion that had come from the east and had roots in Zoroastrianism, Manichaeism, was one of the first Christian philosophers to try and reconcile the now-orthodox Jesus with the theology of the Old Testament. Now that Jesus was the sole and unique son of God, Christianity actually had a major problem: what was the point? Specifically, if Jesus is the son of God, and coequal with God and the Holy Spirit, and the divine savior of all humanity, what could possibly be the point of God incarnating as Jesus only to be killed, and here, over 300 years later, still no sign that the most important dude in the universe hadn't organized his grand come-back tour?

Have a reality problem? No problem! Theology is here to help!

Augustine essentially "invented" a number of theological points to resolve this very real problem. To reconcile not only the failure of the Jesus mythological character, but also his relation to the Jewish Torah or "Old Testament," Augustine got creative. First, he had to reinterpret the *meaning* of the stories of the Old Testament, and here, he primarily focused on the books of *Genesis*, and this is where his creativity shines through. You may be familiar with this strange and enigmatic story of two people living in a garden and interacting with a talking snake that somehow affected all later humans. The story has its roots in the Hebraic tradition, but now that it was adopted into Christianity, its meaning had to change, especially in light of the Jesus myth and orthodoxy. Here's what Augustine added: that bizarre talking snake? That's ... dun, dun, dun ... Satan! This is an important difference between Jewish and Christian theology. There is no Satan in Judaism. There is a title of *satan*, meaning "adversary" or "someone who argues against," but this title isn't attributed to some cosmological being known as Satan or Lucifer, or anyone else in particular. But, this was adopted into Christianity as God's evil opponent. In the book of Genesis, the talking serpent in the story is not given any particular identity in the story itself. It's just a fucking talking snake, for God's sake. But, coming from Manichaeism, where the God of Light is opposed by the God of Darkness, Augustine re-imagined the story of Adam and Eve as their "temptation" by "The Devil himself," and therefore gave an entirely new spin on the ancient story (which itself had been adopted into Hebraic tradition from even earlier Mesopotamian religion and culture).

In Judaism, there is no concept of "original sin" – meaning, that's not how *they read the story*. And because there's no original sin, there's zero need for a savior figure to deliver them from the effects of original sin. However, this is precisely what Augustine decided the story was about. Adam and Eve were tempted by Satan, and therefore created the condition of original sin, which then impacted every human since them.

So, Augustine has now set up the necessary condition that we all suffer from something that we need to be saved from. So far, so good. But, now the next problem is that the so-called savior, Jesus, was a total failure in that he didn't seem to save anyone from anything, got himself killed, and no one has seen or heard anything from him since. Here is where Augustine next introduces his creativity and reinterpretation skills. His solution to this theological (and mythological) problem is that he names Jesus as "The Second Adam," who, through the process of atonement and self-sacrifice, opens the way to salvation from the original sin of Adam. In other words, his crucifixion (which was itself widely-debated in earlier Christianity) now becomes the linchpin that renders Jesus a theological success. If he hadn't been killed, then he couldn't have fulfilled the function of being the Second Adam and there would have been no atonement for original sin.

Problem solved!

However, we can easily see that this is all invention and interpretation. There's no *evidence* for any of this. None of it is connected to observable or experiential reality in any way. It's just the thoughts of some dude about a 300-year old story's relationship to an even older story. But, it went on to become the very bedrock upon which all later Christian theology was built. Interpretations of interpretations of interpretations.

Of note is that later, when Islam came upon the scene, like Judaism, Muslims rejected the invented notion of original sin, and therefore had no need of a savior, and Jesus reverted to the pre-Nicaean version of not only not being the unique son of God and fully divine, but also lost his crucifixion and resurrection and was transformed back to being a prophet, as he was taken as by some, though not most, Jewish groups. However, Islam did import the figure of Satan, here refigured as Shaitan, though the story of Genesis was also reimagined so that Adam and Eve were eventually granted permission back into Paradise and thereby negating the problem of original sin or need for a Savior from Shaitan and his influence, as had become theological doctrine in Christianity via Augustine.

Hinayana to Mahayana in Buddhism:

Let's turn to another tradition to get more examples. This time, we're looking at Buddhism. While Buddhism doesn't necessarily have "theology" per-se, as it is largely a non-theistic (lacking a Creator God) religion, it does have Buddhology, and here we can see similar elements of identity and belief at play.

In early Buddhism, Siddhartha Gautama is a man who became enlightened, and via his enlightenment, decided that the vast majority of what was going on in Hinduism was unnecessary and unrelated to the quest for enlightenment and liberation. Though Buddha rejected most of Hinduism – its ritualism, its reliance on the *Vedas* as revealed religious texts, its social and religious caste system, and essentially all of its theology – he didn't reject the basic assumptions of the Indian worldview that the fundamental *problem* of human existence is that we're trapped in a near-infinite cycle of reincarnation, powered by *karma*, and that the goal of human life is to escape the wheel of *samsara*. This is the unique Indian take on the belief in reincarnation. Other cultures have believed that reincarnation is real, but haven't necessarily deemed it to be a problem that needs a solution. In India, however, virtually all religions that developed there take this problem as a given and a fundamental starting point, so its validity is essentially never questioned. It is merely assumed that this is how thing are. In creating a new religion, Buddha sought to provide a different take, and a different path, on this assumed problem, and thereby created a new identity in Indian culture; that of being Buddhist.

It didn't take long for different Buddhist groups to splinter off and after the Buddha's death, a variety of different schools of thought and practice flourished in early Buddhism. These differences didn't amount to a major reconstruction of Buddhism until several hundred years later with the ascendance of *Mahayana Buddhism*. The self-identified "Great Vehicle" of Buddhism came along, called everything that came before it *Hinayana Buddhism,* or "Little/Lesser Vehicle," and completely reimagined the Buddha. Central to the newly ascendent Mahayana was a completely new Buddhology (their version of theology) of the *Trikaya*. Buddha was no longer merely a man who realized enlightenment and provided a new set of teachings for others to follow, but he was now synonymous with the very nature of reality itself, existing on three different levels of reality simultaneously. In this new Buddhology, the historical Buddha, Siddhartha, was merely "pretending to be a man on the path to enlightenment," and his early teachings were basically for "children," whereas the new Mahayana cosmology and associated practices were for "adults" now that Buddhism had matured. Buddha was recast in more deific terms, was available for new revelations, and stories about his life, teachings, and miracles were completely reformatted, retrofitted, and greatly augmented. Sound vaguely familiar?

It didn't matter that none of the new Buddhist literature had any connection to the earliest teachings of the Buddha as documented in the Pali Canon, because now, in the new Sanskrit Canon, creative Mahayana Buddhists, who saw themselves as superior in insight and knowledge to their predecessors, could claim direct revelation from the Cosmic Buddha, Samantabhadra, or any of the other countless "archetypal" Buddhas that existed across the different levels of the *Trikaya* or three "bodies" of the Buddha: cosmic/universal, visionary, or embodied. Indeed, "there are more Buddhas than there are grains of sand in the Ganges," or so the Mahayana saying goes.

No one could ask Buddha what he thought of all this because he was, well, dead. So again, it came down to what people believed, or wanted to believe, and also identity. Are you one of those stagnant old school Hinayana Buddhists, or are you one of the hip, dynamic, and up-to-date Mahayana Buddhists? Identity and belief win again.

Facilitating 5-MeO-DMT
The Vedantin Schools of Hinduism:

Over a thousand years after the time of the Buddha, when Buddhist philosophical rigor and analysis had become dominant in India, a philosophical and theological rival to Buddhism took shape via Shankara and his articulation of *Advaita Vedanta*. Despite its multi-layered cosmological complexity, Mahayana Buddhism was decidedly nondual in orientation, and this had an impact on Shankara's philosophy. Buddha had rejected a fundamental aspect of Hindu identity: the central importance of the *Vedas* as religious texts. While the *Vedas* were the revealed word of God for Hindus, for Buddhists, they were unimportant ancient literature that could be completely ignored because they had nothing to do with Buddhist non-theology or the Buddhist program of enlightenment. Yet, they retained their significance for Hindus, though the majority of Hindus have never actually read the *Vedas*.

As part of his Hindu philosophical revival, Shankara proclaimed that the *Vedas* were still relevant for, according to his interpretation, they pointed, like the Buddhists, to the nondual nature of reality, and God. In Sanskrit, *Advaita* means precisely this: *a* – non/not, *dvaita* – dual/two. In his interpretation, though Hinduism posits that individual souls are on a journey to reach *moksha* and enlightenment (a doctrine rejected by Buddhism where souls are not thought to exist), there is actually only ONE soul, the soul of God, and as such, there aren't billions of souls on a quest to reach enlightenment but just God in various forms forgetting that it's God in its multitude of manifestations.

By this point, the ancient scriptures of the *Vedas* had been around for thousands of years, first transmitted orally, and then eventually written down and continually recited by the Brahmins, the priestly caste in Hindu society (which is also rejected by Buddhism as being irrelevant for enlightenment). Like Augustine did with ancient Jewish scriptures in Christianity, Shankara put an entirely new spin on these Hindu texts, brought them into alignment with contemporary Buddhist philosophy, and started an entirely new branch of Hindu theology. Outside of this accomplishment, what made Shankara's interpretations of the *Vedas* correct? Well...nothing. That was his interpretation, and it developed a new form of Hindu identity. How could anyone say, with any authority that, after thousands of years, Shankara had *finally* understood the *Vedas* correctly? He certainly felt so, as did his followers.

But it didn't last. Wanting to preserve theological room for individual souls and a creator God, not just some all-pervasive unitary being that was everyone and everything as revealed in ancient texts, the development of devotional *Bhakti* Hinduism had its own, later impact on Hindu philosophy. The next development was the "Qualified Nondual" school of Vedantic philosophy, which taught that yes, everything is God (nonduality), but there *are* individual souls on a quest for enlightenment (qualified), and as you can probably guess, this school said that *this* was the right way to interpret the *Vedas*.

But not even that lasted, because the cultural stream of *Bhakti* devotionalism was strong, and there's still the problem that if God really is you, then what the fuck are you worshiping, praying to, and showing devotion towards? This nonduality stuff just doesn't cut it for anyone who wants to *worship* God. And thus, the 3rd and final school of Vedantic philosophy is . . . can you guess? That's right! *Dvaita Vedanta* – Dual Vedanta! According to this school, individual souls exist, they are different from God and from each other, and God is *other* and *transcendent*. Here, Hinduism has spanned the spectrum from mystical nondual self-realization to numinous worship of a transcendent and superior God. And *this*, according to this school, founded by Vishnu worshipers and devotees, is the proper interpretation of the *Vedas*.

Such diametrically opposed philosophical views and theologies can't all be correct. That's not the way theology works. Theology is all about orthodoxy – correct belief. If two beliefs are opposed to each other in theology, then one is right, the other is wrong. The task of the religious person is to align with *the correct one*. None of the various schools of Vedantin philosophy can *prove* that their *interpretations* of the same text are correct. The interpretations are "correct" because that's what those groups of believers want to believe, and it's how they identify themselves as distinct from others. As is pretty much always the case, differences in theology come down to differences in beliefs and identities, not incontrovertible proof. And, they're always in negotiation with cultural trends at the time they were developed. Hopefully this is clear in all the examples given above. None of these theologies develop in a vacuum. They all develop in a cultural and historical context. That's the way ideas and identities work. It's how religion and culture work, in general.

The Entheology of 5-MeO-DMT:

Elsewhere I've gone into detail into what I've named "the entheological paradigm," which is the understanding I developed of the nature of God, being, and reality as I directly experienced and understood it from my 5-MeO-DMT experiences. What I found in my own experiences was that none of the existing theological or religious traditions really fit with what I was experiencing and concluding myself from my own experience. While there were various aspects of congruency, none were a perfect fit, and some were profoundly off. For example, based on my direct experience,

FACILITATING 5-MEO-DMT

none of the numinous religious traditions were anywhere near correct in their theology. In the discipline of religious studies, numinous can be taken to mean "Holy Other," and this is the predominant theological position of the three Abrahamic religions of Judaism, Christianity, and Islam, though there are mystical exceptions in minority sects within all three religions. However, the depiction of God as being "other" and "transcendent" and as "higher," "above," and "beyond" humanity and as an issuer of commandments, laws, and moral obligations just seemed profoundly incorrect, and obviously so. If I, or anyone else, for that matter, could directly experience myself as God, and this Unitary Being was also simultaneously being everyone and everything else, including all space and time, then there's absolutely nothing "other" about God. Furthermore, if I am God, and each one of us can directly access the profound sense of "I AM," then clearly I'm not some incarnated soul, either living one or multiple lives, because I'm just God acting as the character of "Martin" in this particular body, and doing the same in everyone else simultaneously. And if there are no souls, then there's no reward and punishment, there's no afterlife, there is no spirit world, there's no individual reincarnation. Also, figures like Jesus are no longer unique and special, because everyone is actually "fully God and fully (hu)man," and thus there also is no theological role for a savior, as there's nothing to be saved from. There's also no real escape from *samsara* to pursue because we aren't actually trapped in an endless cycle of individual reincarnation. So, from my personal perspective, as developed from my personal experience, the basic theological foundations of Judaism, Christianity, Islam, Buddhism, and Hinduism just fell away as irrelevant, uninformed, and more expressions of identity than anything that had to do with God, the nature of being, or reality.

All this came from my experience that God was not only *within me* (en-inside, theo-god, logy-logic or understanding), but *was me and all of reality*. And if this is correct, then that means that we all have equal opportunity access to being our own theologians and develop our own personal understanding of the nature of God via direct experience as afforded by 5-MeO-DMT, and we are all free to completely disregard and ignore the theologies of the various religions of the world as they're just not relevant. In my mind, traditional theology is now obsolete.

People who come from a religious background and experience 5-MeO-DMT often reflect that the experience, and what they now understand about themselves, God, and reality, doesn't fit with what they were taught to believe. Myself not coming from a religious background, I didn't have to go through the process of shedding and letting go of my indoctrination, but it did cure me of being Buddhist in philosophical orientation as it now seemed quite clear to me that this whole karma and reincarnation thing *wasn't actually a thing*. However, many people, even if not actively identifying as being one religion or another, were raised within a particular religious tradition, and here they often find that their experience radically challenges what they were raised to believe and hold as true. We're living in the era where more young people self-identify as "spiritual, but not religious," so the adherence to doctrine and dogma isn't as strong as it once was in the modern West, but there are still plenty of spiritual beliefs, practices, and ideas that just don't jive with the 5-MeO-DMT experience. One of the major issues with spirituality is that people use their spirituality to create a self-identity, and this can be shattered by 5-MeO-DMT just as easily as a religious group identity.

It has been my advice that anyone truly serious about self-liberation will eventually abandon and shed off all religious and spiritual identity and embrace the freedom of just being oneself as the unique individual that they are, while simultaneously energetically embodying the reality that they are also the Universal Being as articulated, experienced, and expressed as their unique character, body, and being. However, as is clear in many of the entries in this volume, many people who facilitate 5-MeO-DMT still gravitate toward the language of "the sacred" and see their practice as best held within a ceremonial container. Yet even here, it is generally non-specific, non-dogmatic, and nonsectarian. It is understandable that many people want to create a "sacred" environment around the facilitation and use of 5-MeO-DMT, because using words such as God, the divine, sacred, holy, and other related terms certainly feel like a good fit for the experience. Such can also help create the right receptivity within clients and initiates to consider what they're about to participate in as being of the utmost specialness and value. It's easy to see why people want to treat 5-MeO-DMT in this way. But, there are some things we should be careful of here.

It can be a slippery slope from group ceremonial or temple context to cult and group-think and identity. There are people out there basically running 5-MeO-DMT cults, and some of these have been around since before the contemporary wide-spread awareness and interest in 5-MeO-DMT. There are also relatively brand new "temples" that serve 5-MeO-DMT as a "eucharist" and see it as taking "communion," using language from Christianity. Humans, as social animals, naturally gravitate toward groups and group identities, and running a 5-MeO-DMT church or temple can satisfy this basic, and thoroughly valid, social need. Everyone wants to belong, in some sense. There are now a number of lawyers active in the modern psychedelic movement who are working hard to help those who want to create and safely and securely run entheogenic churches to do so with the maximum possibility for legal protection, even in the face of anti-drug laws. It's a razor's edge, however, as the federal government in the U.S. isn't exactly entheogenic religion-friendly, and the recognized exceptions to

FACILITATING 5-MEO-DMT

drug laws are scant and far outmatched by the prevalence of entheogenic churches and temples on the ground and continually sprouting up across the country and world.

Eventually, the legal and social realities will need to catch up with what's happening out there in the real world. 5-MeO-DMT churches already exist, along with mushroom and ayahuasca churches. Setting anti-drug hysteria, misinformation, and propaganda aside, there are no valid moral, ethical, social, or health reasons for disallowing such establishments, and on a human rights ground, everything is actually in favor of entheogenic churches. Insofar as no one is causing harm to others, then there is no valid argument for denying anyone the basic human right of experiencing their nature as God directly and immediately through entheogenic sacraments, and here, I think we have a special argument in favor of 5-MeO-DMT in particular, as it's "The God Molecule," after all, and presents humanity with a unique possibility: bypassing all religion, all tradition, all arcane arguments over the nature of God and being and going directly to the source in a matter of seconds for self-directed examination, experience, and contemplation. While we may need churches and temples to do this in and have the experienced facilitated, it's the experience itself that's the thing, not the organization or institution, per se.

While I think that legal rights should be extended across the board regarding psychedelics and their use – anything from personal exploration, creativity, general wellbeing, entertainment, therapeutic use, spiritual use, and religious use – 5-MeO-DMT is still exceptional and of special value and importance simply because it goes directly to the heart of the matter and is the most direct route to personal experience of the infinite and unitary nature of being and is more effective than anything else that exists on the planet. The fact that *anyone* can directly experience themselves *as God* via this molecule regardless of background, upbringing, religious or spiritual identity, personal beliefs, identity, or anything else, is pretty damn profound. And more so than any other entheogen, the common take-away by those who have experienced it is that *this is IT!* It's the grand equalizer, and no belief or indoctrination is required.

It's interesting that 5-MeO-DMT seems to be rapidly gaining in popularity and global interest at *precisely the time that we need what it has to offer*. As we balance on the edges of pandemics, social collapse, the resurgence of fascism, nationalism, ethnic and racial superiority, outrageous wealth disparities, religious fundamentalism and fanaticism, environmental destruction, loss of species, and global climate change and the radical societal disruptions and mass migrations it is already causing, this unique molecule comes along and shows us in no uncertain terms that we literally are all one, it's all us, and it's all up to us, because God can't "do" anything for us because God *is* us. There's no one to save us. Either we start taking responsibility for who and what we actually are, and start treating ourselves and each other as such, or it quite possibly could be the end of the party as death and destruction and identity-group violence and partisanship sweep the globe.

What could be more significant to address the current reality of humanity and the state of the globe than a mere molecule that gives us direct access to our unitary nature and clearly reveals that what we do to another, in any form, whether that be someone from a different religion, skin color, place of origin, or social identification, we do to ourselves? 5-MeO-DMT cannot *make us* be one, because we already are, and always have been. But we humans haven't behaved as such, and rather than emphasize our shared identity, we've continually and repeatedly emphasized our differences, and the perception of superiority and correctness within those differences. Theology has been used to determine who is "right" and who is "wrong," and who has a monopoly on truth.

To circle back around to how I started this collection in the introduction, just 14 years ago when I first experienced and started sharing about 5-MeO-DMT, it seemed like virtually no one knew what it was or had really heard about it. Though it had been present for at least a generation in the elite psychedelic underground, there was no real public awareness of it, and even in psychedelic circles, it was either unheard of or misunderstood or misrepresented. It's a different world, now, however, where stories about 5-MeO-DMT and toad secretions regularly show up across the media spectrum, and celebrities, researchers, and medical institutions are all getting on board with 5-MeO-DMT and appreciating its radical potential. For the first time in human history, potentially anyone in the world can learn about this profound molecule and find a way to experience it for themselves. Of course, disparities still exist and it's not the case that there's unlimited access. Interested individuals still have to find some for themselves or find a facilitator and context to take it in, but the potential is there in a way that it never has been before now. And all indications are that this is only going to grow and increase, as interest in 5-MeO-DMT is growing exponentially across the planet. It's a turning point from which humanity might not ever come back, and that, in my mind, is a good thing. And it is my hope that this will grow in ways that are responsible, compassionate, informed, educated, and done with the proper respect for all involved, including the toads.

5-MeO-DMT is not going to fix our problems. It doesn't *make* you enlightened or free or a better person. It's a powerful assist, however, and helps us find the truth of being within ourselves so that we can have greater clarity, resilience, and ability to face the challenges that are arising all around and within us. Its power is that it helps us find *our own answers within our being* to the deepest and most meaningful existential

FACILITATING 5-MEO-DMT

questions humanity has faced throughout its history. It helps us intimately understand who and what we are, and what potential we hold within ourselves. It does this on a person-by-person basis. It might happen in a temple, church, therapist's office, retreat center, or a friend's living room. It doesn't matter where it happens so much as that it happens, and that as many individuals have the opportunity to experience the fullness of themselves as possible in safe, secure, and responsible environments with skilled and conscientious facilitators. 5-MeO-DMT is *already* changing the world. Just imagine what's to come…

It is my hope that one day, perhaps far down the road from now, people will look back on this collection of different ways that people across the globe are facilitating the 5-MeO-DMT experience and say, "And that was just the beginning…"

About the Author/Editor:

Martin W. Ball, Ph.D. is a localized embodiment of the One Universal Consciousness and Being who lives in Ashland, Oregon with his wife, Jessalynn, and son, Jaden, where he writes, makes music, creates art, talks a lot, consults, does photography in his free time, and makes it a habit of being himself. He formerly provided one-on-one 5-MeO-DMT facilitation and now offers individual and private nondual entheogenic integration consultations for those seeking help understanding and integrating their experience, specializing in, but not limited to, 5-MeO-DMT. You can find out more about him at his personal website, www.martinball.net, and you can find his many books in paperback, ebook, and audiobook at Amazon, Kindle, Audible, and the iBookstore.

All of the art featured in this book is by the author. To view his full galleries, visit: www.fractalimagination.com

Amazon author page: www.amazon.com/author/martinwball

Patreon: www.patreon.com/martinwball

The Entheogenic Evolution Podcast: www.entheogenic.podomatic.com

Nondual Entheogenic Integration: www.nondualentheogenicintegration.com

Music: www.martinball.bandcamp.com

Made in the USA
Thornton, CO
02/04/25 16:46:55

6b80e73f-0228-453f-bfea-4cd06d9ad4b9R01